CHRIS BRYANT'S
CCNP

SWITCH 300-115 STUDY GUIDE

CHRIS BRYANT

Table of Contents

A VERY Brief Introduction
Before We Get Started...

Thank you for making The Bryant Advantage part of your CCNP success story! I know you have a lot of training options out there, from books to videos and everything in between, and all of us here at TBA are very appreciative of your purchase.

During your studies, check out my YouTube channel! I'm starting an all-new CCNP SWITCH 300-115 Playlist in October 2015. With over 300 free videos there already, I know there's something there you'll enjoy.

https://www.youtube.com/user/ccie12933

You'll find additional free resources via these links:

Facebook: goo.gl/u72n1M

Google+: https://plus.google.com/+ccie12933

GNS3 (Free CCNP SWITCH Course!): goo.gl/yk2loM

Thanks again for your purchase, and now, *let's get started!*

Chris Bryant

"The Computer Certification Bulldog"

Chapter 1:

SWITCHING FUNDAMENTALS

Your mastery of switching fundamentals can make the difference on exam day, so let's give this material a good going-over before heading on to new material! Before proceeding, let's have a moment of silence for two old friends.

We won't spend any time discussing floppy disks, but the item on the left is a hub, the predecessor to today's switches. (You'll sometimes see a double-headed arrow on top of the icon representing a hub.) Back in the day, our hosts had to share transmission media via a hub.

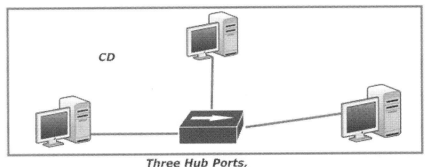

**Three Hub Ports,
One Collision Domain**

Having just one collision domain may sound good, but it's not. With one big collision domain, we must have rules on when a host may transmit data. Otherwise, one host's data

1

will be almost continually colliding with another host's data, rendering the collided signals useless. The hosts then have to retransmit the data, and there's no guarantee that *another* collision won't occur when that retransmission occurs!

The set of rules for transmitting over Ethernet via shared media is *Carrier Sense Multiple Access with Collision Detection*, thankfully referred to as CSMA/CD. Here's the overall process...

A host with data to send must first *listen to the wire*, meaning it checks the shared media to see if another host is currently sending data. If the media is in use, the host backs off for a few milliseconds before listening to the wire again. If the media is not in use, the host sends the data.

If two hosts happen to send data at the exact same time, the voltage on the wire will change, indicating a *data collision*. The hub might as well be a bomb at that point, because the data involved in the collision is going to "explode" when that collision occurs, and all data involved is unusable.

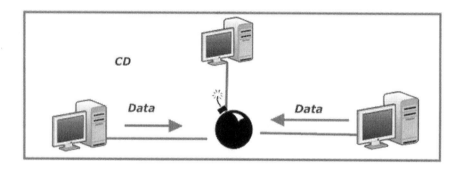

When the sending hosts detect that voltage change, they'll send a *jam signal* indicating to the other hosts that they should not send data right now.

The sending hosts will then invoke a *backoff timer*, set to a random number of milliseconds. When each host's backoff timer expires, they will each begin the CSMA/CD process from the very beginning by listening to the wire. Since that backoff timer is set to a random value, it's unlikely that the data collision will reoccur.

At the time, we were darn glad to have CSMA/CD, and those built-in delays were a small price to pay for sharing media.

You know what wasn't around though? Voice and video conferencing. YouTube. Vimeo. VoIP phones. Cat videos. Dog videos. Donkey videos. In short, all kinds of ultra-delay-sensitive voice and video traffic is present in today's network that we were only dreaming about back in the days of the hub. Having one big collision domain just would *not* do today.

One reason we love switches is the creation of smaller collision domains. Today's networks typically have each host connected to their own individual port on a switch, and by doing so, a separate collision domain is created for each host. Collisions literally cannot occur!

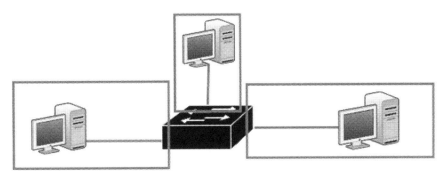

*Three hosts, three collision domains --
thanks to one switch!*

Some Cisco documentation refers to this "one host, one collision domain" setup as *microsegmentation*. It's not a term you hear often, but it's certainly a good one to know when you're reading Cisco docs.

Thanks to our switch, we also get a lot more bandwidth! When hosts are connected to individual switch ports, they no longer have to share bandwidth with other hosts. With the right switch config and network cards, each host can theoretically run at 200 Mbps (100 sending and 100 receiving), assuming FastEthernet ports.

That takes care of the collision domain issue, but we still have one large broadcast domain. By default, a broadcast or multicast sent by any host connected to that switch will be received by every *other* host on that switch. That's a lot of unnecessary broadcasts flying around our network, which in turn means unnecessary work for the switch and for the hosts. We'll start breaking up those broadcast domains in the Virtual LAN (VLAN) section of the course.

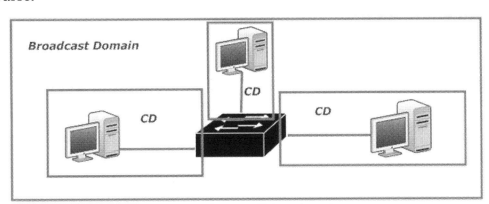

*Three hosts, three collision domains --
but still one big broadcast domain.*

3

"Decisions, Decisions"

When a switch receives a frame, that switch will forward it, filter it, or flood it. We'll take a look at each process right after this pop quiz!

When a frame enters a switch, what common value does the switch look at first?

It makes perfect sense that the switch would look at the frame's destination address first. After all, the only way for the switch to get the frame where it needs to go is to look at its intended destination, right?

Wrong! The switch will actually look at the source MAC address before any other value. The logical question to that answer would be: "Why does the switch even care where the frame came from?" The answer: "Because source addresses of incoming frames are how the switch builds and maintains its MAC address table." That's not the only reason for this behavior, but it's the major reason.

Our routing table is helped along by dynamic routing protocols like EIGRP and OSPF. There is no equivalent to those protocols at Layer 2, so the switches have to build their MAC address tables in another fashion (or fashions).

We could build a MAC address table with all static entries, but that approach has a serious drawback. Every time you add a host to a switch, you'd have to make a static MAC entry for that host. The more information you add statically, the greater the chance of a mistyped entry, which in turn leads to unnecessary troubleshooting.

If a port goes down and you switch the host connected to the bad port to a good port, you won't have full connectivity until you add a new static entry for that host's MAC address. In the heat of battle, it's easy to forget to remove the old entry, which leads to even more unnecessary troubleshooting when the bad port is fixed and another host is eventually connected to it.

When I have a choice between letting the hardware do the work and me doing the work, I'll let the hardware do it every time. That doesn't mean I'm lazy, it means I'm smart. It's much more efficient to let the hardware carry out dynamic operations rather than forcing you and I, the network admins, to handle everything statically.

Let's take a look at how a switch builds that all-important MAC address table, and we'll also see each of those frame forwarding options in action. We'll start with four hosts and one switch, using an odd topology to illustrate one forwarding option in particular. Hosts A and B are connected to a hub, which in turn is connected to a switch.

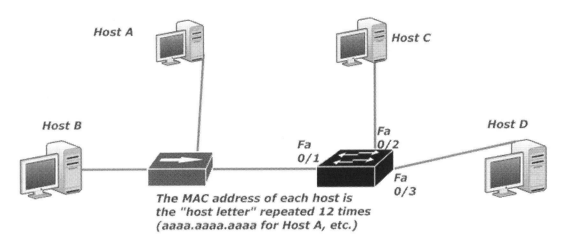

The MAC address of each host is
the "host letter" repeated 12 times
(aaaa.aaaa.aaaa for Host A, etc.)

For clarity, switchport numbers are
not repeated in subsequent illustrations.

We'll assume the switch has just been added to the network, which brings up another important point. When you first boot a switch, the MAC address table isn't empty. There will be some entries for the CPU, and they'll look something like this:

```
MLS _ 1#show mac address-table
        Mac Address Table



Vlan     Mac Address      Type       Ports
---      -----------      --------
All      0100.0ccc.cccc   STATIC     CPU
All      0100.0ccc.cccd   STATIC     CPU
```

The only way the switch can learn where the hosts are is for you and I to add a bunch of static entries (clumsy, not scalable) or let the switch learn their addresses dynamically. We'll start our walkthrough with Host A sending a frame to Host C. The frame enters the switch on fast0/1; the switch then looks at the source MAC address of the frame and asks itself one simple question: "Do I have an entry for this address in my MAC address table?" There's no grey area here – the answer is either yes or no!

Since we just turned the switch on, there's no entry for Host A's address in the MAC table, so the switch makes one. Our dynamic entries in that table are as follows:

```
MLS _ 1#show mac address-table dynamic
        Mac Address Table



Vlan     Mac Address      Type       Ports
---      -----------      --------
  1      aaaa.aaaa.aaaa   DYNAMIC    Fa0/1
```

ong last, we get to the frame forwarding decision! Will this frame be *forwarded*, *filtered*, or *flooded*? That depends on the answer to the next question the switch asks itself: "Do I have an entry for this destination address in my MAC address table?" The answer is no, so the switch floods the frame, sending a copy of the frame out of every single port on the switch except the port the frame rode in on. This is an *unknown unicast frame*, since the frame is a unicast (destined for one particular host), but there is no entry for this address in the MAC table.

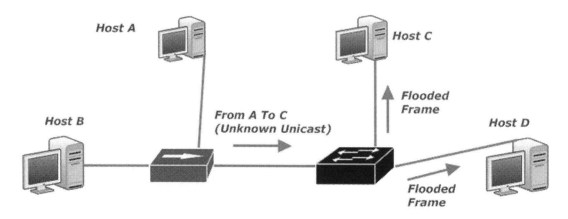

This flooding ensures the frame will go out the port leading to the correct host, and it also guarantees the other hosts will get the frame, which is a huge waste of bandwidth, host resources, and switch resources. If this is a 64-port switch and there's a host on every port, the switch has to send 63 copies of the frame – 62 of which are totally unnecessary!

There's nothing wrong with a little frame flooding as you add a host or switch to a network – it really can't be avoided – but after the initial add, we'd rather not have much flooding.

Host C will now respond to Host A with a frame of its own. We know what happens when the switch receives that frame, but will there be an entry for the source MAC of that frame?

```
MLS _ 1#show mac address-table dynamic
        Mac Address Table


Vlan      Mac Address       Type          Ports
  1       aaaa.aaaa.aaaa    DYNAMIC       Fa0/1
```

No entry for cccc.cccc.cccc, so the switch will create one.

```
MLS _ 1#show mac address-table dynamic
        Mac Address Table


Vlan      Mac Address       Type          Ports
  1       aaaa.aaaa.aaaa    DYNAMIC       Fa0/1
  1       cccc.cccc.cccc    DYNAMIC       Fa0/2
```

The dynamic entries in the table will now start to work in our favor. The switch checks for the frame's destination address of aaaa.aaaa.aaaa in that table, and since there is one, the switch will forward the frame via Fa0/1.

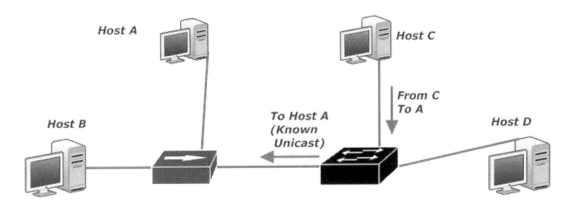

If Host A responds to Host C, the switch will have an entry for Host C's MAC address where it didn't have one earlier. Frames flowing from Host A to Host C will now be forwarded out Fa0/2 rather than being flooded.

Let's jump ahead to a scenario where the topology is the same and the switch has a dynamic MAC entry for each host. Please note that this is not a topology you're going to see in many production networks (if at all). I'm strictly presenting it to you to illustrate the switch's third option for frame forwarding.

We have an unusual setup where Hosts A and B are connected to a hub that is in turn connected to a switch. From the switch's point of view, both of those hosts are found off port Fa0/1. When Host A sends a frame to Host B, B will get a copy of it through the hub, as will the switch. The switch checks for the source addresses in its MAC address table, and sees that they're both found off the same port!

```
MLS _ 1#show mac address-table dynamic
         Mac Address Table


Vlan     Mac Address         Type        Ports
---      ----------          -------     -------
   1     aaaa.aaaa.aaaa      DYNAMIC     Fa0/1
   1     bbbb.bbbb.bbbb      DYNAMIC     Fa0/1
   1     cccc.cccc.cccc      DYNAMIC     Fa0/2
   1     dddd.dddd.dddd      DYNAMIC     Fa0/3
```

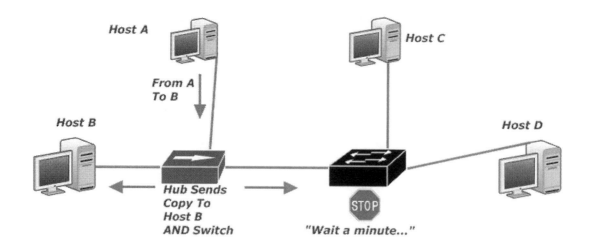

This messes with the switch's mind for just a moment, and the switch then filters the frame. "Filter" is a fancy big-city way of saying "the frame is dropped".

Let's review those decisions and add a little broadcast / multicast discussion.

Flooding occurs when the switch has no entry for the frame's destination MAC. When a frame is flooded, a copy of it is sent out of every port on the switch except the one it came in on. Unknown unicast frames are always flooded.

Frames with a destination MAC of all Fs (ffff.ffff.ffff) are called *broadcast frames*, and are treated in the same manner as unknown unicast frames. Broadcast frames are actually intended for all hosts, where unknown unicast frames are sent to all hosts as a side effect of the frame flooding.

Multicast frames have a destination MAC in the range 0100.5e00.0000 – 0100.5e7f.ffff and are treated in the same fashion as broadcast frames.

Forwarding happens when the switch has an entry for the frame's destination MAC. Forwarded frames are sent out only via the port indicated by the MAC address table.

Filtering happens when the source and destination MAC addresses are found off the same port. Technically, filtering also occurs when a frame is not sent out of a port because the destination is a known unicast.

More About That MAC Address Table

When I was waxing poetic about dynamically learned MAC addresses, I'm sure you wondered how long those addresses stay in the table. The default aging time for dynamically learned MAC addresses is 300 seconds, and that timer is reset when a frame comes in with that particular source MAC address. In short, as long as the switch hears from a host within any five-minute period, that host's MAC address stays in the table.

With time-based IOS commands, be sure to use IOS Help to check the unit of time that particular command uses. For example, if I asked you to set the MAC address aging time to 10 minutes, and you already knew that the command to change that value is mac address-table aging-time, you might be tempted to enter the following:

```
MLS_1(config)#mac address-table aging-time 10
```

Not only is that wrong, it's *really* wrong. IOS Help reveals that the time unit for this commands is seconds...

```
MLS_1(config)#mac address-table aging-time ?
  <0-0>         Enter 0 to disable aging
  <10-1000000>  Aging time in seconds

MLS_1(config)#mac address-table aging-time
```

... so our dynamic entries are now aging out in just 10 seconds. Let's fix that:

```
MLS_1(config)#mac address-table aging-time 600
```

Verify with *show mac address-table aging-time.*

```
MLS_1#show mac address-table aging-time
Global Aging Time: 600
```

I strongly urge you to use IOS Help to check any numeric value. Time-related commands use different combinations of seconds, milliseconds, hours, days, and minutes. Data-based commands use megabits, kilobits, gigabits – you get the idea. Use IOS Help, my friends – that's why it's there!

I shall now hop down from Ye Olde Soapbox and we'll march forward!

Another factor in favor of dynamic MAC address table entries is the switch's ability to dynamically adapt to a change in physical ports. To demo this, I'll need to know the port ROUTER_3 is connected to.

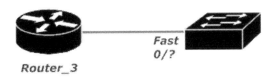

Fast
0/?

Router_3

Do *you* know a command that will give us information about directly connected Cisco devices?

```
MLS_1#show cdp neighbor
Capability Codes: R - Router, T - Trans Bridge, B - Source Route Bridge
                  S - Switch, H - Host, I - IGMP, r - Repeater, P - Phone,
                  D - Remote, C - CVTA, M - Two-port Mac Relay
```

```
Device ID        Local Intrfce      Holdtme    Capability  Platform  Port ID
ROUTER _ 1       Fas 0/1            177              R  S  I   2801      Fas 0/0
ROUTER _ 3       Fas 0/3            136              R  S  I   2801      Fas 0/0
```

Right! More about CDP later in the course. Right now, let's use *show mac address-table dynamic interface* to get info about only that particular port. (When you have 48 or so dynamically learned addresses, you'll want to use this filter.)

```
MLS _ 1#show mac address-table int fast 0/3
            Mac Address Table


Vlan      Mac Address        Type          Ports
---       ----------         -------
 13       001f.ca96.2754     DYNAMIC       Fa0/3
Total Mac Addresses for this criterion: 1
```

So far, so good! But now... port Fa0/3 goes BAD.

Router_3

With dynamically learned addresses, all we need to do is move that cable to a port that's working. I'll move it to Fast0/11 and check the full dynamic address table.

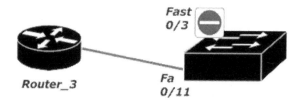

Fast 0/3

Router_3   **Fa 0/11**

```
MLS _ 1#show mac address-table dynamic
            Mac Address Table


Vlan      Mac Address        Type          Ports
---       ----------         -------
  1       001f.ca96.2754     DYNAMIC       Fa0/13
 13       0017.59e2.474a     DYNAMIC       Fa0/1
Total Mac Addresses for this criterion: 2
```

Success! ROUTER_3's MAC address is correctly listed in the table. No aging was necessary – once the switch saw frames from ROUTER_3 come in on a new port, the entry for that address on Fa0/3 was removed.

There is one thing you have to do manually in this situation, and that's changing the VLAN membership of that port. Earlier *show* commands told us that the previous port belonged to VLAN 13, and our Cisco switch ports belong to VLAN 1 by default. You likely remember how to change a port's VLAN membership. If not, here's a reminder, and there's plenty of additional work with VLANs ahead!

```
MLS _ 1(config)#int fast 0/13
MLS _ 1(config-if)#switchport access vlan 13


MLS _ 1#show vlan brief

VLAN Name                              Status    Ports
---  ------------------------------    --------- 
  1  default                           active    (All ports except those in
                                                 #13)
 13  VLAN0013                          active    Fa0/1, Fa0/3, Fa0/13
```

We've been working with the MAC address table for a while now, so it's good time to tell you the other name for this table. The MAC address table is also known as the Content Addressable Memory (CAM) table, and for Layer 2 switching, having "just" the CAM table is enough to get the job done. Multilayer switches have other challenges and tasks besides switching – routing, advanced security, and Quality of Service (QoS) to name just a few!

For these tasks, we'll need the help of a Ternary Content Addressable Memory (TCAM) table. While CAM table lookups use two values (no surprise, they're 0 and 1), TCAM tables have three values – 0, 1, and "x" for "don't care". It's common for multilayer switches to have multiple TCAM tables to go along with the multiple functions an MLS must handle.

You'll find more info on the TCAM in the Multilayer Switching portion of the course.

Switch Roles And The SDM

The great thing about multilayer switches is their ability to fit almost any role in your network. You may have an MLS that spends most of its time routing, while others act pretty much as L2 switches. The default allocation of switch resources may not fit the role of the switch; by default, the resources are split up pretty much evenly between routing, switching, and security. Wouldn't it be great if we could allocate more system resources to routing if the MLS is primarily going to route? How about making a larger MAC address table possible for an MLS that's primarily going to switch?

Thanks to SDM, we can do just that on many Cisco switches. Some switches have default source allocations that can't be changed, but when they can be changed, SDM does that for us with ease! (This is not the Security Device Manager that you may have used and studied previously; this SDM is the Switching Database Manager.)

SDM uses templates to allocate system resources, and if you cringe when you hear the word "template", you may un-cringe – these templates are already created! Let's see the SDM templates available on my switch:

```
MLS_1(config)#sdm prefer ?
  Access              Access bias
  Default             Default bias
  dual-ipv4-and-ipv6  Support both IPv4 and IPv6
  routing             Unicast bias
  vlan                VLAN bias
```

When IOS Help says "bias", it means business! Here's a quick look at each template and its capabilities:

Access – If your MLS is running a whoooole lot of ACLs, this template can come in handy, as it will allocate resources to handle the maximum number of ACLs.

Default – That's the default template, and it treats all functions more or less equally

Dual-ipv4-and-ipv6 – Great for an MLS running dual stack (both IPv4 and v6 at the same time). This template doesn't support everything IPv6-wise, including IPv6 multicast, so do your homework before applying this template.

Routing – Enhances the environment for IPv4 unicast routing.

VLAN – Supports the CAM table's growth to contain the maximum number of unicast MAC addresses. Very important: This template disables hardware routing.

To see the currently loaded template and its allocation settings, run *show sdm prefer*.

```
MLS_1#show sdm prefer
   The current template is "desktop default" template.
   The selected template optimizes the resources in
   the switch to support this level of features for
   8 routed interfaces and 1024 VLANs.

   number of unicast mac addresses:                 6K
   number of IPv4 IGMP groups + multicast routes:   1K
   number of IPv4 unicast routes:                   8K
     number of directly-connected IPv4 hosts:       6K
     number of indirect IPv4 routes:                2K
   number of IPv4 policy based routing aces:        0
   number of IPv4/MAC qos aces:                     0.5K
   number of IPv4/MAC security aces:                1K
```

Let's load the VLAN template and see what happens.

```
MLS_1(config)#sdm prefer vlan
 Changes to the running SDM preferences have been stored, but cannot take
effect
```

```
until the next reload.
Use 'show sdm prefer' to see what SDM preference is currently active.
```

Well, the first thing that's going to happen is you and I being told we have to reload the switch for the template switch to take effect. There's no workaround for this one, we really do have to reload the switch! I'll do so now and run *show sdm prefer* after the reload.

```
MLS_1#show sdm prefer
   The current template is "desktop vlan" template.
   The selected template optimizes the resources in
   the switch to support this level of features for
   8 routed interfaces and 1024 VLANs.

   number of unicast mac addresses:              12K
   number of IPv4 IGMP groups + multicast routes: 1K
   number of IPv4 unicast routes:                 0
   number of IPv4 policy based routing aces:      0
   number of IPv4/MAC qos aces:                   0.5K
   number of IPv4/MAC security aces:              1K
```

Quite a difference! We now have twice the space for unicast mac addresses, but look at that tradeoff! There's no room for IPv4 unicast routes or PBR. Something to keep in mind when using the SDM vlan template!

Let's load the routing template and check the results.

```
MLS_1(config)#sdm prefer vlan
Changes to the running SDM preferences have been stored, but cannot take effect
until the next reload.
Use 'show sdm prefer' to see what SDM preference is currently active.
```

After the reload:

```
MLS_1#show sdm prefer
   The current template is "desktop routing" template.
   The selected template optimizes the resources in
   the switch to support this level of features for
   8 routed interfaces and 1024 VLANs.

   number of unicast mac addresses:              3K
   number of IPv4 IGMP groups + multicast routes: 1K
   number of IPv4 unicast routes:                 11K
     number of directly-connected IPv4 hosts:    3K
     number of indirect IPv4 routes:             8K
   number of IPv4 policy based routing aces:      0.5K
   number of IPv4/MAC qos aces:                   0.5K
   number of IPv4/MAC security aces:              1K
```

Additional resources are indeed reserved for IPv4 unicast and PBR, but we still have some room for MAC addresses. The SDM routing template doesn't disable switching, but the SDM vlan template does disable routing. Important stuff to keep in mind!

Before we move on, just for shiggles, here's the allocation when the access template is in use.

```
MLS_1#show sdm prefer
    The current template is "desktop access IPv4" template.
    The selected template optimizes the resources in
    the switch to support this level of features for
    8 routed interfaces and 1024 VLANs.

    number of unicast mac addresses:                    4K
    number of IPv4 IGMP groups + multicast routes:      1K
    number of IPv4 unicast routes:                      6K
      number of directly-connected IPv4 hosts:          4K
      number of indirect IPv4 routes:                   2K
    number of IPv4 policy based routing aces:           0.5K
    number of IPv4/MAC qos aces:                        0.5K
    number of IPv4/MAC security aces:                   2K
```

Just Some Reminders...

The Ethernet types and speeds we'll see in this course:

Ethernet: 10 Mbps. The original, but not the best.

FastEthernet: 100 Mbps. Can run in half- or full-duplex mode. Most Cisco switch ports we'll use in this course are FE ports.

Gig Ethernet: 1 Gbps (1000 Mbps). Also expressed as GbE. Wikipedia: "Half-duplex gigabit links connected through hubs are allowed by the specification, but the specification is not updated anymore and full-duplex usage with switches is used exclusively."

10 Gig Ethernet: 10 Gbps (10,000 Mbps). Does not support half-duplex links. Can be run on copper cables, but requires higher-grade cables (Cat 6a or Cat7).

Port Speed, Duplex, And Autonegotiation

In the real world, use autonegotiation on both ends of a connection and you're gold. With that in mind, let's discuss some things that can go wrong with autonegotiation, port speeds, and port duplex settings.

Here, ROUTER_3's Fast 0/0 interface is connected to 0/7 on MLS_1.

Router_3   MLS_1

With both interfaces enabled for autonegotiation, both devices will send *fast link pulses* to the other. The obvious question is: "Fast compared to what?" They're fast compared to normal link pulses (NLPs):

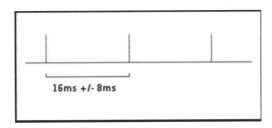

As expected, our FLPs give more pulses in the same amount of time. (Both drawings courtesy of Wikipedia; both are in the public domain.)

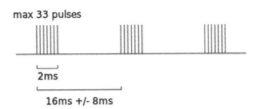

The FLP is basically a declaration of the capabilities of the sending device with regards to speed and duplex, allowing a decision as to speed and duplex that is as fast and efficient as possible without exceeding device capabilities.

The fundamental autonegotiation rules:

If both ports support half- and full-duplex, full-duplex is (thankfully) always preferred.

If both ports support different speeds, the highest common speed is preferred.

Now, back to the demo...

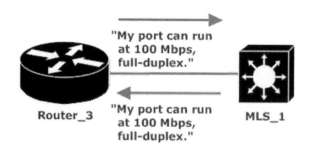

Not much to decide here, since the max capabilities are the same on both sides! Both involved ports end up running at FastEthernet speed, set to full-duplex. But what happens if MLS_1 is not running autonegotiation at all? Let's find out while hardcoding the speed and duplex settings on MLS_1.

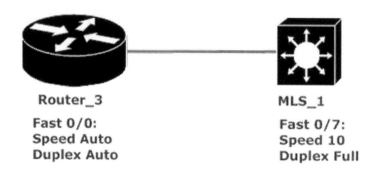

Router_3	MLS_1
Fast 0/0:	Fast 0/7:
Speed Auto	Speed 10
Duplex Auto	Duplex Full

```
MLS _ 1(config)#int fast 0/7
MLS _ 1(config-if)#speed ?
   10     Force 10 Mbps operation
   100    Force 100 Mbps operation
   Auto   Enable AUTO speed configuration

MLS _ 1(config-if)#speed 10
MLS _ 1(config-if)#duplex ?
   Auto   Enable AUTO duplex configuration
   Full   Force full duplex operation
   Half   Force half-duplex operation

MLS _ 1(config-if)#duplex full

ROUTER _ 3(config)#int fast 0/0
ROUTER _ 3(config-if)#speed auto
ROUTER _ 3(config-if)#duplex auto
```

With one endpoint running autonegotiation and the other end not, we end up with *parallel detection*. PD brings us some good news: The device running autonegotiation can detect the speed of the remote device and adjust its speed accordingly. ROUTER_3 detects the 10 Mbps speed on the remote endpoint and sets its own speed accordingly.

```
ROUTER_3#show int fast 0/0
FastEthernet0/0 is up, line protocol is up
   Hardware is Gt96k FE, address is 001f.ca96.2754 (bia 001f.ca96.2754)
   MTU 1500 bytes, BW 10000 Kbit/sec, DLY 1000 usec,
      reliability 255/255, txload 1/255, rxload 1/255
   Encapsulation ARPA, loopback not set
   Keepalive set (10 sec)
   Half-duplex, 10Mb/s, 100BaseTX/FX
```

Sadly, it's not all good with PD, as Router_3 will be unable to detect the remote endpoint's duplex setting. The router can't assume full-duplex on that remote endpoint, so it must set its own port to the dreaded half-duplex. (That's verified by the *show interface* output just above.)

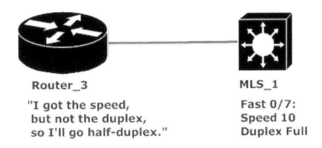

Router_3
"I got the speed,
but not the duplex,
so I'll go half-duplex."

MLS_1
Fast 0/7:
Speed 10
Duplex Full

Now we have a problem, and it's a problem that's not always easy to spot. The physical interfaces and line protocols are still up on both devices:

```
MLS_1#show int fast 0/7
FastEthernet0/7 is up, line protocol is up (connected)

ROUTER_3#show int fast 0/0
FastEthernet0/0 is up, line protocol is up
```

ROUTER_3 is running at half-duplex, so that interface will transmit *or* receive, but it will not do both at the same time. MLS_1 will go at data transmission with all guns blazing, since it's running at full-duplex. ROUTER_3 will see data coming in at the same time it's transmitting, and will think a data collision has occurred when in reality no such collision has.

In short, you end up with a real mess, and a totally unnecessary one at that.

These duplex mismatches can be tough to spot just by looking at the config, but our old pal CDP will let you know about 'em in a heartbeat:

```
*Apr 11: %CDP-4-DUPLEX_MISMATCH: duplex mismatch discovered on FastEthernet0/0
(not full duplex), with MLS_1 FastEthernet0/7 (full duplex).
```

That's about as self-explanatory as a console message can get!

Coming up next: The wonderful world of VLANs!

Chapter 2:

THE WHEN, WHERE, AND HOW OF VLANS

Even if you've just earned your CCNA, don't breeze through this section. VLANs are the core of your switching network, and they're going to be all over your SWITCH exam. We're in the exam room to score points, not give them away, and part of scoring points is mastering VLAN fundamentals.

Speaking of that, let's jump to the most fundamental of fundamentals by answering these questions: "Why don't we just use physical LANs? Why do we need virtual ones?"

One great use for VLANs is to limit the scope of our old pal, the *broadcast*. By default, a switch will take an incoming broadcast and send a copy of it out of every single port *except* the port that received the original broadcast. In the following example, the switch will forward a copy of the incoming broadcast to every other host. (For clarity, cabling is not shown.) Our hosts are all in the same broadcast domain, making this a *flat network topology*.

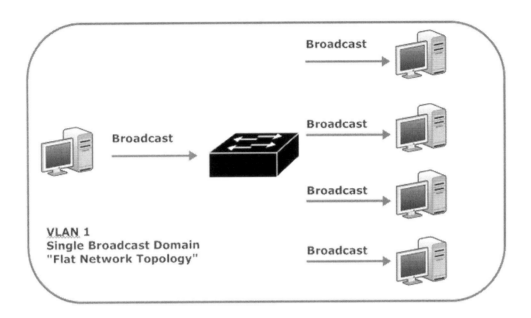

I pride myself on presenting as many real-world networking examples as possible in my books. Rest assured that this is *not* one of them. Broadcast propagation wouldn't be a huge deal in a 5-host network, but we don't run into many 5-host networks in the real world. On a switch with 24, 48, or 60+ ports, this *broadcast flooding* would have a negative impact on overall switch operation, and your available bandwidth would start to get sucked up by a bunch of unnecessary broadcasts. It's doubtful that every host connected to your switch actually *needs* the broadcast.

We limit the overall number of broadcasts by *limiting their scope*, a fancy way of saying "let's only send the broadcasts where they need to go rather than just sending them everywhere."

That's where VLANs come in. When you create VLANs, you're creating multiple, smaller broadcast domains, which in turn lowers the number of overall broadcasts. Broadcasts are forwarded only to hosts in the same VLAN as the original sender of the broadcast.

Cisco's best practice is to have one VLAN per IP subnet, and this is a best practice that works really well in real-world networking. Cisco also recommends that a VLAN doesn't reach beyond the distribution layer in its 3-layer switching model. (More on that in the design section of this course.)

The method used to determine a host's VLAN membership depends on the kind of VLAN you're using. In this course, we'll concentrate on *static VLANs*, and static VLAN membership is dependent on the port the host is connected to.

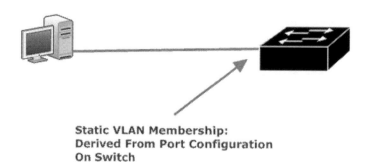

**Static VLAN Membership:
Derived From Port Configuration
On Switch**

With dynamic VLANs, the membership depends on the host's MAC address. The actual VLAN membership determination is still done by the switch.

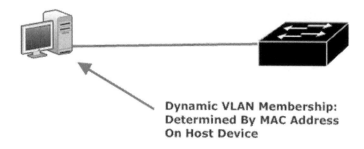

**Dynamic VLAN Membership:
Determined By MAC Address
On Host Device**

The terms "static" and "dynamic" refer to how the host is assigned VLAN membership, not to how the VLAN is actually created. Whether you're using static or dynamic VLANs, the host doesn't care about its VLAN membership. It's only important to the port to which the host is connected.

Let's take our first look at *show vlan*. The five VLANs shown are default VLANs and cannot be deleted. All 12 ports on this particular switch are in the default VLAN, VLAN 1.

```
SW1#show vlan
```

VLAN	Name	Status	Ports			
1	default	active	Fa0/1,	Fa0/2,	Fa0/3,	Fa0/4
			Fa0/5,	Fa0/6,	Fa0/7,	Fa0/8
			Fa0/9,	Fa0/10,	Fa0/11,	Fa0/12
1002	fddi-default	act/unsup				
1003	token-ring-default	act/unsup				
1004	fddinet-default	act/unsup				
1005	trnet-default	act/unsup				

VLAN	Type	SAID	MTU	Parent	RingNo	BridgeNo	Stp	BrdgMode	Trans1	Trans2
1	enet	100001	1500	-	-	-	-	-	0	0
1002	fddi	101002	1500	-	-	-	-	-	0	0
1003	tr	101003	1500	-	-	-	-	-	0	0

```
1004  fdnet 101004  1500   -        -        -        -        -        0       0
1005  trnet 101005  1500   -        -        -        ibm      -        0       0


Remote SPAN VLANs



Primary Secondary Type            Ports
------ --------- -----------------
```

You may never use VLANs 1002 – 1005 in real-world networking. They're legacy VLANs designed for use with FDDI and Token Ring. (Never say "old" in networking, always say "legacy".) Keep them in mind for the exam.

To be blunt, while this is an important command to know, it gives you a lot of info you really don't need to start troubleshooting or to verify your work. I prefer *show vlan brief.*

```
SW1#show vlan brief


VLAN Name                           Status      Ports
---  ------------------------------ ---------
1    default                        active      Fa0/1,  Fa0/2,  Fa0/3,  Fa0/4,
                                                Fa0/5,  Fa0/6,  Fa0/7,  Fa0/8,
                                                Fa0/9,  Fa0/10, Fa0/11, Fa0/12
1002 fddi-default                   act/unsup
1003 token-ring-default             act/unsup
1004 fddinet-default                act/unsup
1005 trnet-default                  act/unsup
```

This command shows you only the port memberships, which is all we need to get started. As your studies and career progress, you'll be surprised at how often a host-to-host communications issue comes down to a port being in a different VLAN than you thought it was!

I occasionally hear a network admin say "we don't use VLANs," and while that admin may not have *configured* VLANs, VLANs are always in use. Cisco switch ports are in VLAN 1 by default. Each VLAN is its own broadcast domain, and right now, all hosts are in one single broadcast domain. We know what that means – a broadcast that comes in on any of these ports will be forwarded out every other port on the switch.

Let's practice limiting the broadcast scope, using this four-host network for a lab. To meet Cisco's best practices, we'll use the single IP subnet 10.1.1.0 /24, and the host number will serve as the last octet in the host's IP address. The ping results will look different than they would on a PC, as I'm using Cisco routers as my hosts.

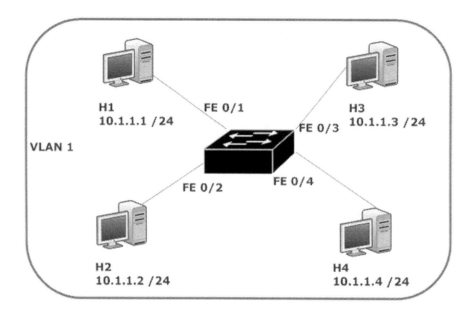

I've used *ping* to test connectivity in the lab, and every host can ping every other host. (Always test your basic connectivity before starting a lab.) I'll show the ping results here only from H1 to save a little space. I know you'll take my word on the others!

```
HOST1#ping 10.1.1.2
Type escape sequence to abort.
Sending 5, 100-byte ICMP Echos to 10.1.1.2, timeout is 2 seconds:
!!!!!
Success rate is 100 percent (5/5), round-trip min/avg/max = 4/6/8 ms

HOST1#ping 10.1.1.3
Type escape sequence to abort.
Sending 5, 100-byte ICMP Echos to 10.1.1.3, timeout is 2 seconds:
!!!!!
Success rate is 100 percent (5/5), round-trip min/avg/max = 4/4/8 ms

HOST1#ping 10.1.1.4
Type escape sequence to abort.
Sending 5, 100-byte ICMP Echos to 10.1.1.4, timeout is 2 seconds:
!!!!!
Success rate is 100 percent (5/5), round-trip min/avg/max = 4/10/32 ms
```

Right now, any broadcast sent by any host will be received by all of our other hosts. (I know I'm hitting you over the head with this. The pain will stop soon.) Let's configure our switch to allow broadcasts sent by H1 to be forwarded only to H2 by putting them in their own little broadcast domain – that is, their own VLAN!

We'll place those two hosts into the not-yet-existent VLAN 12 with *switchport mode access* and *switchport access vlan 12*. The first command puts the port into access mode, which means it can belong to one and only one VLAN. The second command defines VLAN membership.

```
SW1(config)#int fast 0/1
SW1(config-if)#switchport mode access
SW1(config-if)#switchport access ?
  vlan Set VLAN when interface is in access mode

SW1(config-if)#switchport access vlan ?
  <1-1005> VLAN ID of the VLAN when this port is in access mode
  dynamic When in access mode, this interfaces VLAN is controlled by VMPS

SW1(config-if)#switchport access vlan 12
% Access VLAN does not exist. Creating vlan 12
```

If you try to put ports into a non-existent VLAN, the switch will do it for you. This dynamic creation of a VLAN does NOT make this a dynamic VLAN. The terms "static" and "dynamic" refer to the method used to place hosts into a VLAN, not the method of VLAN creation.

To create a VLAN manually, use the *vlan* command. I'll create VLAN 20 on this switch, name it ACCOUNTING, and then we'll leave that VLAN alone for the duration of the lab. The *name* command is the only one of these options we need to concern ourselves with.

```
SW1(config)#vlan 20
SW1(config-vlan)#?
VLAN configuration commands:
  Are            Maximum number of All Route Explorer hops for this VLAN (or
                 zero if none specified)
  Backupcrf      Backup CRF mode of the VLAN
  bridge         Bridging characteristics of the VLAN
  exit           Apply changes, bump revision number, and exit mode
  media          Media type of the VLAN
  mtu            VLAN Maximum Transmission Unit
  name           Ascii name of the VLAN
  no             Negate a command or set its defaults
  parent         ID number of the Parent VLAN of FDDI or Token Ring type VLANs
  private-vlan   Configure a private VLAN
  remote-span    Configure as Remote SPAN VLAN
  ring           Ring number of FDDI or Token Ring type VLANs
  said           IEEE 802.10 SAID
  shutdown       Shutdown VLAN switching
  state          Operational state of the VLAN
  ste            Maximum number of Spanning Tree Explorer hops for this VLAN
                 (or zero if none specified)
  stp            Spanning tree characteristics of the VLAN
```

```
tb-vlan1       ID number of the first translational VLAN for this VLAN (or
               zero if none)
tb-vlan2       ID number of the second translational VLAN for this VLAN (or
               zero if none)
```

If you earned your CCNA with me, you know what I'm going to say. *Trust your config, but verify it!*

```
SW1#show vlan brief

VLAN Name                             Status     Ports
---- ----------------------------     --------
1    default                          active     Fa0/3,   Fa0/4,   Fa0/5,   Fa0/6
                                                 Fa0/7,   Fa0/8,   Fa0/9,   Fa0/10
                                                 Fa0/11,  Fa0/12
12   VLAN0012                         active     Fa0/1,   Fa0/2
20   ACCOUNTING                       active
1002 fddi-default                     act/unsup
1003 token-ring-default               act/unsup
1004 fddinet-default                  act/unsup
1005 trnet-default                    act/unsup
```

Bingo! VLAN 20 sits empty, and VLAN 12 contains fast 0/1 and 0/2. I'll rename VLAN 12 "SUCCESS", and then we'll move on.

```
SW1(config)#vlan 12
SW1(config-vlan)#name SUCCESS

SW1#show vlan brief

VLAN Name                             Status     Ports
---- ----------------------------     --------
1    default                          active     Fa0/3,   Fa0/4,   Fa0/5,   Fa0/6
                                                 Fa0/7,   Fa0/8,   Fa0/9,   Fa0/10
                                                 Fa0/11,  Fa0/12
12   SUCCESS                          active     Fa0/1,   Fa0/2
20   ACCOUNTING                       active
1002 fddi-default                     act/unsup
1003 token-ring-default               act/unsup
1004 fddinet-default                  act/unsup
1005 trnet-default                    act/unsup
```

Congratulations! Assuming all hosts are sending roughly the same number of broadcasts, you just cut broadcast traffic in your network by 66%, and all is well!

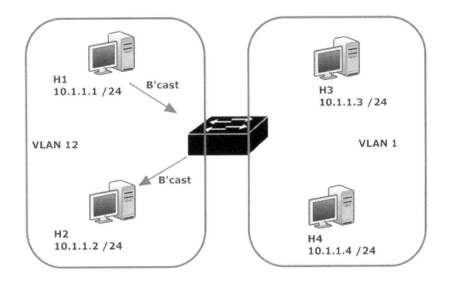

Or... IS it?

Let's ping the network from H1. For brevity's sake, for the rest of this section I'll show only the ping and ping result.

```
HOST1#ping 10.1.1.2
!!!!!

HOST1#ping 10.1.1.3
.....

HOST1#ping 10.1.1.4
.....
```

Sometimes, in networking, a solution leads to another issue.

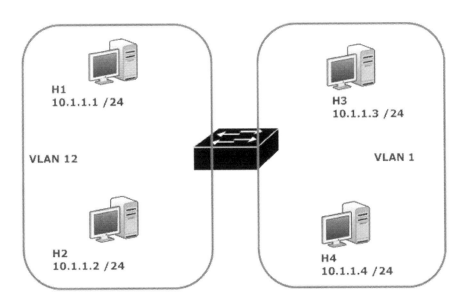

The good news is that broadcasts from H1 aren't going to H3 or H4. The bad news is that *no* traffic is going from H1 to H3 or H4, even though they're in the same IP subnet.

Inter-VLAN traffic requires the routing layer of the OSI model to get involved. If this is a Multi-Layer Switch (MLS), we could enable IP routing on the switch and then work something out. If this is strictly a Layer 2 switch, we'll need to get a router involved. We'll look at using an MLS in this situation later in the course. For now, keep in mind that inter-VLAN traffic requires Layer 3 involvement.

Before we hit dynamic VLANs, let me give you a real-world networking tip that's saved my hash on more than one occasion. When you have one or two VLANs, the output of *show vlan brief* is easy to read. Once you get more VLANs, and ports spread out among them, it's easy to misread, as in the following:

```
SW1#show vlan brief

VLAN Name                             Status    Ports
---- -------------------------------- --------- 
1    default                          active    Fa0/3,  Fa0/4,  Fa0/5,  Fa0/7
                                                Fa0/11, Fa0/12
10   KANSASCITY                       active    Fa0/6
12   SUCCESS                          active    Fa0/1,  Fa0/2
20   OREGON                           active    Fa0/9
35   GREENBAY                         active    Fa0/10
42   OHIOSTATE                        active    Fa0/8
1002 fddi-default                     act/unsup
1003 token-ring-default               act/unsup
1004 fddinet-default                  act/unsup
1005 trnet-default                    act/unsup
```

It's *really* easy for the eye to skip up a line as you read this output. If you read fast0/10 as belonging to VLAN 42, that's just going to make your troubleshooting harder! To see the ports in one particular VLAN, use *show vlan id* followed by the VLAN number.

```
SW1#show vlan id 35

VLAN Name                             Status    Ports
---- -------------------------------- --------- 
35   GREENBAY                         active    Fa0/10
```

Dynamic VLANs

The actual configuration of dynamic VLANs is *way* out of the CCNP SWITCH exam scope, but you should be familiar with the basics of the *VLAN Membership Policy Server* (VMPS), the core of dynamic VLAN configuration.

One of the painful things about static VLANs becomes apparent when you need to move a host from one port to another. Let's say a problem has arisen with 0/4 on our current switch, and we need to move that host to 0/5. We'd need to manually configure 0/5 for that host, and as good network admins, we'd keep up with our network housekeeping and remove the config from 0/4. (I'll leave 0/4 as an access port.)

```
SW1(config)#int fast 0/4
SW1(config-if)#no switchport access vlan 12
SW1(config-if)#int fast 0/5
SW1(config-if)#switchport mode access
SW1(config-if)#switchport access vlan 12
```

You're likely thinking "Hey Chris, what's the big deal?" I admit that it's not a ton of work, but the more manual configuration you do, the larger the chance of a simple **mis**configuration, especially when one of your company's VPs is yelling at you while you write the config. All you have to do is enter "21" for "12" on that 0/5 config and you have more trouble than you started with.

Wouldn't it be great if you could just detach the cable from 0/4 and plug it into 0/5, and the VLAN membership adjusted automatically? That's what VMPS brings to the table. VMPS uses the source MAC address of incoming frames to determine the VLAN membership of the port receiving those frames, so moving the cable is all we have to do.

When the switch sees frames coming in on 0/5 with a source MAC address that was in its MAC address table as belonging to 0/4...

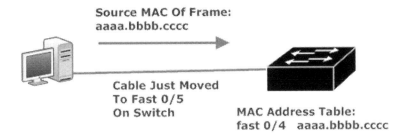

...the switch will realize what's happened, and will then dynamically change the VLAN membership of 0/5 and update its MAC address table.

Some VMPS notes:

A somewhat odd default of VMPS is that PortFast is automatically enabled for a port when it receives its VLAN membership dynamically. It can then be disabled if you like.

A quick reminder: PortFast allows a port to go straight from blocking mode to forwarding mode. Using this can be a big help with host DHCP issues.

The VMPS Server must be configured before you can dynamically assign any VLAN membership. (Yeah, I know, "duh".)

Port security and dynamic VLAN memberships don't play well together. Actually, they don't play together at all. You have to disable port security on a port in order for that port to get a dynamic VLAN assignment.

Trunk ports can't receive a dynamic VLAN assignment, since by definition trunk ports already belong to all VLANs.

A Word Or Two On Voice VLANs

Cisco IP Phones have three ports. One will be connected to a switch, another to a PC, and the third is an internal connection to an Application-Specific Integrated Circuit (ASIC).

With Cisco IP phones, there is no special config needed on the PC. As far as the PC is concerned, it is attached directly to that switch. As far as the direct connection to the IP phone is concerned, the PC is unaware and it doesn't care!

The key to keeping end users happy with voice-based traffic is to deliver it without *jitter*. Jitter is defined by Wikipedia as "the deviation from true periodicity of a presumed signal in electronics and telecommunications, often in relation to a reference clock source." Chris Bryant defines jitter as "that really annoying continual interruption in a voice stream that makes you want to tear your own eardrums out."

Whichever definition you use, it's *really* annoying.

The link between the switch and the IP phone can be configured as either an 802.1q trunk or access link. Using a trunk gives us the advantage of creating a voice VLAN (VVID), a VLAN dedicated to carrying voice traffic. The VVID allows the highest Quality of Service available, giving the delay-sensitive voice traffic priority over normal, non-voice data streams.

Can Be Trunk
Or Access Link

Using an access link results in voice and data traffic being carried in the same VLAN, which can lead to time-related delivery issues with the voice traffic. The human ear will only accept 140 – 150 milliseconds of delay before it notices a problem with voice delivery. Should the voice traffic start to be delayed, your end users begin to get annoyed, and your support center phones start to ring!

We have four options for the switch-to-phone link:

Use an access link

Use a trunk and use 802.1p

Use a trunk without tagging voice traffic

Use a trunk and specify a VVID

The question "*Who's The Boss?*" has stumped the great scholars and live-in housekeepers of eras past and present, but in this situation the boss is the switch, which tells the phone which of those four options will be used.

"Here's what we're
gonna do."

The interface is using VLAN 100 for normal data, and the native VLAN is unchanged from the default, verified by this partial output of *show interface switchport*.

```
SW1#show int fast 0/1 switchport
Access Mode VLAN: 100 (VLAN0100)
Trunking Native Mode VLAN: 1 (default)
Administrative Native VLAN tagging: enabled
Voice VLAN: none
```

The PVID shown in the following options is the port VLAN ID, the number identifying the non-voice VLAN.

```
SW1(config)#int fast 0/1
SW1(config-if)#switchport voice vlan ?
```

```
<1-4094> Vlan for voice traffic
dot1p    Priority tagged on PVID
none     Don't tell telephone about voice vlan
untaggedUntagged on PVID
```

The *<1 – 4094>* option creates a voice VLAN and a dot1q trunk between the switch and IP phone. As with data VLANs, if the VVID has not been previously created, the switch will create it for you.

```
SW1(config-if)#switchport voice vlan 10
% Voice VLAN does not exist. Creating vlan 10
```

Verify with *show interface switchport*. The output of this command is huge, so I'll show only the VLAN information here.

```
SW1#show int fast 0/1 switchport
Access Mode VLAN: 100 (VLAN0100)
Trunking Native Mode VLAN: 1 (default)
Administrative Native VLAN tagging: enabled
Voice VLAN: 10 (VLAN0010)
```

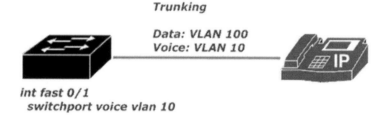

```
int fast 0/1
switchport voice vlan 10
```

Using *dot1p* results in the IP phone granting voice traffic high priority, and voice traffic will be sent through VLAN 0.

```
SW1(config-if)#switchport voice vlan dot1p

SW1#show int fast 0/1 switchport
Access Mode VLAN: 100 (VLAN0100)
Trunking Native Mode VLAN: 1 (default)
Administrative Native VLAN tagging: enabled
Voice VLAN: dot1p
```

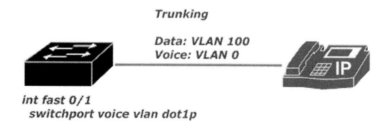

```
int fast 0/1
switchport voice vlan dot1p
```

Using *untagged* results in voice packets being placed into the native VLAN.

```
SW1(config-if)#switchport voice vlan untagged

SW1#show int fast 0/1 switchport
Access Mode VLAN: 100 (VLAN0100)
Trunking Native Mode VLAN: 1 (default)
Administrative Native VLAN tagging: enabled
Voice VLAN: untagged
```

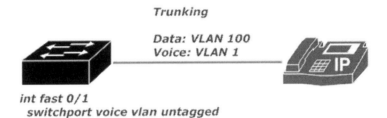

Trunking

Data: VLAN 100
Voice: VLAN 1

int fast 0/1
switchport voice vlan untagged

Finally, *none* sets the port back to its default, where a trunk is not used and the voice and non-voice traffic use the access VLAN.

```
SW1(config-if)#switchport voice vlan none

SW1#show int fast 0/1 switchport
Access Mode VLAN: 100 (VLAN0100)
Trunking Native Mode VLAN: 1 (default)
Administrative Native VLAN tagging: enabled
Voice VLAN: untagged
```

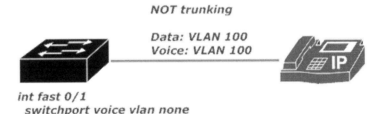

NOT trunking

Data: VLAN 100
Voice: VLAN 100

int fast 0/1
switchport voice vlan none

A quick Portfast note to end our VVID discussion: Portfast is automatically enabled on a port when a voice VLAN is created, verified by *show config* and *show spanning interface portfast*. Here's that info for 0/2, which is using VLAN 100 for data and VLAN 11 for voice. I didn't manually enable portfast, but there it is!

```
interface FastEthernet0/2
    switchport access vlan 100
    switchport mode access
    switchport voice vlan 11
    spanning-tree portfast
```

```
SW1#show spanning int fast 0/2 portfast
VLAN0011          enabled
VLAN0100          enabled
```

You're unlikely to find all ports in a given VLAN to be on the same switch. With that in mind, let's head to the next section!

Chapter 3:

TRUNKING

It's nice and neat to have all hosts in a VLAN connected to a single switch. It's also unlikely. In the next example, we have hosts in VLANs 1 and 12 connected to separate switches. The switches are connected via two crossover cables. Trunks do not require you to use the identically numbered port on each switch (port 0/11 on each switch, for example), but in labs it's a great organizational tool.

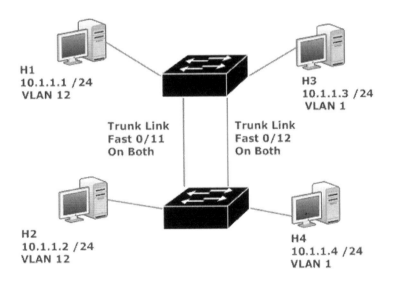

For frames to flow flawlessly and freely between two switches, a *trunk* must be established. Sometimes all it takes to create a trunk is physically connecting the switches. On occasion, it takes a little fine-tuning to get the job done. It's a safe bet that your CCNP SWITCH exam will test you on both scenarios!

A trunk is a member of all VLANs by default, allowing traffic for any and all VLANs to cross the trunk (good idea). That includes broadcast traffic (not-so-good idea).

Theoretically, you need a crossover cable for a switch-to-switch connection, and that's what I'm using here. Some Cisco switch models allow you to use a straight-through cable for trunking. In any case, verify with *show interface trunk*.

```
SW2#show int trunk

Port            Mode            Encapsulation  Status        Native vlan
Fa0/11          auto            n-802.1q       trunking      12
Fa0/12          auto            n-802.1q       trunking      12


Port            Vlans allowed on trunk
Fa0/11          1-4094
Fa0/12          1-4094


Port            Vlans allowed and active in management domain
Fa0/11          1,12
Fa0/12          1,12


Port            Vlans in spanning tree forwarding state and not pruned
Fa0/11          none
Fa0/12          1,12
```

From left to right, that command shows us...

> The ports attempting to trunk (if none are shown, none are trunking)

> The trunking mode each port is using

> The encapsulation type

> The status of the trunk (either "trunking" or "not trunking")

> The "native vlan"

Know where you will *not* find your trunk ports?

```
SW2#show vlan brief

VLAN Name                             Status    Ports
---- -------------------------------- --------- -----------
1    default                          active    Fa0/1,  Fa0/2,  Fa0/3,  Fa0/4
                                                Fa0/5,  Fa0/6,  Fa0/7,  Fa0/8
                                                Fa0/9, Fa0/10, Fa0/13, Fa0/14,
                                                Fa0/15, Fa0/16, Fa0/17, Fa0/18,
                                                Fa0/19,   Fa0/20,    Fa0/21,
                                                Fa0/22, Fa0/23, Fa0/24, Gi0/1,
                                                Gi0/2
1002 fddi-default                     act/unsup
1003 token-ring-default               act/unsup
```

```
1004   fddinet-default                      act/unsup
1005   trnet-default                        act/unsup
```

Our pal *show vlan brief* will not show ports that are trunking, since trunk ports are members of *all* VLANs. If you're looking for a specific port's VLAN membership and you don't see it here, check to see if the port is trunking.

Our trunk is up and running, so let's make sure we can ping between hosts in the same VLAN. We'll start by pinging H2 from H1 and then H4 from H3.

HOST1#ping 10.1.1.2

!!!!!

Success rate is 100 percent (5/5), round-trip min/avg/max = 4/5/8 ms

HOST3#ping 10.1.1.4

!!!!!

Success rate is 100 percent (5/5), round-trip min/avg/max = 4/6/8 ms

Aaaaaand it's *good*!

Trunking is a beautiful thing, but as with everything good in networking, there's a little overhead involved. The overhead here involves *frame tagging*, where the frame has a VLAN ID attached by the sending switch. In turn, that VLAN ID is read by the receiving switch, and that switch knows that the VLAN ID indicates the destination VLAN.

The amount of overhead involved depends on whether ISL or IEEE 802.1q ("dot1q") is used as the trunking protocol. While most Cisco switches no longer support ISL, we need to be *very* clear on the features and drawbacks of each for our CCNP SWITCH exam.

The similarities end pretty quickly. Both of these trunking protocols are point-to-point protocols, with a switch at each endpoint.

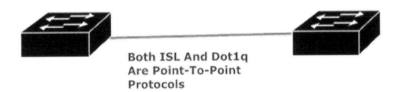

Both ISL And Dot1q
Are Point-To-Point
Protocols

So much for the similarities! Now, for the differences...

ISL is Cisco-proprietary; only Cisco switches understand ISL. You can't use ISL in a multi-vendor switching environment.

ISL will encapsulate *every frame* going across the trunk, placing both a header and trailer onto the frame ("double tagging"). That doesn't sound like a big deal, but the cumulative effect of adding that overhead to every frame adds up to a lot of extra effort on the part of both the sender and the receiver, which has to remove the encapsulation.

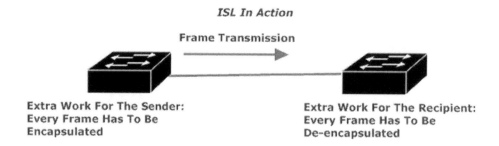

Everything we do on a Cisco switch has a cost in terms of time and effort, and that includes encapsulation and de-encapsulation. Double tagging means double the workload on the switches!

There's even *more* to dislike regarding ISL. ISL doesn't understand the concept of the native VLAN (the default VLAN). We'll see why that's so important in just a moment.

ISL adds a total overhead of 30 bytes. 26 bytes of that is in the header, which includes the VLAN ID. The 4-byte trailer contains a Cyclic Redundancy Check (CRC) value. The CRC is a frame validity scheme that checks the frame's integrity.

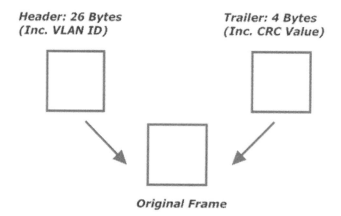

Using IEEE 802.1Q ("dot1q") results in much less overhead on our frames. Dot1q places only a 4-byte header on each frame, and if the frame is destined for the native VLAN, even *that* header isn't put on the frame! When the receiving switch sees a frame with no VLAN ID, that switch assumes the native VLAN *is* the destination VLAN. This is an excellent reason to make sure your switches agree on the native VLAN.

A few more dot1q tidbits for you:

> Dot1q embeds the tagging information into the frame itself. For this reason, you'll sometimes hear dot1q referred to as "internal tagging".

Dot1q is the industry-standard trunking protocol, making it suitable for use in a multi-vendor switching environment.

Dot1q adds only one tag, so it's often referred to as "single tagging".

Both ISL and dot1q bring a 4-byte addition to a frame, but they're in different locations:

ISL's 4-byte trailer is just that – a trailer.

Dot1q's 4-byte addition is in the form of a tag inserted into the frame.

No need to tag frames traversing access ports. An access port belongs to one and only one VLAN, so there's no need for any VLAN ID info.

Now, about that native VLAN...

Verifying And Changing The Native VLAN

When dot1q is our trunking protocol, as it likely is, frames destined for the native VLAN are not tagged. That saves a little bit of overhead per frame, which in turn saves a great deal of *overall* overhead. Those little overhead savings add up!

If there is a particular VLAN responsible for a majority of traffic, we might want to change the native VLAN. (VLANs 1002 – 1005 not shown in following lab.)

```
SW1#show vlan brief

VLAN Name                             Status     Ports
---- -------------------------------- ---------  ---------
1    default                          active
12   ACCOUNTING                       active     Fa0/1,  Fa0/2,  Fa0/3,  Fa0/4,
                                                 Fa0/5,  Fa0/6,  Fa0/7,  Fa0/8,
                                                 Fa0/9,  Fa0/10


SW2#show vlan brief

VLAN Name                             Status     Ports
---- -------------------------------- ---------  ---------
1    default                          active     Fa0/22, Fa0/23, Fa0/24, Gi0/1,
                                                 Gi0/2
12   ACCOUNTING                       active     Fa0/1,  Fa0/2,  Fa0/3,  Fa0/4,
                                                 Fa0/5,  Fa0/6,  Fa0/7,  Fa0/8,
                                                 Fa0/9,  Fa0/10, Fa0/13, Fa0/14,
                                                 Fa0/15, Fa0/16, Fa0/17, Fa0/18,
                                                 Fa0/19, Fa0/20, Fa0/21
```

Assume an analysis of traffic going over the trunk has revealed that most frames are destined for VLAN 12. It would make sense to make that our native VLAN. We'll use *switchport trunk native vlan* on both switches to make that happen.

I'll use IOS Help to illustrate the options (or lack of) with this command, followed by the error message you can expect to see after you change the native VLAN on one switch and before you change it on the other switch. I'll use the always-handy *interface range* config option to change the native VLAN on both trunking ports on SW1 at one time.

```
SW1(config)#int range fast 0/11 - 12
SW1(config-if-range)#switchport trunk ?
  allowed   Set allowed VLAN characteristics when interface is in trunking mode
  native    Set trunking native characteristics when interface is in trunking
            mode
  pruning   Set pruning VLAN characteristics when interface is in trunking mode

SW1(config-if-range)#switchport trunk native ?
  vlan      Set native VLAN when interface is in trunking mode

SW1(config-if-range)#switchport trunk native VLAN ?
  <1-1005>  VLAN ID of the native VLAN when this port is in trunking mode

SW1(config-if-range)#switchport trunk native VLAN 12 ?
  <cr>

SW1(config-if-range)#switchport trunk native VLAN 12
```

After completing that config, I received this stack of messages on SW1:

```
 08:14:55: %SPANTREE-2-RECV_PVID_ERR: Received BPDU with inconsistent peer
vlan id 1 on FastEthernet0/12 VLAN12.
 08:14:55: %SPANTREE-2-BLOCK_PVID_PEER: Blocking FastEthernet0/12 on VLAN0001.
Inconsistent peer vlan.
 08:14:55: %SPANTREE-2-BLOCK_PVID_LOCAL: Blocking FastEthernet0/12 on VLAN0012.
Inconsistent local vlan.
 08:14:55: %SPANTREE-2-RECV_PVID_ERR: Received BPDU with inconsistent peer
vlan id 1 on FastEthernet0/11 VLAN12.
 08:14:55: %SPANTREE-2-BLOCK_PVID_PEER: Blocking FastEthernet0/11 on VLAN000
 SW1#1. Inconsistent peer vlan.
 08:14:55: %SPANTREE-2-BLOCK_PVID_LOCAL: Blocking FastEthernet0/11 on VLAN0012.
Inconsistent local vlan.
```

It can panic even the calmest network admin when six error messages come up at once, along with all the talk of blocking ports! No worries, just finish your config and all will be well. I'll finish the config here and then hop back to SW1.

```
SW2(config)#int range fast 0/11 - 12
SW2(config-if-range)#switchport trunk native vlan 12

SW1#
08:15:26: %SPANTREE-2-UNBLOCK_CONSIST_PORT: Unblocking FastEthernet0/12 on
VLAN0001. Port consistency restored.
08:15:26: %SPANTREE-2-UNBLOCK_CONSIST_PORT: Unblocking FastEthernet0/12 on
VLAN0012. Port consistency restored.
08:15:26: %SPANTREE-2-UNBLOCK_CONSIST_PORT: Unblocking FastEthernet0/11 on
VLAN0001. Port consistency restored.
08:15:26: %SPANTREE-2-UNBLOCK_CONSIST_PORT: Unblocking FastEthernet0/11 on
VLAN0 012. Port consistency restored.
```

All looks well, but verify with *show interface trunk*.

```
SW1#show int trunk

Port        Mode        Encapsulation   Status      Native vlan
Fa0/11      desirable   802.1q          trunking    12
Fa0/12      desirable   802.1q          trunking    12

SW2#show int trunk

Port        Mode        Encapsulation   Status      Native vlan
Fa0/11      auto        n-802.1q        trunking    12
Fa0/12      auto        n-802.1q        trunking    12
```

Should Trunking Negotiate?

For this section, I've erased the previous switch configs and reloaded both switches, so they're now both running at their defaults. We'll again concentrate on the top of the output of *show interface trunk*, shown here on both switches.

```
SW1#show int trunk

Port        Mode        Encapsulation   Status      Native vlan
Fa0/11      desirable   802.1q          trunking    1
Fa0/12      desirable   802.1q          trunking    1

SW2#show int trunk

Port        Mode        Encapsulation   Status      Native vlan
Fa0/11      auto        n-802.1q        trunking    1
Fa0/12      auto        n-802.1q        trunking    1
```

Note the default trunk modes are different. "Desirable" used to be the default for all Cisco switches, but that's no longer the case. Here's a review of the trunking modes:

Trunk mode is unconditional trunking.

Dynamic desirable (shown as "desirable") means that the port is actively attempting to form a trunk with the port at the remote end of the point-to-point connection. If the remote port is running *trunk, desirable,* or *auto* mode, a trunk will form.

Dynamic auto (shown as "auto") is the wallflower of trunking modes. A port in auto mode will not initiate a trunk, but if the remote port initiates trunking, the auto port will accept that. In other words, the remote port has to ask a port in auto mode to trunk.

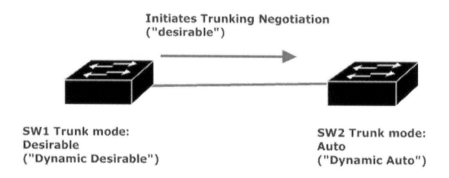

Did you notice the *n-* in front of the encapsulation type on SW2? That means the encapsulation type was negotiated rather than manually configured. Oddly enough, SW1 doesn't show the encap type as negotiated. Here's why...

If your switch is capable of running both ISL and dot1q, as SW2 is, you can configure the encap type with *switchport trunk encapsulation*. If the encap type is configured and you want the port to negotiate instead, use this command with the *negotiate* option. I'm not going to change the setting here – I just want to show you the options on this particular switch, which can run either ISL or dot1q.

```
SW2(config)#int fast 0/11
SW2(config-if)#switchport trunk encapsulation ?
  dot1q      Interface uses only 802.1q trunking encapsulation when trunking
  isl        Interface uses only ISL trunking encapsulation when trunking
  negotiate  Device will negotiate trunking encapsulation with peer on
             interface
```

That's all fine, but what does that have to do with the "n-" not being on SW1?

Some Cisco switches only support dot1q, including 2950 switches. In that case, the IOS will not recognize this command, as shown on this Cisco 2950. The *encapsulation* option won't even be available!

```
SW1(config-if)#switchport trunk    encapsulation
                                        ^
% Invalid input detected at '^' marker.

SW1(config-if)#switchport trunk ?
  allowed   Set allowed VLAN characteristics when interface is in trunking
            mode
  native    Set trunking native characteristics when interface is in trunking
            mode
  pruning   Set pruning VLAN characteristics when interface is in trunking
            mode
```

To DTP Or Not To DTP

The *Dynamic Trunking Protocol* (DTP) handles the actual trunk negotiation workload. When this Cisco-proprietary point-to-point protocol is in action, it attempts to negotiate a trunk with the remote port. As with everything in networking, DTP comes with a cost. A port running DTP will send DTP frames out every 30 seconds.

When a port is configured as an unconditional trunk port, there's no need for that same port to send DTP frames. Also, if there's a device on the other end of the p-t-p connection that literally can't trunk (a firewall, for example), why have the DTP overhead?

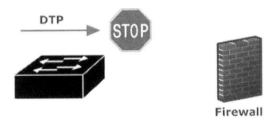

Firewall

Leaving DTP running on ports that aren't actually trunking is a BIG security risk. Leaving DTP on such ports makes it easier for an intruder to introduce a rogue switch to our network. (A rogue switch looks like a legit part of the network, but it's under the intruder's control, nor ours.) It's generally recommended that all ports have DTP disabled, and trunking mode be set to unconditional trunking.

We'll do just that in our next lab, starting with SW1. We'll disable DTP at the interface level with switchport nonegotiate. If the ports are not in unconditional trunking mode, they must be configured as such before using switchport nonegotiate, as the switch is kind enough to tell us!

```
SW1(config)#interface range fast 0/11 - 12
SW1(config-if-range)#switchport nonegotiate
Command rejected: Conflict between 'nonegotiate' and 'dynamic' status.
```

```
Command rejected: Conflict between 'nonegotiate' and 'dynamic' status.
SW1(config-if-range)#switchport mode trunk
SW1(config-if-range)#switchport nonegotiate
```

You'll get slightly different messages from the IOS in this situation depending on the switch model and IOS version. We had the same command rejected twice since that's how many ports we had in our interface range. We had no issue moving the interfaces from desirable to trunk mode, not with disabling DTP.

Verify DTP settings with *show interface switchport*. I highly recommend that you use the pipe option to skip to the interface you want, because this is one verbose command when left on its own! There's some handy info in this output, and we're most interested in the "Negotiation Of Trunking" setting, which is now off.

```
SW1#show interface switchport | begin Fa0/11
Name: Fa0/11
Switchport: Enabled
Administrative Mode: trunk
Operational Mode: trunk
Administrative Trunking Encapsulation: dot1q
Operational Trunking Encapsulation: dot1q
Negotiation of Trunking: Off
Access Mode VLAN: 1 (default)
Trunking Native Mode VLAN: 12 (VLAN0012)

SW1#show interface switchport | begin Fa0/12
Name: Fa0/12
Switchport: Enabled
Administrative Mode: trunk
Operational Mode: trunk
Administrative Trunking Encapsulation: dot1q
Operational Trunking Encapsulation: dot1q
Negotiation of Trunking: Off
Access Mode VLAN: 1 (default)
Trunking Native Mode VLAN: 1 (default)
```

While we're here, let's verify the trunks on SW1.

```
SW1#show int trunk

Port        Mode        Encapsulation  Status      Native vlan
Fa0/11      on          802.1q         trunking    1
Fa0/12      on          802.1q         trunking    1
```

The mode has changed to "on", indicating that the port is in unconditional trunking mode. Let's head to SW2 and repeat the process.

```
SW2(config)#int range fast 0/11 - 12
SW2(config-if-range)#switchport mode trunk
Command rejected: An interface whose trunk encapsulation is "Auto" cannot be
configured to "trunk" mode.
% Range command terminated because it failed on FastEthernet0/11
SW2(config-if-range)#
```

This particular switch IOS rejected the command once and then terminated the *range* command. No big deal, but I just want to point out why we only received one rejection when two ports are in the range.

There's a good reason you can't go straight from *auto* to *trunk* mode. As we saw earlier, SW2 is capable of both ISL and dot1q encapsulation. We need to define which encapsulation protocol the port is going to use, and then we can go from *auto* to *trunk*.

```
SW2(config-if-range)#switchport trunk encapsulation ?
  dot1q      Interface uses only 802.1q trunking encapsulation when trunking
  isl        Interface uses only ISL trunking encapsulation when trunking
  negotiate  Device will negotiate trunking encapsulation with peer on
             interface

SW2(config-if-range)#switchport trunk encapsulation dot1q
SW2(config-if-range)#switchport mode trunk
SW2(config-if-range)#switchport nonegotiate
```

Verify the trunk mode with *show interface trunk* and then verify DTP has been disabled with *show interface switchport*. Port 0/11 no longer has the "n-" in front of the encap type, since negotiation is no longer involved. The mode for 0/11 is now "on", which indicates that the port is unconditionally trunking.

```
SW2#show int trunk

Port        Mode        Encapsulation  Status      Native vlan
Fa0/11      on          802.1q         trunking    1
Fa0/12      on          802.1q         trunking    1

SW2#show interface switchport | begin Fa0/11
Name: Fa0/11
Switchport: Enabled
Administrative Mode: trunk
Operational Mode: trunk
Administrative Trunking Encapsulation: dot1q
Operational Trunking Encapsulation: dot1q
Negotiation of Trunking: Off
```

```
Name: Fa0/12
Switchport: Enabled
Administrative Mode: trunk
Operational Mode: trunk
Administrative Trunking Encapsulation: dot1q
Operational Trunking Encapsulation: dot1q
Negotiation of Trunking: Off
```

There's an oddity in the *switchport mode* options:

```
SW2(config-if)#switchport mode ?
  access       Set trunking mode to ACCESS unconditionally
  dot1q-tunnel set trunking mode to TUNNEL unconditionally
  dynamic      Set trunking mode to dynamically negotiate access or trunk
               mode
  private-vlan Set private-vlan mode
  trunk        Set trunking mode to TRUNK unconditionally
```

We have an option for "off", but not for "on". Setting a port to access mode turns trunking off. When I change 0/11's mode to access, the trunk is immediately lost.

```
SW2(config)#int fast 0/11
SW2(config-if)#switchport mode access

SW2#show int trunk

Port        Mode          Encapsulation  Status        Native vlan
Fa0/12      trunk         802.1q         trunking      1
```

To see trunk settings for a particular port, even one that isn't showing up in *show interface trunk*, run *show interface (interface type and number) trunk*. That's where you'll see the trunk mode actually set to *off*.

```
SW2#show interface fast 0/11 trunk

Port        Mode          Encapsulation  Status        Native vlan
Fa0/11      off           802.1q         not-trunking  12
```

Filtering The VLANs Allowed To Use The Trunk

For our next lab, I've erased the config on both switches and set them back to their default settings. After a reload, here's the full output of *show interface trunk* on SW2.

```
SW2#show int trunk

Port          Mode              Encapsulation   Status        Native vlan
Fa0/11        auto              n-802.1q        trunking      1
Fa0/12        auto              n-802.1q        trunking      1


Port          Vlans allowed on trunk
Fa0/11        1-4094
Fa0/12        1-4094


Port          Vlans allowed and active in management domain
Fa0/11        1,12
Fa0/12        1,12


Port          Vlans in spanning tree forwarding state and not pruned
Fa0/11        none
Fa0/12        1,12
```

When I first saw "VLANs allowed on trunk", I immediately wondered why you would *want* to disable some VLANs on a trunk. Here's one great reason:

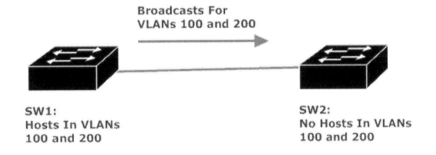

The broadcast rears its ugly head yet again! There are no hosts on SW2 in VLAN 100 or 200, but since trunk ports belong to all VLANs, broadcast traffic for all VLANs will be sent from SW1 to SW2 (and vice versa). We can eliminate unnecessary broadcasts by not allowing traffic for VLANs 100 and 200 to go from SW1 to SW2.

We filter the list of VLANs allowed to send traffic across the trunk with *switchport trunk allowed*. The command and the options in all their splendor:

```
SW1(config-if)#switchport trunk allowed vlan ?
  WORD    VLAN IDs of the allowed VLANs when this port is in trunking mode
  add     add VLANs to the current list
  all     all VLANs
  except  all VLANs except the following
  none    no VLANs
  remove  remove VLANs from the current list
```

The *except* option is excellent when you need to exclude just one or a few VLANs. I'll use it here to exclude VLANs 100 and 200 on both 0/11 and 0/12.

```
SW1(config)#interface range fast 0/11 - 12
SW1(config-if-range)#switchport trunk allowed vlan except 100,200
```

Verify with *show interface trunk*. As expected, VLANs 100 and 200 are no longer allowed on the trunk.

```
SW1#show int trunk

Port          Mode            Encapsulation  Status        Native vlan
Fa0/11        auto            n-802.1q       trunking      1
Fa0/12        auto            n-802.1q       trunking      1


Port          Vlans allowed on trunk
Fa0/11        1-99,101-199,201-4094
Fa0/12        1-99,101-199,201-4094
```

I'll use the *add* option to add VLAN 100 back to the allowed list.

```
SW1(config)#int range fast 0/11 - 12
SW1(config-if-range)#switchport trunk allowed vlan add 100


SW1#show int trunk

Port          Mode            Encapsulation  Status        Native vlan
Fa0/11        auto            n-802.1q       trunking      1
Fa0/12        auto            n-802.1q       trunking      1


Port          Vlans allowed on trunk
Fa0/11        1-199,201-4094
Fa0/12        1-199,201-4094
```

We just got word from our bosses that VLAN 100 *should* be on the disallowed list, so let's put it there with the *remove* option.

```
SW1(config)#int range fast 0/11 - 12
SW1(config-if-range)#switchport trunk allowed vlan remove 100


SW1#show int trunk

Port          Mode            Encapsulation  Status        Native vlan
Fa0/11        auto            n-802.1q       trunking      1
Fa0/12        auto            n-802.1q       trunking      1
```

```
Port            Vlans allowed on trunk
Fa0/11          1-99,101-199,201-4094
Fa0/12          1-99,101-199,201-4094
```

If I wanted to remove all VLANs from the allowed list, I'd use the *none* option.

```
SW1(config)#int range fast 0/11 - 12
SW1(config-if-range)#switchport trunk allowed vlan none

SW1#show int trunk

Port          Mode            Encapsulation  Status      Native vlan
Fa0/11        auto            n-802.1q       trunking    1
Fa0/12        auto            n-802.1q       trunking    1


Port          Vlans allowed on trunk
Fa0/11        none
Fa0/12        none
```

We can quickly reinstate all VLANs on the trunk with the *all* option, and we're right back to where we began!

```
SW1(config)#int range fast 0/11 - 12
SW1(config-if-range)#switchport trunk allowed vlan all

SW1#show int trunk

Port          Mode            Encapsulation  Status      Native vlan
Fa0/11        auto            n-802.1q       trunking    1
Fa0/12        auto            n-802.1q       trunking    1


Port          Vlans allowed on trunk
Fa0/11        1-4094
Fa0/12        1-4094
```

You'll usually have more than one combination of these commands that will filter the VLANs on the allowed list the way you want them filtered. There's no "right" or "wrong" way to get the job done, as long as you filter only the VLANs you want filtered.

What happens to traffic destined for a given VLAN when that same VLAN has already been removed from the allowed list? Let's find out! I've placed H1 and H4 into VLAN 14, changing nothing else, and pings go through just fine.

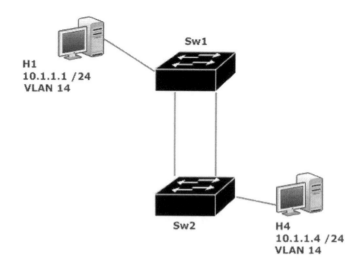

```
HOST1#ping 10.1.1.4
!!!!!
Success rate is 100 percent (5/5), round-trip min/avg/max = 4/4/4 ms

HOST4#ping 10.1.1.1
!!!!!
Success rate is 100 percent (5/5), round-trip min/avg/max = 4/5/8 ms
```

Let's see what happens when VLAN 14 is removed from the allowed list on both of SW1's trunk ports. Before sending the pings, I'll run *debug ip packet* on both hosts.

```
SW1(config)#int range fast 0/11 - 12
SW1(config-if-range)#switchport trunk allowed vlan except 14

SW1#show int trunk
```

Port	Mode	Encapsulation	Status	Native vlan
Fa0/11	desirable	802.1q	trunking	1
Fa0/12	desirable	802.1q	trunking	1

Port	Vlans allowed on trunk
Fa0/11	1-13,15-4094
Fa0/12	1-13,15-4094

```
HOST1#ping 10.1.1.4
Type escape sequence to abort.
Sending 5, 100-byte ICMP Echos to 10.1.1.4, timeout is 2 seconds:
1d01h: IP: s=10.1.1.1 (local), d=10.1.1.4 (Ethernet0), len 100, sending
1d01h: IP: s=10.1.1.1 (local), d=10.1.1.4 (Ethernet0), len 100, sending
1d01h: IP: s=10.1.1.1 (local), d=10.1.1.4 (Ethernet0), len 100, sending
```

```
1d01h: IP: s=10.1.1.1 (local), d=10.1.1.4 (Ethernet0), len 100, sending
1d01h: IP: s=10.1.1.1 (local), d=10.1.1.4 (Ethernet0), len 100, sending
Success rate is 0 percent (0/5)


HOST1#undebug all
All possible debugging has been turned off


HOST4#ping 10.1.1.1
Type escape sequence to abort.
Sending 5, 100-byte ICMP Echos to 10.1.1.1, timeout is 2 seconds:
1d01h: IP: s=10.1.1.4 (local), d=10.1.1.1 (Ethernet0), len 100, sending.
1d01h: IP: s=10.1.1.4 (local), d=10.1.1.1 (Ethernet0), len 100, sending.
1d01h: IP: s=10.1.1.4 (local), d=10.1.1.1 (Ethernet0), len 100, sending.
1d01h: IP: s=10.1.1.4 (local), d=10.1.1.1 (Ethernet0), len 100, sending.
1d01h: IP: s=10.1.1.4 (local), d=10.1.1.1 (Ethernet0), len 100, sending.
Success rate is 0 percent (0/5)


HOST4#undebug all
All possible debugging has been turned off
```

The pings are leaving the hosts, but they're failing. We know why, since we caused the problem as part of the lab. This is an excellent reminder that when pings fail, it may not be the fault of the sender or intended recipient. It may very well be a device in the middle. A switch, perhaps!

Adding VLAN 14 back to the allowed list resolves the issue.

```
SW1(config)#int range fast 0/11 - 12
SW1(config-if-range)#switchport trunk allowed vlan add 14


SW1#show int trunk

Port        Mode              Encapsulation  Status       Native vlan
Fa0/11      desirable         802.1q         trunking     1
Fa0/12      desirable         802.1q         trunking     1


Port        Vlans allowed on trunk
Fa0/11      1-4094
Fa0/12      1-4094


HOST4#ping 10.1.1.1
!!!!!


HOST1#ping 10.1.1.4
!!!!!
```

49

With VLANs and trunking down, we need to spread the word throughout the network about the VLANs we create. That's what the *VLAN Trunking Protocol* is all about, and that's the subject of the next chapter!

<h1 style="text-align:center">Chapter 4:</h1>

<h1 style="text-align:center">THE VLAN TRUNKING PROTOCOL (VTP)</h1>

We'll start this section with our two-switch network and won't even worry about the connected hosts. VTP deals exclusively with trunking, and we'll do the same!

SW1   SW2

VTP allows each switch to have a synchronized view of the network's active VLANs without necessarily having ports in every VLAN. I'll create VLAN 100 on SW1, and then run *show vlan brief* for both switches. Both switches are at their default settings, and any config from previous chapters or labs has been removed. (I've removed VLANs 1002 – 1005 from the output of *show vlan brief* and will do so throughout this section.)

```
SW1#show vlan brief

VLAN Name                             Status    Ports
---  ------------------------------   --------- 
 1   default                          active    Fa0/1,  Fa0/2,  Fa0/3,  Fa0/4,
                                                Fa0/5,  Fa0/6,  Fa0/7,  Fa0/8,
                                                Fa0/9,  Fa0/10

100  VLAN0100                         active

SW2#show vlan brief
```

```
VLAN Name                            Status    Ports
---  ------------------------------  --------
  1  default                         active    Fa0/1,  Fa0/2,  Fa0/3,  Fa0/4,
                                                Fa0/5,  Fa0/6,  Fa0/7,  Fa0/8,
                                                Fa0/9,     Fa0/10,    Fa0/13,
                                                Fa0/14,    Fa0/15,    Fa0/16,
                                                Fa0/17,    Fa0/18,    Fa0/19,
                                                Fa0/20,    Fa0/21,    Fa0/22,
                                                Fa0/23, Fa0/24, Gi0/1, Gi0/2
```

Right now, SW2 can only learn about VLAN 100 by manually creating that same VLAN on SW2 or to place a port on SW2 into VLAN 100. SW2's ignorance of VLAN 100 isn't hurting anything now, but as our little network grows just a bit larger, it *does* become a problem.

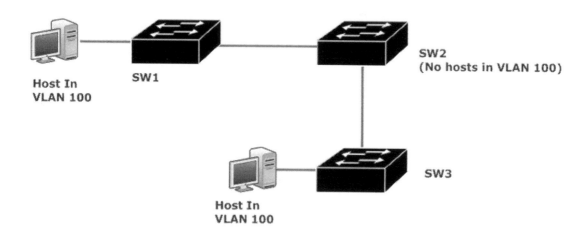

The only way for the two hosts in VLAN 100 to communicate is through SW2, and since SW2 doesn't know VLAN 100 exists, that communication can't happen. SW2 doesn't know how to handle incoming frames marked with VLAN ID 100, so they're dropped.

You and I, the network admins, could certainly create VLAN 100 manually on SW2. That would work well in a 3-switch network, but what about a 300-switch network? Statically creating VLANs simply isn't a scalable solution. Of course, the more manual configuration you have, the more time it takes and the larger the chances of *mis*configuration.

When we place all three of these switches into the same *VTP management domain* (generally referred to as a "VTP domain"), they'll exchange information about the VLANs they know about and all three switches will have a like view of the VLANs on the network. Our hosts in VLAN 100 can then communicate with no manual VLAN creation necessary on SW2.

Better yet, as VLANs are created and deleted, these switches will be happy to let their neighbors in the same VTP domain know about these changes via *VTP advertisements*. The key phrase: "in the same VTP domain". Switches in one VTP domain will not exchange VLAN info with switches in another VTP domain.

Let's step back to the two-switch network and put both switches into the VTP domain **CCNP.** Before doing so, let's run *show vtp status* on both.

```
SW1#show vtp status
VTP Version                       : 2
Configuration Revision            : 0
Maximum VLANs supported locally : 64
Number of existing VLANs          : 5
VTP Operating Mode                : Server
VTP Domain Name                   :
VTP Pruning Mode                  : Disabled
VTP V2 Mode                       : Disabled
VTP Traps Generation              : Disabled


SW2#show vtp status
VTP Version capable               : 1 to 3
VTP version running               : 1
VTP Domain Name                   :
VTP Pruning Mode                  : Disabled
VTP Traps Generation              : Disabled
Device ID                         : 0017.9466.f780
Configuration last modified by 0.0.0.0 at 0-0-00 00:00:00
Local updater ID is 0.0.0.0 (no valid interface found)


Feature VLAN:

VTP Operating Mode                : Server
Maximum VLANs supported locally : 1005
Number of existing VLANs          : 5
Configuration Revision            : 0
```

The *VTP Domain Name* field is blank, which simply means that the switches haven't joined a VTP domain...yet!

```
SW1(config)#vtp domain CCNP
Changing VTP domain name from NULL to CCNP

SW1#show vtp status
VTP Version                       : 2
Configuration Revision            : 0
Maximum VLANs supported locally : 64
Number of existing VLANs          : 5
VTP Operating Mode                : Server
VTP Domain Name                   : CCNP
VTP Pruning Mode                  : Disabled
VTP V2 Mode                       : Disabled
VTP Traps Generation              : Disabled
```

```
SW2#show vtp status
VTP Version capable                 : 1 to 3
VTP version running                 : 1
VTP Domain Name                     : CCNP
VTP Pruning Mode                    : Disabled
VTP Traps Generation                : Disabled
Device ID                           : 0017.9466.f780
Configuration last modified by 0.0.0.0 at 0-0-00 00:00:00
Local updater ID is 0.0.0.0 (no valid interface found)


Feature VLAN:


VTP Operating Mode                  : Server
Maximum VLANs supported locally : 1005
Number of existing VLANs            : 5
Configuration Revision              : 0
```

After placing SW1 into that VTP domain, that event triggers a VTP advertisement to SW2. That VTP ad contains info about the VTP domain, and SW2 will then join that domain as a VTP Server.

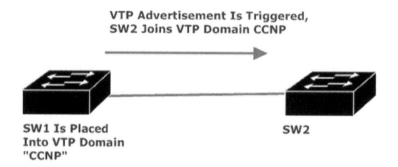

Should you put SW1 into the domain **CCNP** and SW2 into the domain **ccnp** …

```
SW2(config)#vtp domain ccnp
Changing VTP domain name from CCNP to ccnp
*Mar  1 00:29:00.896:  %SW_VLAN-6-VTP_DOMAIN_NAME_CHG:  VTP  domain  name
changed to ccnp.
*Mar 1 00:29:02.020: %DTP-5-DOMAINMISMATCH: Unable to perform trunk negotiation
on port Fa0/12 because of VTP domain mismatch.
*Mar 1 00:29:02.078: %DTP-5-DOMAINMISMATCH: Unable to perform trunk negotiation
on port Fa0/11 because of VTP domain mismatch.
```

… you end up with a mess. Moral of the story: VTP domain names are case-sensitive!

After switching (no pun intended – happy accident!) SW2 back to the VTP domain CCNP, we get the lay of the land via *show vtp status*. The output will be slightly different on each switch, but the most important VTP values are in each. We'll follow this output by discussing the VTP Operating Mode info for each switch.

```
SW1#show vtp status
VTP Version                    : 2
Configuration Revision         : 2 Maximum VLANs supported locally  : 64
Number of existing VLANs       : 7
VTP Operating Mode             : Server
VTP Domain Name                : CCNP
VTP Pruning Mode               : Disabled
VTP V2 Mode                    : Disabled
VTP Traps Generation           : Disabled
MD5 digest                     : 0x87 0xA7 0x10 0x69 0x58 0xA8 0x12 0x72
Configuration last modified by 0.0.0.0 at 3-1-93 00:30:42
Local updater ID is 0.0.0.0 (no valid interface found)


SW2#show vtp status
VTP Version capable            : 1 to 3
VTP version running            : 1
VTP Domain Name                : CCNP
VTP Pruning Mode               : Disabled
VTP Traps Generation           : Disabled
Device ID                      : 0017.9466.f780
Configuration last modified by 0.0.0.0 at 3-1-93 00:30:42
Local updater ID is 0.0.0.0 (no valid interface found)


Feature VLAN:
--------------

VTP Operating Mode             : Server
Maximum VLANs supported locally : 1005
Number of existing VLANs       : 7
Configuration Revision         : 2
MD5 digest                     : 0x87 0xA7 0x10 0x69 0x58 0xA8 0x12 0x72 0x5D
                                 0x74 0x8A 0xED 0x1F 0xE1 0x67 0xE2
```

The default VTP operating mode is *server*, with the options illustrated by *vtp mode*.

```
SW2(config)#vtp mode ?
  client      Set the device to client mode.
  off         Set the device to off mode.
  server      Set the device to server mode.
  Transparent Set the device to transparent mode.
```

There are times that IOS Help gives us wonderful descriptions for our options. This is *not* one of those times. IOS Help pretty much tells us what we already know, and I have a feeling we need to know a little more about each mode!

The VTP Modes

In *VTP server mode*, a switch can create, delete, and modify VLANs. By "modify", we mean "change the name of the VLAN". We do NOT mean "add ports to a VLAN", which can be done in server, client, and transparent modes. We must have at least one switch in any given VTP domain running in server mode, or we couldn't create new VLANs or delete previously existing ones.

Switches running in *VTP client mode* cannot create, modify, or delete VLANs. Clients listen for VTP advertisements and update their databases appropriately when those ads arrive. Let's see what happens after I make SW2 a VTP client and then try to create a VLAN on that same switch – or more accurately, what *doesn't* happen.

```
SW2(config)#vtp mode client
Setting device to VTP Client mode for VLANS.
SW2(config)#vlan 100
   VTP VLAN configuration not allowed when device is in CLIENT mode.
```

'Nuff said!

Switches in *VTP transparent mode* aren't fully participating in the VTP domain. (Hang in there with me on this one.) VTP transparent switches do not synch their VTP databases with other VTP speakers in the same domain. They don't even advertise their own VLAN information! VLANs created on a transparent VTP switch will not be advertised to other VTP speakers in the same domain, making them *locally significant only*.

When a transparent switch receives VTP advertisements, it will ignore the ads but forward them out its other trunks.

The fourth mode, "off", disables VTP on the switch, and the switch will not forward VTP advertisements. (This mode was one of the improvements that came along with VTP v3, and isn't available on previous versions.)

Another major difference between the modes is how they handle VTP advertisements. VTP servers originate VTP advertisements, and accept advertisements from other VTP servers and clients in the same domain. We must have at least one VTP server in our domain, or we're going to have a bunch of clients just looking at each other (and transparent switches just ignoring each other).

VTP Clients do not originate VTP ads, but will pass them across their trunks.

As you'd expect, VTP Transparent switches take a slightly more complicated approach. If a Transparent switch is running VTP v1, the switch will only forward incoming VTP ads if the VTP version number and domain name is the same as those switches that would receive the forwarded advertisement.

If the Transparent switch is running VTP v2, that switch will forward VTP advertisements via its trunk ports even if the domain name of the downstream switches doesn't match.

The VTP Advertisement Process & Config Revision Number

VTP advertisements are multicasts that are sent out only over trunk links. Makes sense, since the only devices that need the advertisements are other switches!

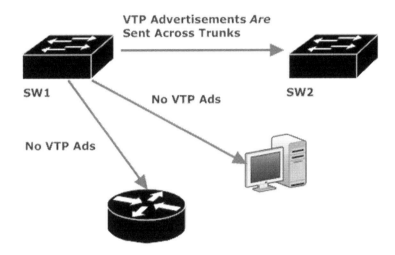

VTP advertisements carry a *configuration revision number* (CRN) that enables VTP-enabled switches to ensure they have the latest VTP information, and that they're not overwriting their current VLAN database to make room for *old* information!

One VTP ad type is the *subset advertisement*, sent anytime there's a change in the VLAN landscape. That change doesn't have to be a VLAN addition or deletion. It could be something as simple as renaming a VLAN, which is what we'll do in this lab.

On some switches, you'll see the CRN near the top of the *show vtp status* output...

```
SW1#show vtp status
VTP Version                     : 2
Configuration Revision          : 2
Maximum VLANs supported locally : 64
Number of existing VLANs        : 7
VTP Operating Mode              : Server
VTP Domain Name                 : CCNP
VTP Pruning Mode                : Disabled
VTP V2 Mode                     : Disabled
VTP Traps Generation            : Disabled
```

... and on others, you'll see it near the bottom of that same command's output.

```
SW2#show vtp status
VTP Version capable            : 1 to 3
VTP version running            : 1
VTP Domain Name                : CCNP
VTP Pruning Mode               : Disabled
VTP Traps Generation           : Disabled
Device ID                      : 0017.9466.f780
Configuration last modified by 0.0.0.0 at 3-1-93 00:30:42

Feature VLAN:

VTP Operating Mode             : Client
Maximum VLANs supported locally : 1005
Number of existing VLANs       : 7
Configuration Revision         : 2
```

Both switches have a CRN of 2. I'll add a VLAN to SW1 and then recheck the CRN on each switch, also checking to be sure the VLAN is visible in SW2's *show vlan brief* output.

```
SW1(config)#vlan 300

SW1#show vtp status
Configuration Revision         : 3

SW2#show vtp status
Configuration Revision         : 3

SW2#show vlan brief

VLAN Name                           Status
---  ------------------------------ 
1    default                        active
100  VLAN0100                       active
200  VLAN0200                       active
300  VLAN0300                       active
```

VLAN 300 is in SW2's database, and the CRN incremented on both switches. What happened on each switch to make the CRN increment? Let's take a behind-the-scenes look...

The creation of VLAN 300 on SW1 triggers a subset advertisement from SW1, and the CRN increments *before* that ad is sent across the trunk to SW2.

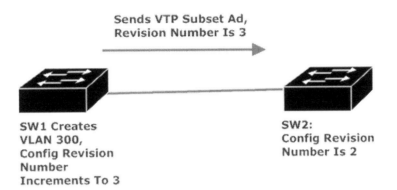

SW2 receives the subset ad with a CRN of 3. SW2 compares the incoming CRN to its own CRN (2). When an incoming subset ad's CRN is larger than the one on the receiving switch, the contents of the ad are accepted and used to overwrite the receiving switch's existing VTP database. Once that's done, SW2 will increment its own CRN.

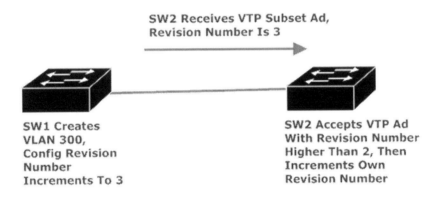

We *love* the CRN! The switches make sure they're accepting only the latest VLAN revision information, and you and I don't have to do a thing. (That doesn't make us lazy, that makes us smart.)

You have to be *sure* to set the CRN to zero in one particular scenario, or you'll have a *real* mess on your hands. We have a simple three-switch network with two Clients and one Server. SW2 is busy sending an advertisement with CRN 300. The domain is CCNP, and the non-default VLANs in use are VLANs 10, 20, 30, 40, and 50.

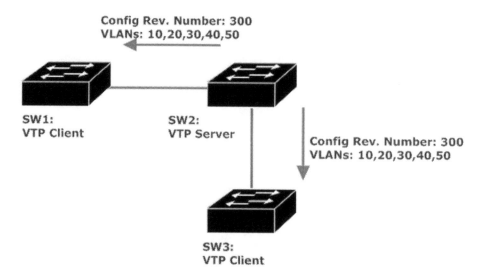

A switch that was at another physical location is brought to this client site and installed in the CCNP domain. The problem: the CRN on that switch is 500, and this switch only knows about VLAN 1.

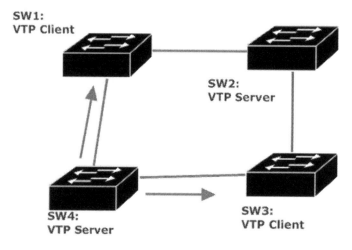

The other switches will receive a VTP advertisement with a higher CRN than the one currently in their VTP database, so they synch their databases in accordance with this new advertisement. Since that new advertisement only includes VLAN 1, connectivity for the other five VLANs is lost. (The VTP Clients will forward the VTP ad to SW2.)

SW4 doesn't even have to be in Server mode to ruin things. While a Client generally spends its time listening for and forwarding VTP ads, it does send a full Summary ad when it first comes online. That's enough to cause a lot of trouble here.

This is most likely to happen when a switch goes down and is replaced in a hurry with a switch from another client site, or even from a CCNP / CCIE practice lab! No matter the source of the switch, the CRN MUST be set to zero before it's inserted into the new network. Just bouncing the switch isn't enough, since the CRN is kept in NVRAM. Cisco theory says that there are two ways to ensure the CRN is set to zero:

Change the VTP domain name to a nonexistent domain, then change it back to the original name.

Change the VTP mode from server to transparent, then back to server.

Whichever you choose, just be sure to verify the zero before you proceed. The official name of this issue is "VTP synch issue", but you'll call it something *much* more profane if it happens to your network.

The Three VTP Advertisement Types (And Two Directions!)

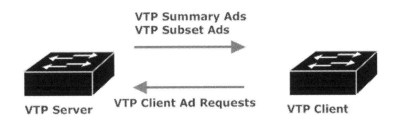

Summary Advertisements are sent by VTP Servers every 5 minutes OR upon a change in the VLAN database. Included in this ad type are the VTP domain name and version, CRN, MD5 hash code, a timestamp, and the number of Subset Advertisements that will follow this Summary ad.

Subset Advertisements are sent by VTP Servers when there's a VLAN configuration change. Subset ads give more specific info about the VLAN that's been changed, including whether the VLAN was actually created, deleted, or suspended, the VLAN type (Ethernet, Token Ring, FDDI, etc.), and the new VLAN name and/or MTU (if those values were changed).

Client Advertisement Requests are requests from VTP Clients for VLAN information, which may seem unnecessary. If those Summary Ads are coming every 5 minutes, and both Summary and Subset ads are sent when there's a VLAN change, why does the client ever have to request info?

These requests come in handy should the client's VLAN database become corrupt or if it's deleted. Rather than wait for the Server's ads to be triggered, the Client can explicitly request VLAN info, and the Server will answer with a series of Summary and Subset ads that will allow the Client to rebuild its VLAN database.

VTP Versions

The available VTP versions are 1, 2, and 3, and a Cisco switch will run Version 1 by default. Use *vtp version* to change versions.

```
SW2#show vtp status
VTP Version capable             : 1 to 3
VTP version running             : 1
VTP Domain Name                 : CCNP
VTP Pruning Mode                : Disabled
VTP Traps Generation            : Disabled

SW2(config)#vtp version ?
  <1-3> Set the administrative domain VTP version number
```

As you'd expect, there were some improvements when VTP v2 came along:

VTP v2 supports Token Ring VLANs and Token Ring switching, where v1 does not.

VTP v2 performs a consistency check when changes are made to VLANs or the VTP configuration at the command-line interface (CLI). The consistency check is performed on the VLAN names and numbers, which helps to prevent incorrect names from propagation throughout the network.

A transparent VTP switch running VTP v2 will forward VTP advertisements via its trunk ports, even if the VTP domain name is different on the switches it's trunking with. With v1, the domain *and* version number of the trunking switches had to match that of the transparent switch. (Whew!)

Those were solid improvements, but *serious* improvements came along with the introduction of VTP v3. VTP v3 introduced the VTP mode *off* we saw earlier. If you're on a switch that can't run VTP version 3, you will not see the *off* option.

```
SW1(config)#vtp mode ?
  client       Set the device to client mode.
  server       Set the device to server mode.
  transparent  Set the device to transparent mode.
```

VTP v3 can be enabled and disabled at the port level, rather than only at the switch level.

The VTP Password ("Secure Mode")

With previous versions of VTP, it was easy to compromise the password. I'll configure SW2 to run VTP v2, and then set a password.

```
SW2(config)#vtp version 2
VTP version is already in V2. (Hey, I was already there!)

SW2(config)#vtp password CCNP
Setting device VTP password to CCNP

SW2#show vtp password
VTP Password: CCNP
```

You could also spot the VTP password in the *vlan.dat* file.

```
SW2#more vlan.dat
00000000: BADB100D 00000002 02044343 4E500000 :[.. .... ..CCNP..
```

Improvement was needed, and VTP v3 brought it. Let's upgrade SW2 to VTP v3 and then view our options for the VTP password. I'll do that after removing the previous password.

```
SW2(config)#no vtp password CCNP
Clearing device VTP password.

SW2#show vtp password
The VTP password is not configured.

SW2(config)#vtp version 3
Mar 1 00:06:32.318: %SW_VLAN-6-OLD_CONFIG_FILE_READ: Old version 2 VLAN
   configuration file detected and read OK. Version 3 files will be written in
the future.
SW2(config)#vtp password ?

SW2(config)#vtp password CCNP ?
hidden Set the VTP password hidden option
secret Specify the vtp password in encrypted form
<cr>

SW2(config)#vtp password CCNP secret ?
VTP secret has to be 32 characters in length

SW2(config)#vtp password CCNP hidden
Setting device VTP password

SW2#show vtp password
VTP Password: 50EF55299259C91C41DDF825699A177D
```

I just didn't feel up to a 32-character password, so I went with *hidden*, which really is the best option. Cisco's website documentation on VTP v3 mentions that *show* commands can't be used to see the password, nor is it visible in the *vlan.dat* file, and that is indeed the case!

The vlan.dat file is HUGE, so I'm not showing the entire thing here. Suffice to say I looked for the password and it wasn't there, as it was with VTP v2.

VTP v3 vs. The Synch Problem

Remember the VTP synch problem we saw earlier in this chapter? VTP v3 helps us prevent that problem (proactively!) by introducing the *primary server* concept. When you configure a VTP Server as the primary server, that's the only device that can actually update other switches in the VTP domain. Use *vtp primary* to make a VTP server the primary server. You need the VTP password to do so, and you'll be prompted one more time to *ensure* you're sure about making this switch the primary server.

```
SW2#vtp primary vlan
This system is becoming primary server for feature vlan
Enter VTP Password:
No conflicting VTP3 devices found.
Do you want to continue? [confirm]
SW2#
*Mar 1 00:24:17.629: %SW _ VLAN-4-VTP _ PRIMARY _ SERVER _ CHG: 0017.9466.f780 has
become the primary server for the VLAN VTP feature
```

A Final Word About VTP Versions

According to Cisco website documentation, VTP v3 is friendly to VTP v2, but v3 will not work with v1. If a switch running v1 detects a v3 switch, the switch running v1 will attempt to upgrade to v2. Naturally, if the switch can only run v1, you're stuck.

Another major difference between versions to watch out for: VTP v1 and v2 support only VLANs 1 – 1005, where v3 supports the full range of extended VLANs (1 – 4094).

Cisco strongly recommends that you determine whether your current switches are v2-capable before introducing v3 to your network. You're better off if all your current switches are v3-capable.

VTP Pruning

Trunk ports are members of all VLANs, which leads to an issue involving broadcasts, unknown unicasts, and multicasts.

A trunk port will forward broadcasts and multicasts for all VLANs it knows about, regardless of whether the switch at the other end of the trunk actually has ports in those VLANs. This means that the sending switch is likely sending unnecessary traffic, and the recipient is receiving totally unnecessary traffic.

Here, SW1 has hosts in VLANs 2 – 19. That switch is trunking with SW2, which has hosts in VLANs 2 – 10. There's no reason to send broadcast, unknown unicast, or multicast traffic belonging to VLANs 11 – 19 to SW2.

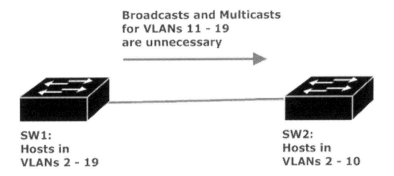

With VTP pruning, a switch will send a message to its trunking partners, identifying the VLANs in use by the switch sending the message.

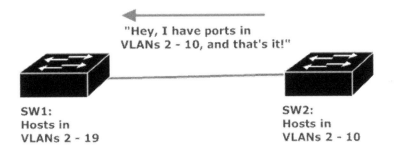

SW1 now knows which multicasts, broadcast, and unknown unicasts should and should not be sent across the trunk to SW2.

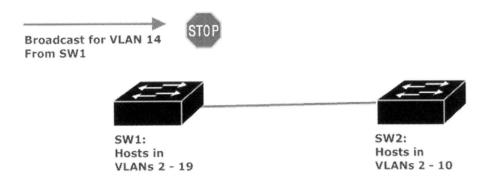

Enabling VTP pruning is just as easy. You don't even have to type "on"!

```
SW2(config)#vtp pruning ?
  <cr>

SW2(config)#vtp pruning
Pruning switched on
```

That simple command makes VLANs 2 – 1001 eligible for pruning. You can't prune the default VLANs! If you want to make some of those VLANs "prune-proof", use the *switch-port trunk pruning vlan* command.

```
SW1(config)#int range fast 0/11 - 12
SW1(config-if-range)#switchport trunk pruning vlan ?
  WORD    VLAN IDs of the allowed VLANs when this port is in trunking mode
  add     add VLANs to the current list
  except  all VLANs except the following
  none    no VLANs
  remove  remove VLANs from the current list
```

Enough of VLANs – for now! Let's get started with the Spanning Tree Protocol!

Chapter 5:

THE FUNDAMENTALS OF STP

Whether it's Layer 2 or Layer 3, we love redundancy. A single point of failure for *anything* in today's networks just isn't acceptable. Redundancy works just a *bit* differently at L2 than L3, however.

L3 routing protocols such as EIGRP and OSPF allow us to use secondary paths *in addition* to the primary paths, making equal- and unequal-cost load balancing possible. With routing, we want to use as many of those paths as is feasible. (More on that in your ROUTE studies!)

At Layer 2, our redundant paths need to be ready for action in case the primary path fails, but they will *not* be used in addition to the primary path. The basic purpose of the Spanning Tree Protocol (STP) is to identify valid loop-free paths and then choose the best of those paths for use. STP will then block ports on the valid but less desirable paths, holding those paths in standby. Should a primary path become unavailable, STP will realize this and begin to unblock the necessary ports to put the next best path into action.

This becomes a *lot* clearer with examples and lab work, which we have plenty of in the next few sections of the course!

So that's all fine, you say, but what about those redundant paths? Why can't we use every single path from "A" to "B" for switching, as we like to do for routing? The problem at L2 is the possibility of switching loops. Here's an example of such a loop where STP is not in action.

Note: Switching loops are sometimes called "bridging loops", even in networks that don't have bridges. It's a legacy term, and we always say "legacy" because we don't like to say "old".

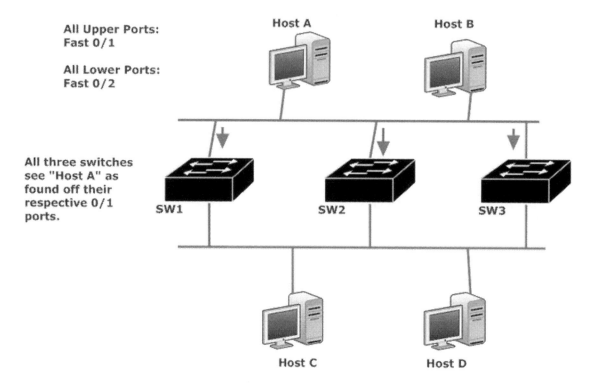

Now this is redundancy! We have three switches connecting two Ethernet segments, so if two switches go down, each host would still be able to reach every other host. Having STP on would help prevent switching loops, but in this example, it's not on.

Let's say all three switches have just been turned on, and Host A sends a frame to Host C. With this topology, all three switches would receive the frame on their Fast0/1 interfaces. Before making a forwarding decision regarding the incoming frame, each switch will check its own MAC address table regarding an entry for the source MAC address of the frame. None of the switches have such an entry, so they'll each make an entry in their respective MAC tables, listing Host A as reachable via Fast0/1.

On to the forwarding decision! None of the switches have an entry for the frame's destination, Host 3, so each switch will follow the default behavior for an unknown unicast address. They'll flood the frame out all ports except the one it came in on. In our example, the frames will be flooded out Fast0/2 on each switch.

Just that quickly, without STP, we're about to experience a switching loop. Each switch will see the frame just flooded by the other two switches. The problem is the source MAC address of each flooded frame, which is still Host A's MAC address. When each switch receives a frame on Fast 0/2 with Host A's MAC address as the source, each switch will then change the MAC address table setting for Host A to Fast 0/2. As those frames are flooded in turn, the switches will keep going back and forth on the MAC address table entry for Host A.

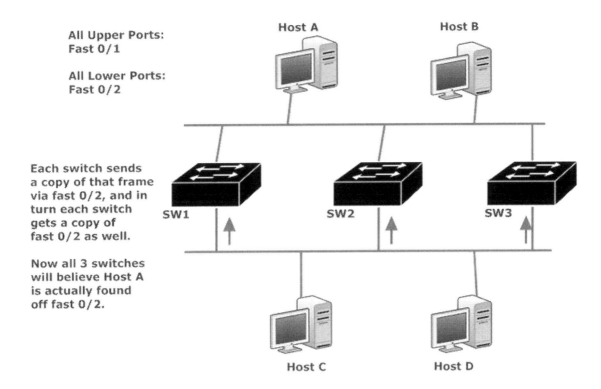

All Upper Ports:
Fast 0/1

All Lower Ports:
Fast 0/2

Each switch sends
a copy of that frame
via fast 0/2, and in
turn each switch
gets a copy of
fast 0/2 as well.

Now all 3 switches
will believe Host A
is actually found
off fast 0/2.

If you think that's bad (and it is!), just wait until the other hosts start sending traffic! Slowly but surely (don't call me Shirley), more and more broadcast traffic is forwarded by the switches. Finally, the switch is overwhelmed by those broadcasts and we have a broadcast storm. In short, switching loops cause three major problems:

Frames can't reach their intended destination, either in full or in part

There's an unnecessary strain put on the switch CPU

A lot of bandwidth is unnecessarily sucked up by all those broadcasts

Luckily for us, switching loops don't occur often, because STP does a great job of preventing switching loops before they happen. It all begins with the exchange of Bridge Protocol Data Units (BPDUs).

The Bridge Protocol Data Unit Types and The Root Bridge Election

We have two BPDU types, both multicast to the well-known MAC address 01-80-c2-00-00-00. We're going to concentrate on Configuration BPDUs, the BPDUs that are used in STP calculations. TCN BPDUs will be covered later in this section.

Only the root bridge will originate Configuration BPDUs. The non-roots will receive and forward a copy of that BPDU, but non-root bridges do not actually create this BPDU type. The root bridge is also the switch that decides what the STP timers will be, and we'll see that in action after we have an election.

Each switch has a Bridge ID Priority value, commonly referred to as a BID. The BID is a combination of a 2-byte Priority value and the switch's 6-byte MAC address. The Priority value comes first in the BID. If a Cisco switch has the default priority 32768 and a MAC address of 11-22-33-44-55-66, the resulting BID is 32768:11-22-33-44-55-66. If the Priority is left at the default on all switches, the MAC address is the deciding factor in the root bridge election, and the switch with the lowest MAC address wins.

In any network, you'll have switches that are more powerful than others in terms of processing power and speed. In general, you should ensure that your primary and secondary root bridges are your more powerful switches. We don't want to leave those roles to chance – or the lowest MAC address!

I'll show you exactly how to be deterministic about root bridge elections after we walk through an example of a root bridge election using only the defaults.

The Default Root Bridge Election Process

Switches are a lot like people. When they first arrive, they announce to everyone around them that they are the center of the universe.

Unlike some people, the switches get over it.

But seriously folks, Config BPDUs will be exchanged between our switches until one switch is elected root bridge. The switch with the lowest BID will win that coveted role.

We're about to walk through a root bridge election on a three-switch network, and we'll take a look at the election from each switch's point of view. Each switch has the default priority 32768, and the MAC address of each switch is the switch's number repeated 12 times. All three switches are coming online at the same time, so all three believe they are the root bridge, and all three of them get very busy announcing that fact.

Since each switch believes it's the root, all six ports in this example will go to the listening state, allowing it to hear BPDUs from other switches. (Much more on these STP port states later in this section.)

Here's our network and the root bridge election from SW1's perspective.

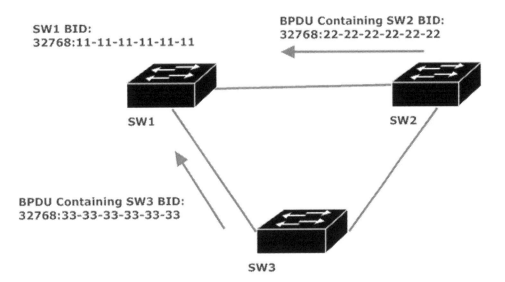

SW1 is receiving BPDUs from both SW2 and SW3, both containing BIDs higher than SW1's own BID. While higher BIDs are winners in auctions, they're losers in root bridge elections. SW1 continues to believe that it's the root bridge and will continue to announce itself as such.

Here's the election from SW2's perspective:

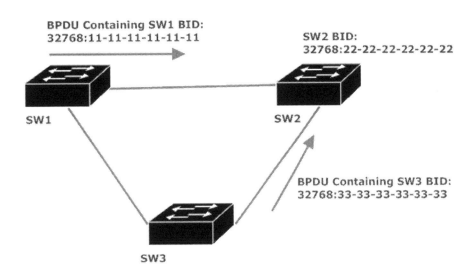

SW2 believes it's the root, and the BPDU from SW3 will not change its mind. However, the BPDU from SW1 will! When SW2 sees the BID inside the BPDU from SW1, SW2 will realize it is not the root bridge for this network. SW2 will stop originating Configuration BPDUs, and will instead begin to relay those sent by SW1.

The election from SW3's point of view:

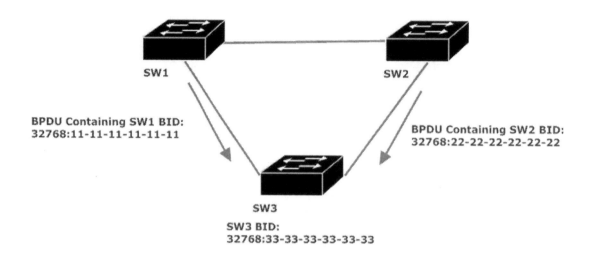

BPDU Containing SW1 BID:
32768:11-11-11-11-11-11

BPDU Containing SW2 BID:
32768:22-22-22-22-22-22

SW3 BID:
32768:33-33-33-33-33-33

SW3 is about to develop a *massive* inferiority complex! Both incoming BPDUs contain BIDs superior to that of SW3. SW3 recognizes that the BPDU containing the best BID is coming from SW1. Just that quickly, SW2 and SW3 recognize SW1 as the root – for now!

Root bridge elections never really end. SW1 is currently recognized as the root for this network, but if another switch comes along that advertises a superior BID, that switch would then become the root!

SW4 has now come on board, and is advertising a BID lower than that of SW1. SW4 will advertise this BID via a Configuration BPDU, and when SW1 sees that BPDU, SW1 will realize it's no longer the root bridge. SW4 will then take over that role, and SW1 will begin forwarding the Configuration BPDUs it receives from SW4. These Config BPDUs go out every 2 seconds, so this process takes very little time.

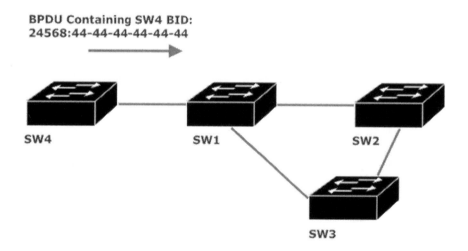

BPDU Containing SW4 BID:
24568:44-44-44-44-44-44

This example allowed you to see the details of a root bridge election, but in your production network, that election's already taken place. It's a good idea to know how to see the BIDs of your live switches as well as spot the winner of a root bridge election that's already taken place. For this lab, we'll use a two-switch network, with the switches trunking on their 0/11 and 0/12 ports.

To see the BID of both the local switch and the root switch for a particular VLAN, run *show spanning-tree vlan*. (Each VLAN will have its own root switch.) Let's take a look at the root bridge info for our default VLAN.

```
SW1#show spanning vlan 1


VLAN0001
  Spanning tree enabled protocol ieee
  Root ID    Priority    32769
             Address     000f.90e2.2540
             This bridge is the root
             Hello Time   2 sec   Max Age 20 sec  Forward Delay 15 sec

  Bridge ID  Priority    32769     (priority 32768 sys-id-ext 1)
             Address     000f.90e2.2540
             Hello Time   2 sec   Max Age 20 sec  Forward Delay 15 sec
             Aging Time 15


Interface          Role Sts Cost      Prio.Nbr  Type
---------------    ---- --  --------- --------   --------
Fa0/11             Desg FWD 19        128.11     P2p
Fa0/12             Desg FWD 19        128.12     P2p
```

There are four different ways to tell you're on the root switch. The most obvious is the phrase "This bridge is the root". The other three ways:

The MAC address of the Root ID (the info for the root) and the Bridge ID (the info for the local switch) is the same.

As odd as it sounds, the root bridge will have no root port. The root port is the port a switch will use to reach the root bridge, so the root bridge doesn't need one!

All ports on the root bridge will be in forwarding mode (FWD). No ports on the root bridge will be in blocking mode (BLK).

What do things look like on the non-root bridge, you ask?

```
SW2#show spanning vlan 1
VLAN0001
  Spanning tree enabled protocol ieee
  Root ID    Priority    32769
             Address     000f.90e2.2540
             Cost        19
             Port        13 (FastEthernet0/11)
             Hello Time   2 sec  Max Age 20 sec  Forward Delay 15 sec

    Bridge ID  Priority    32769 (priority 32768 sys-id-ext 1)
               Address     0017.9466.f780
               Hello Time   2 sec Max Age 20 sec Forward Delay 15 sec
               Aging Time 300 sec


Interface         Role Sts Cost        Prio.Nbr  Type
--------------    ---- -- ---------    --------  --------
Fa0/11            Root FWD 19           128.13    P2p
Fa0/12            Altn BLK 19           128.14    P2p
```

There are four ways to tell you're *not* on the root bridge. The first listed here isn't highlighted, since it doesn't exist, but the other three are in bold.

No "This bridge is the root" message

The MAC address under the Root ID and Bridge ID fields are different

The switch has a root port (Fa0/11)

There is a port in blocking mode

STP prevents switching loops by putting some ports into blocking mode. In the end, STP allows only one path between "Point A" and "Point B" – in this case, our two switches – and disallows the others by putting the minimum number of ports necessary into blocking mode. In our two-switch network, one path between the switches is open and the other is closed. Only one is in blocking mode, rather than the two you might expect.

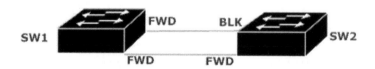

STP puts the minimum number of ports into blocking mode in order to speed up the process of bringing a new path up when the currently open one becomes unavailable. The fewer ports that need to reopen, the faster that new path will be available.

Root Port Selection, Path Costs, and Root Path Costs

Wondering how SW2 chose 0/11 as its root port, instead of 0/12?

Every port on our switches has an assigned *path cost*, and that cost is used to arrive at the port's *root path cost*. The path cost is strictly a local value and is not advertised to upstream or downstream switches. The faster the port, the lower the path cost.

The *root path cost* is a cumulative value reflecting the overall cost for a given port to reach the root. The Configuration BPDU carries the root path cost, and that cost increments as that BPDU is forwarded throughout the network.

These terms will become much clearer after the upcoming example!

It all begins with the root bridge transmitting a Configuration BPDU with the root path cost set to zero. When SW2 receives that BPDU, it will add the cost of the port the BPDU was received upon to the root path cost found in that incoming BPDU. It's important to note that the root path cost increments as BPDUs are *received*, not *sent*.

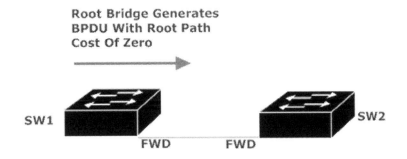

The root path cost goes from 0 to 19 (when received by SW2) to 38 (when received by SW3).

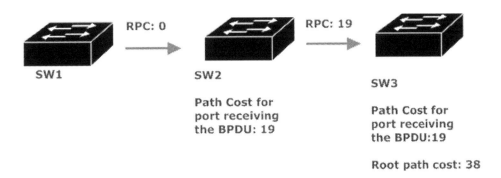

Let's zip back to our two-switch example.

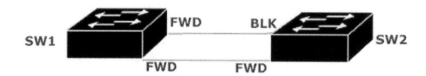

The incoming root path cost should be the same for both ports on SW2, since every port involved here is a Fast Ethernet port. Let's run *show spanning-tree vlan* to see what the deciding factor was.

```
SW2#show spanning vlan 1

< Some config removed for clarity >

Interface         Role Sts Cost      Prio.Nbr   Type
---------------   ---- --  --------- --------
Fa0/11            Root FWD 19        128.13     P2p
Fa0/12            Altn BLK 19        128.14     P2p
```

The path cost is 19 for each port, but 0/11 was chosen as the root port over 0/12. Here's the process for choosing the root port:

First, choose the port receiving the *superior BPDU*, the BPDU containing the lowest BID. 0/11 and 0/12 are both receiving BPDUs from SW1, so this is a tie.

Next, choose the port with the lowest root path cost. That's a tie, as both ports will have a root path cost of 19. It was zero on SW1 and incremented as the BPDUs were received by SW2.

Next tiebreaker: choose the port receiving the BPDU with the lowest Sender BID. Since both ports received their BPDUs directly from SW1, this is also a tie.

Finally, the lowest sender Port ID wins. There's our tiebreaker, and fast 0/11 is your winnah!

Let's head back to our three-switch network and identify the root ports. All ports are Fast Ethernet ports with a path cost of 19.

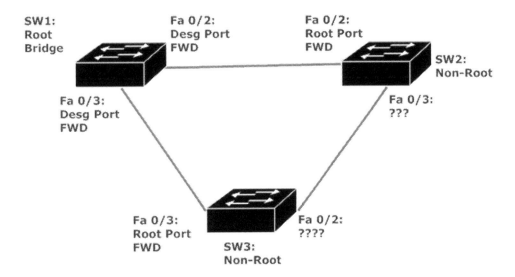

With all path costs the same, we can quickly identify the root ports on SW2 and SW3, and root ports will always be in forwarding mode (FWD). We know that the ports on the root bridge aren't root ports. They're *designated ports*, and they'll also be in forwarding mode. We have four ports in forwarding mode, so STP better put a port or two in blocking mode soon!

Speaking of designated ports, we need one of those for the segment connecting SW2 and SW3. We need one and only one designated port on that segment, just in case that ends up being a shared network segment.

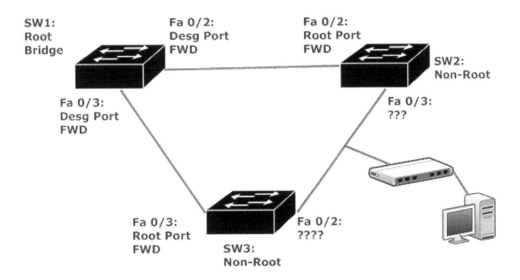

In this admittedly unlikely-to-be-seen-in-the-real-world scenario, frames coming from that host onto the segment shared by SW2 and SW3 might cause a switching loop if both switches could forward frames from that host to SW1. That's where the designated port

(DP) comes in. The switch with the lowest root path cost will have its port on this shared segment named as the designated port.

In this scenario, both switches will have the exact same root path cost, so we need a tie-breaker. The port belonging to the switch with the lowest BID will become the designated port, along with all ports on the root bridge. We saw earlier that SW2's BID is 32768:22-22-22-22-22-22 and SW3's is 32768:33-33-33-33-33-33, so SW2's port on that shared segment becomes the DP.

Here's the final result:

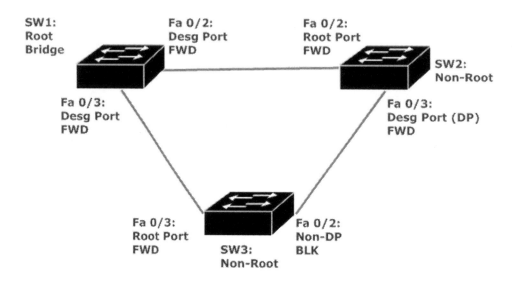

Of the six ports, five of them are in forwarding mode and only one is blocked, but placing that one particular port into blocking mode prevents switching loops from forming. Putting just one of the two ports on the SW2–SW3 shared segment into blocking mode makes the cutover to that path for SW3 a little quicker, should the current path from SW2 to SW1 become unavailable.

Luckily, that only happens now and Zen. And speaking of Zen...

The Shortest Path Is Not Always The Shortest Path

We know the STP path costs are determined by port speed, and it couldn't hurt to be familiar with the following port speeds. (These port costs have changed over time, and these values are from the most recent list on Cisco's website.) This is not a list of every possible speed, but lists the more common speeds you'll bump into on Cisco switches.

10 Gbps	2
1 Gbps	4

100 Mbps	19
16 Mbps	62
10 Mbps	100
4 Mbps	250

Keep STP costs in mind when eyeballing a network map on your CCNP SWITCH exam, job interview, or during your network admin duties. Do not jump to the conclusion that the *physically* shortest path is the *logically* shortest path.

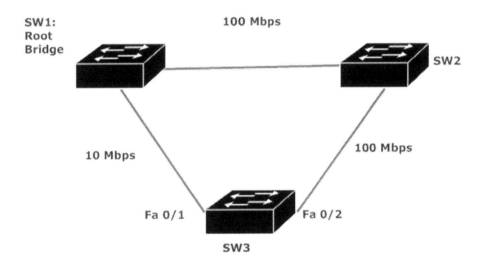

If you were asked which of SW3's two ports would become its root port, it would be really easy to say 0/1. It would also be really *wrong*.

SW3-to-SW1 root path cost: 100 (One 10 Mbps link)

SW3-to-SW2-to-SW1 root path cost: 38 (Two 100 Mbps links)

Fast 0/2 becomes the root port. The root path using that port has a cost of 38, while the more physically direct path has a root path cost of 100. Whether it's in the exam room or your server room, be sure to double-check the port speeds. Some of the network maps I've looked at over the years have a font size of about 0.5, and it's really easy to miss a zero – or think one is there that isn't!

Changing A Port's Path Cost

We'll verify port path cost changes with *show spanning-tree vlan*. We need only the information at the bottom of that command's output in this lab, so I'll edit the "Root ID" and "Bridge ID" fields from the output. Let's verify!

```
SW2#show spanning vlan 1

Interface         Role Sts Cost
---------------   ---- --  ---------
Fa0/11            Root FWD 19
Fa0/12            Altn BLK 19
```

We want 0/12 to be the root. Lowering its path cost to 9 for all VLANs should do it!

```
SW2(config)#int fast 0/12
SW2(config-if)#spanning-tree ?
   bpdufilter      Don't send or receive BPDUs on this interface
   bpduguard       Don't accept BPDUs on this interface
   cost            Change an interface's spanning tree port path cost
   guard           Change an interface's spanning tree guard mode
   link-type       Specify a link type for spanning tree protocol use
   mst             Multiple spanning tree
   port-priority   Change an interface's spanning tree port priority
   portfast        Enable an interface to move directly to forwarding on link
   stack-port      Enable stack port
   vlan            VLAN Switch Spanning Tree

SW2(config-if)#spanning-tree cost ?
   <1-200000000> port path cost
SW2(config-if)#spanning-tree cost 9
```

Just a few seconds after changing the cost, we get this little message:

```
*Mar 2 05:31:08.510: %LINEPROTO-5-UPDOWN: Line protocol on Interface Vlan1,
changed state to down
```

Doesn't sound good! Our management interface, Vlan1, has gone down. Let's see if it comes back up while we check in on our root port situation!

```
SW2#show spanning vlan 1
Interface         Role Sts Cost
---------------   ---- --  ---------
Fa0/11            Altn BLK 19
Fa0/12            Root LIS 9
```

The change to 0/12's path cost is immediate, as is the transition of 0/11 from forwarding to blocking. What *isn't* immediate is the transition of 0/12 from blocking to forwarding. More on that shortly, but trust me – there's a really good reason that change isn't immediate. Right now, 0/12 is in listening mode. About 15 seconds after that output, I ran the same command:

```
SW2#show spanning vlan 1

Interface          Role  Sts  Cost
---------------    ----  --   ---------
Fa0/11             Altn  BLK  19
Fa0/12             Root  LRN  9
```

0/12 is now in learning mode. About 15 seconds later...

```
*Mar 2 05:35:41.802: %LINEPROTO-5-UPDOWN: Line protocol on Interface Vlan1,
changed state to up

SW2# show spanning vlan 1

Interface          Role  Sts  Cost
---------------    ----  --   ---------
Fa0/11             Altn  BLK  19
Fa0/12             Root  FWD  9
```

... the VLAN1 interface comes back up and 0/12 is in forwarding mode. That's just what we wanted – we just had to be a little patient!

Load Balancing On A Per-VLAN Basis

Using *cost* is an all-or-nothing deal. What if we want to change the cost for some VLANs while leaving it alone for others?

In the following lab, all VLANs are using the top trunk (Fa 0/11 on both switches). We're just wasting the other path! We want VLANs 10 and 20 to continue to use the top path, but VLANs 30 and 40 should use the bottom trunk (Fa 0/12 on both switches). This is *per-VLAN load balancing*, and while it's not *perfect* load balancing, it's better than sending all our traffic across one trunk while treating the other trunk as strictly a backup.

Requirements:

VLANs 10 and 20: Use Fast 0/11

VLANs 30 and 40: Use Fast 0/12

We'll make this happen with *spanning-tree vlan*, using the *cost* option. We'll change the path cost for 0/12 on SW2 to 9 for VLANs 30 and 40 while leaving it alone for VLANs 10 and 20. Note the option to specify a range of VLANs.

```
SW2(config)#int fast 0/10
SW2(config-if)#spanning vlan ?
   WORD vlan range, example: 1,3-5,7,9-11

SW2(config-if)#spanning vlan 30,40 ?
   cost            Change an interface's per VLAN spanning tree path cost
   port-priority   Change an interface's spanning tree port priority

SW2(config-if)#spanning vlan 30,40 cost ?
   <1-200000000>   Change an interface's per VLAN spanning tree path cost

SW2(config-if)#spanning vlan 30,40 cost 9
```

The port begins to transition from blocking to forwarding for VLANs 30 and 40...

```
SW2#show spanning vlan 30

Interface       Role Sts Cost
--------------- ---- -- ---------
Fa0/11          Altn BLK  19
Fa0/12          Root LIS  9


SW2#show spanning vlan 40

Interface       Role Sts Cost
--------------- ---- -- ---------
Fa0/11          Altn BLK  19
Fa0/12          Root LIS  9
```

... but there's no transition for VLANs 10 and 20.

```
SW2#show spanning vlan 10

Interface       Role Sts Cost
--------------- ---- -- ---------
Fa0/11          Root FWD  19
Fa0/12          Altn BLK  19


SW2#show spanning vlan 20

Interface       Role Sts Cost
--------------- ---- -- ---------
Fa0/11          Root FWD  19
```

```
Fa0/12                 Altn BLK  19
```

Thirty seconds or so later, the transition has completed, and 0/12 is now the root port for both VLANs 30 and 40.

```
SW2#show spanning vlan 30

Interface          Role Sts Cost
--------------     ---- --  ---------
Fa0/11             Altn BLK  19
Fa0/12             Root FWD  9

SW2#show spanning vlan 40

Interface          Role Sts Cost
--------------     ---- --  ---------
Fa0/11             Altn BLK  19
Fa0/12             Root FWD  9
```

All VLAN 30 and 40 traffic will now use the trunk that was previously unused. Pretty cool!

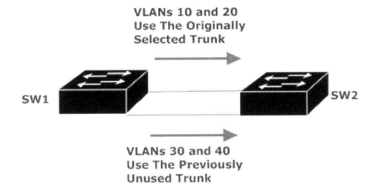

Let's quickly review those STP port states.

The STP port state *disabled* is a little odd in that you won't see "DIS" next to a port in the output of *show spanning vlan*. Cisco does consider this to be an official STP state, so we will too! A disabled port is simply a port that's been administratively shut down. A disabled port isn't forwarding frames or even officially running STP.

Once that port is administratively enabled, the port goes into blocking state (BLK). The port still can't do much. No frame forwarding, no frame receiving, and therefore no dynamic learning of MAC addresses. About the only thing a blocked port can do is accept BPDUs from neighboring switches.

```
SW2#show spanning vlan 40

Interface        Role Sts Cost
--------------   ---- --  ---------
Fa0/11           Root FWD 19
Fa0/12           Altn BLK 19
```

When a port starts the transition from blocking to forwarding, it enters listening mode (LIS).

```
SW2# show spanning vlan 40

Interface        Role Sts Cost
--------------   ---- --  ---------
Fa0/11           Altn BLK 19
Fa0/12           Root LIS 9
```

The obvious question: "Listening for *what?*" A listening port is listening for BPDUs. A listening port can send BPDUs as well, allowing the port to participate in the root bridge election. A port in listening mode still can't forward or receive frames, and as a result the port can't learn MAC addresses.

As the transition continues, the port goes from listening to learning (LRN) mode.

```
SW2#show spanning vlan 40

Interface        Role Sts Cost
--------------   ---- --  ---------
Fa0/11           Altn BLK 19
Fa0/12           Root LRN 9
```

A learning port isn't forwarding frames, but it is learning MAC addresses and adding them to the switch's MAC address table. A port in learning mode continues to send and receive BPDUs.

Finally, the port goes from learning to forwarding mode. Forwarding mode allows a port to forward and receive frames, send and receive BPDUs, and continue to learn MAC addresses. This is the only state where the port is actually forwarding frames!

Let's review that list we used for root port selection:

First, choose the port receiving the superior BPDU.

Tie? Choose the port with the lowest root path cost.

Still tied? Choose the port receiving the BPDU with the lowest Sender BID.

Still tied? Choose the port receiving a frame from the lowest **sender** Port ID.

That port ID is a combination of port priority and port number. During that lab, we had the following ports sending BPDUs on SW1:

```
SW1#show spanning vlan 1


Interface         Role Sts Cost         Prio.Nbr
---------------   ---- --  ---------
  Fa0/11          Desg FWD 19           128.11
  Fa0/12          Desg FWD 19           128.12
```

There's another cute little way of performing per-VLAN load balancing on our switches, and that's by manipulating the port priority. In this lab, we'll change the port priority of 0/12 to make it lower than that of 0/11 for *some* VLANs, while leaving it the same for others. We'll have VLANs 10 and 20 use the trunk over 0/12. VLANs 30 and 40 will continue to use the trunk over 0/11. (The commands from the previous load-balancing lab have been removed.)

Requirements:

VLANs 10 and 20: Use Fast 0/12

VLANs 30 and 40: Use Fast 0/11

Configure SW1 only!

The edited readout of *show spanning vlan* for each VLAN on SW1 reflects the default port priority of 128 on ports 0/11 and 0/12.

```
SW1#show spanning vlan 10


Interface         Role Sts Cost         Prio.Nbr   Type
---------------   ---- --  ---------    --------
  Fa0/11          Desg FWD 19           128.13     P2p
  Fa0/12          Desg FWD 19           128.14     P2p


SW1#show spanning vlan 20


Interface         Role Sts Cost         Prio.Nbr Type
---------------   ---- --  ---------    --------
  Fa0/11          Desg FWD 19           128.13     P2p
  Fa0/12          Desg FWD 19           128.14     P2p
```

```
SW1#show spanning vlan 30

Interface       Role Sts Cost        Prio.Nbr    Type
--------------- ---- --- ---------   --------    --------
Fa0/11          Desg FWD 19          128.13      P2p
Fa0/12          Desg FWD 19          128.14      P2p


SW1#show spanning vlan 40

Interface       Role Sts Cost        Prio.Nbr    Type
--------------- ---- --- ---------   --------    --------
Fa0/11          Desg FWD 19          128.13      P2p
Fa0/12          Desg FWD 19          128.14      P2p
```

The same commands on SW2 show the same port priority for each VLAN.

```
SW2#show spanning vlan 10


VLAN0010
  Spanning tree enabled protocol ieee
  Root ID      Priority      24586
               Address    001c.0fbf.2f00
               Cost       19
               Port       12 (FastEthernet0/12)
               Hello Time 2 sec   Max Age 20 sec  Forward Delay 15 sec

   Bridge ID   Priority      32778 (priority 32768 sys-id-ext 10)
               Address    000e.84ae.3600
               Hello Time 2 sec   Max Age 20 sec  Forward Delay 15 sec
               Aging Time   300

Interface       Role Sts Cost        Prio.Nbr  Type
--------------- ---- --- ---------   --------  --------
Fa0/11          Altn BLK 19          128.11    P2p
Fa0/12          Root FWD 19          128.12    P2p


SW2#show spanning vlan 20

Interface       Role Sts Cost        Prio.Nbr  Type
--------------- ---- --- ---------   --------  --------
Fa0/11          Altn BLK 19          128.11    P2p
Fa0/12          Root FWD 19          128.12    P2p



SW2#show spanning vlan 30
```

```
Interface          Role Sts Cost        Prio.Nbr  Type
---------------    ---- --  ---------   --------
Fa0/11             Altn BLK 19          128.11    P2p
Fa0/12             Root FWD 19          128.12    P2p


SW2#show spanning vlan 40


Interface          Role Sts Cost        Prio.Nbr  Type
---------------    ---- --  ---------   --------
Fa0/11             Altn BLK 19          128.11    P2p
Fa0/12             Root FWD 19          128.12    P2p
```

For VLANs 30 and 40 to start using fast 0/11, we'll decrease the port priority for those VLANs on fast 0/12. The new port priority must be set in increments of 16, and the switch doesn't like it when you do not do so.

```
SW1(config)#int fast 0/12
SW1(config-if)#spanning vlan 30 ?
   Cost            Change an interface's per VLAN spanning tree path cost
   port-priority   Change an interface's spanning tree port priority

SW1(config-if)#spanning vlan 30 port-priority ?
   <0-240> port priority in increments of 16

SW1(config-if)#spanning vlan 30 port-priority 35
% Port Priority in increments of 16 is required

SW1(config-if)#spanning vlan 30 port-priority 64
SW1(config-if)#spanning vlan 40 port-priority 64
```

show spanning vlan 30 and *show spanning vlan 40* verify the change.

```
SW1#show spanning vlan 30


Interface          Role Sts Cost        Prio.Nbr  Type
---------------    ---- --  ---------   --------
Fa0/11             Desg FWD 19          128.13    P2p
Fa0/12             Desg FWD 19          64.14     P2p


SW1#show spanning vlan 40


Interface          Role Sts Cost        Prio.Nbr  Type
---------------    ---- --  ---------   --------
Fa0/11             Desg FWD 19          128.13    P2p
Fa0/12             Desg FWD 19          64.14     P2p
```

When it comes to VLANs 30 and 40, the BPDU going from SW1 to SW2 over fast 0/11 is now superior to that over fast 0/12. As a result, VLANs 30 and 40 are now using the trunk over fast 0/11, verified by *show spanning vlan 30* and *show spanning vlan 40* on SW2.

```
SW2#show spanning vlan 30

Interface        Role Sts Cost        Prio.Nbr  Type
--------------   ---- --  ---------   --------  --------

Fa0/11           Root FWD 19          128.11    P2p
Fa0/12           Altn BLK 19          128.12    P2p


SW2#show spanning vlan 40

Interface        Role Sts Cost        Prio.Nbr  Type
--------------   ---- --  ---------   --------  --------

Fa0/11           Root FWD 19          128.11    P2p
Fa0/12           Altn BLK 19          128.12    P2p
```

VLANs 10 and 20 continue to use the trunk over fast 0/12, verified by *show spanning vlan 10* and *show spanning vlan 20* on SW2.

```
SW2#show spanning vlan 10

Interface        Role Sts Cost        Prio.Nbr  Type
--------------   ---- --  ---------   --------  --------

Fa0/11           Altn BLK 19          128.11    P2p
Fa0/12           Root FWD 19          128.12    P2p


SW2#show spanning vlan 20

Interface        Role Sts Cost        Prio.Nbr  Type
--------------   ---- --  ---------   --------  --------

Fa0/11           Altn BLK 19          128.11    P2p
Fa0/12           Root FWD 19          128.12    P2p
```

Now, I already know what you're gonna ask. Could we have raised the port priority on 0/11 rather than decreasing it on 0/12? Let's find out! First, I'll remove the two lab commands from fast 0/12 on SW1.

```
SW1(config)#int fast 0/12
SW1(config-if)#no spanning vlan 40 port-priority 64
SW1(config-if)#no spanning vlan 30 port-priority 64
```

On SW2, *show spanning vlan 30* and *show spanning vlan 40* verify the change back to fast 0/12.

```
SW2#show spanning vlan 30

Interface        Role  Sts Cost       Prio.Nbr   Type
---------------  ----  --  ---------  --------
Fa0/11           Altn  BLK 19         128.11     P2p
Fa0/12           Root  FWD 19         128.12     P2p


SW2#show spanning vlan 40

Interface        Role  Sts Cost       Prio.Nbr   Type
---------------  ----  --  ---------  --------
Fa0/11           Altn  BLK 19         128.11     P2p
Fa0/12           Root  FWD 19         128.12     P2p
```

On fast 0/11, we'll raise the port priority for VLANs 30 and 40 to 160 (a multiple of 160!).

```
SW1(config)#int fast 0/11
SW1(config-if)#spanning vlan 30 port-priority 160
SW1(config-if)#spanning vlan 40 port-priority 160
```

Raising the port priority on fast 0/11 has the same effect as reducing it on fast 0/12, verified by show spanning vlan on SW2. VLANs 30 and 40 are using the trunk over fast 0/11…

```
SW2#show spanning vlan 30

Interface        Role  Sts Cost       Prio.Nbr   Type
---------------  ----  --  ---------  --------
Fa0/11           Root  FWD 19         128.11     P2p
Fa0/12           Altn  BLK 19         128.12     P2p


SW2#show spanning vlan 40

Interface        Role  Sts Cost       Prio.Nbr   Type
---------------  ----  --  ---------  --------
Fa0/11           Root  FWD 19         128.11     P2p
Fa0/12           Altn  BLK 19         128.12     P2p
```

… while VLANs 10 and 20 continue to use the trunk over fast 0/12.

```
SW2#show spanning vlan 10

Interface        Role  Sts Cost       Prio.Nbr   Type
---------------  ----  --  ---------  --------
Fa0/11           Altn  BLK 19         128.11     P2p
Fa0/12           Root  FWD 19         128.12     P2p
```

```
SW2#show spanning vlan 20

Interface        Role Sts Cost        Prio.Nbr  Type
---------------  ---- --  ---------   --------
Fa0/11           Altn BLK 19          128.11    P2p
Fa0/12           Root FWD 19          128.12    P2p
```

Whether you choose to lower or raise a port priority to get VLAN load balancing going is really up to you when it comes to real-world networking. For CCNP SWITCH exam success, as with all Cisco exams, it's great to know more than one way to get something done!

STP Timers

These timers are so important, you'll see them twice when you run *show spanning vlan*! (That's not the real reason, but you *will* see them twice.)

```
SW1#show spanning vlan 1


VLAN0001
  Spanning tree enabled protocol ieee
  Root ID    Priority    32769
             Address     000f.90e2.2540
             This bridge is the root
             Hello Time  2 sec  Max Age 20 sec   Forward Delay 15 sec

  Bridge ID Priority     32769 (priority 32768 sys-id-ext 1)
             Address     000f.90e2.2540
             Hello Time  2 sec  Max Age 20 sec   Forward Delay 15 sec
             Aging Time  15

Interface        Role Sts Cost        Prio.Nbr  Type
---------------  ---- --  ---------   --------
Fa0/11           Desg FWD 19          128.11    P2p
Fa0/12           Desg FWD 19          128.12    P2p
```

Hello Time defines how often the root bridge originates Config BPDUs. Default setting: 2 seconds.

Forward Delay is the length of the listening and learning port stages, with a default of 15 seconds for each individual stage.

Maximum Age (Max Age) is how long a switch will retain the superior BPDU's contents before discarding it. Default setting: 20 seconds.

Those are important values to know, but why do we see each one listed twice in that output? The first set of timers is in the *Root ID* field. It's this set of timers that is actually used by the root and all switches that receive a Configuration BPDU that originated with that particular root. The second set of timers is found in the *Bridge ID* field, and those are the local switch's setting for the timers. Unless you're on the root, frankly, those timers under *Bridge ID* do not matter.

Use *spanning vlan* to change these timers. For the change to take effect throughout the VLAN, always use these commands on your primary and secondary roots. IOS shows us the ranges of allowable settings for each command. None of them can be set to zero.

```
SW1(config)#spanning vlan 1 ?
   forward-time   Set the forward delay for the spanning tree
   hello-time     Set the hello interval for the spanning tree
   max-age        Set the max age interval for the spanning tree
   priority       Set the bridge priority for the spanning tree
   root           Configure switch as root
   <cr>

SW1(config)#spanning vlan 1 Hello ?
  <1-10> number of seconds between generation of config BPDUs

SW1(config)#spanning vlan 1 Hello 5
SW1(config)#spanning vlan 1 forward ?
  <4-30> number of seconds for the forward delay timer

SW1(config)#spanning vlan 1 forward 16
SW1(config)#spanning vlan 1 max-age ?
  <6-40> maximum number of seconds the information in a BPDU is valid

SW1(config)#spanning vlan 1 max-age 25
```

Verify with *show spanning vlan*.

```
SW1#show spanning vlan 1

VLAN0001
   Spanning tree enabled protocol ieee
   Root ID    Priority    32769
              Address     000f.90e2.2540
              This bridge is the root
              Hello Time   5 sec  Max Age 25 sec   Forward Delay 16 sec

   Bridge ID  Priority    32769 (priority 32768 sys-id-ext 1)
              Address     000f.90e2.2540
              Hello Time   5 sec  Max Age 25 sec   Forward Delay 16 sec
              Aging Time  300
```

On the root bridge, we expect the timers in the Root ID and Bridge ID fields to be identical. What about the downstream, non-root switch though?

```
SW2#show spanning vlan 1

VLAN0001
Spanning tree enabled protocol ieee
Root ID Priority 32769
Address 000f.90e2.2540
Cost 19
Port 13 (FastEthernet0/11)
Hello Time 5 sec Max Age 25 sec Forward Delay 16 sec

Bridge ID Priority 32769 (priority 32768 sys-id-ext 1)
Address 0017.9466.f780
Hello Time 2 sec Max Age 20 sec Forward Delay 15 sec
Aging Time 300 sec
```

As always, the settings in use are the ones under Root ID!

Root Switch Selection: Be Deterministic

If we leave STP to its own devices, a single switch is going to be the root bridge for every VLAN in our network. That might not be so bad, depending on your network topology, but the default root switch selection is left up to chance. The switch with the lowest MAC address will be crowned as the root, and that's not always best for our network.

We can choose another particular switch to be the root bridge for all VLANs, or we can spread the workload around a bit and let one switch be the root for some VLANs while another switch is the root for the rest of the VLANs. You can spread the root switch role around as much as you like. If you have 50 VLANs and five switches, you could make each switch the root for 10 VLANs. It's up to you!

Before this lab, I did a *write erase* and *delete vlan.dat* on both switches, reloaded, and created VLANs 10, 20, and 30 for our next lab. Please note that the cabling has changed, and we'll be adding a switch and two cables as this lab progresses.

As expected, SW1 is the root for all four VLANs.

SW1
Root for
All VLANs
(1,10,20,30)

Fast 0/10   Fast 0/10   SW2

We'd like SW2 to be the root for VLANs 20 and 30 while leaving SW1 the root for VLANs 1 and 10. Let's use *spanning vlan root primary* to make SW2 the root for VLAN 20.

```
SW2(config)#spanning vlan 20 root ?
   Primary    Configure this switch as primary root for this spanning tree
   Secondary  Configure switch as secondary root

SW2(config)#spanning vlan 20 root primary

SW2#show spanning vlan 20


VLAN0020
   Spanning tree enabled protocol ieee
   Root ID    Priority    24596
              Address     0017.9466.f780
              This bridge is the root
              Hello Time   2 sec  Max Age 20 sec   Forward Delay 15 sec
```

Done and done! The new root's priority is 24596. That's certainly good enough to make it the root, but where exactly did that priority come from? It depends...

Current root priority greater than 24576? Result: priority of new root is 24576 (plus the VLAN ID in this case, since system extension ID is running).

Current root priority less than 24576? Result: subtract 4096 from that root priority and you have the new root priority!

We'll now make SW2 the root for VLAN 30.

```
SW2(config)#spanning vlan 30 root primary

SW2#show spanning vlan 30


VLAN0030
   Spanning tree enabled protocol ieee
   Root ID    Priority    24606
              Address     0017.9466.f780
              This bridge is the root
              Hello Time   2 sec   Max Age 20 sec  Forward Delay 15 sec
```

I'm sure you noticed the *secondary* option. If you want a certain switch to take over as root bridge if the current root goes down, run *show spanning vlan root secondary* on the desired secondary bridge. That command will adjust the switch's priority enough to make it the *backup* root, but not enough to make it the *primary* root.

Let's see that in action! SW2 is still the root for VLANs 20 and 30, and we've added a third switch to the lab. We'll concentrate on those two VLANs from here on out.

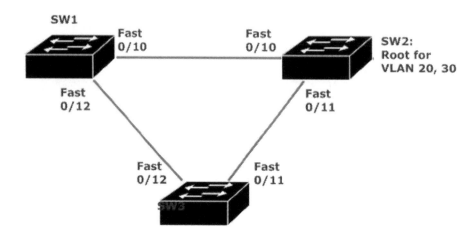

Here's the Bridge ID info for both SW1 and SW2, and here's a pop quiz: Which one of these would take over as the root for VLAN 20 if SW2 went down?

```
SW1#show spanning vlan 20
    Bridge ID   Priority    32788 (priority 32768 sys-id-ext 20)
                Address     000f.90e2.2540
                Hello Time   2 sec  Max Age 20 sec   Forward Delay 15 sec
                Aging Time   300

SW3#show spanning vlan 20
    Bridge ID   Priority    32788 (priority 32768 sys-id-ext 20)
                Address     001c.0fbf.2f00
                Hello Time   2 sec  Max Age 20 sec   Forward Delay 15 sec
                Aging Time   300 sec
```

They both have the default priority, so it comes down to MAC address, and SW1's MAC is lower than that of SW3. SW1's address begins with "000", and SW3's begins with "001", so nothing after that matters. I'll reload SW2 and we'll see if SW1 becomes the root in SW2's absence.

```
SW2#reload
Proceed with reload? [confirm]

*Mar 1 01:27:11.899: %SYS-5-RELOAD: Reload requested by console.

SW1#show spanning vlan 20
```

```
VLAN0020
   Spanning tree enabled protocol ieee
   Root ID     Priority      32788
               Address       000f.90e2.2540
               This bridge is the root
```

In SW2's absence, SW1 is now the root for VLANs 20 and 30.

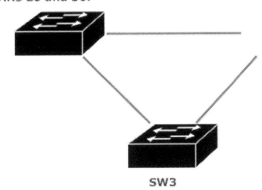

SW3

It does indeed! (*show spanning vlan 30* isn't shown, but we know SW1 is the root for that VLAN as well.) SW2 will become the root for VLAN 20 again once it comes back up...

```
SW2#show spanning vlan 20


VLAN0020
   Spanning tree enabled protocol ieee
   Root ID     Priority      24596
               Address       0017.9466.f780
               This bridge is the root
```

... but we'd like SW3 to take over as the root for VLAN 20 when SW2 is unavailable, while keeping SW1 as the root for VLAN 30 in that circumstance.

Let's make it happen. Note the change to SW3's priority.

```
SW3(config)#spanning vlan 20 root ?
   Primary    Configure this switch as primary root for this spanning tree
   Secondary  Configure switch as secondary root

SW3(config)#spanning vlan 20 root secondary

SW3#show spanning vlan 20


VLAN0020
   Spanning tree enabled protocol ieee
   Root ID     Priority      24596
```

When SW2 goes offline, SW1 will again take over the root bridge role for VLAN 30, but now SW3 will take that role for VLAN 20.

```
SW2#reload
Proceed with reload? [confirm]

SW1#show spanning vlan 30
            This bridge is the root

SW3#show spanning vlan 20
            This bridge is the root
```

With SW2 down, SW1 becomes the root for VLAN 30.

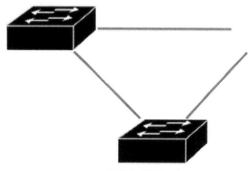

With SW2 down, SW3 becomes the root for VLAN 20.

SW2 will again take over as the primary root for both VLANs when it comes back online. SW3 remains the secondary for VLAN 20 and SW1 the secondary for VLAN 30.

If SW1 is the desired secondary root for VLAN 30, you're fine right now, but what if another switch is added to the network? That new switch might have a lower MAC than that of SW1. In this situation, I would manually configure SW1 as the secondary root for VLAN 30.

Of the two methods to configure primary and secondary roots, I prefer the one we just used. You can change the priority manually with *spanning vlan priority*, but the switch isn't going to help you by saying "Hey, the priority you set isn't low enough for this switch to become the primary / secondary!" There's one more thing that makes this method a tad complicated:

```
SW1(config)#spanning vlan 20 priority ?
  <0-61440> bridge priority in increments of 4096

SW1(config)#spanning vlan 20 priority 7000
% Bridge Priority must be in increments of 4096.
% Allowed values are:
    0       4096  8192   12288  16384  20480  24576  28672
    32768   36864 40960  45056  49152  53248  57344  61440
```

Hey, I *tried* using a non-4096 multiple!

By the way, we just got a call from the other BPDU type, demanding semi-equal time!

The Topology Change Notification BPDU

TCN BPDUs are generated by a switch when a port goes into forwarding mode *or* when a port goes from forwarding or learning into blocking mode. The TCN doesn't say exactly what happened, just that *something* happened.

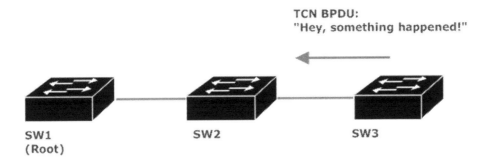

Each switch receiving the TCN will send an ACK back, and the TCN continues to be forwarded until it reaches the root.

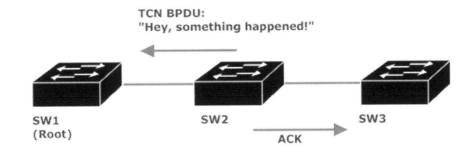

When the root receives the TCN, the root will acknowledge it in the form of a Configuration BPDU with the Topology Change bit set.

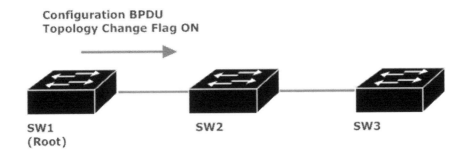

That BPDU with the TC bit set tells the receiving switches to change the aging time for their MAC tables from the default of 300 seconds to the duration of the Forward Delay timer. By default, that's just 15 seconds! This allows the switch to quickly rid itself of now-invalid MAC address table entries while keeping entries for hosts that are currently sending frames to that switch.

The aging time will stay at the new value for (Forward Delay + Max Age), and if the timers haven't been changed, that's 35 seconds.

Exception time! Changes to Portfast-enabled ports cannot result in the generation of a TCN BPDU. That makes sense, since the most common use of Portfast is when a single PC is directly connected to a switch port. When a port connected to a host goes into forwarding mode, it doesn't really affect STP operation, so there's no need to alert the entire network about it. If you're fuzzy on Portfast or any other advanced STP features, we'll take care of that in the very next section!

Chapter 6:

STP — ADVANCED FEATURES AND VERSIONS

Putting these features into operation is easy. Knowing where to run them and why is another matter. Let's jump right in!

Portfast

Portfast allows a port running STP to go directly from blocking to forwarding mode. And I can hear you now…"We spent all that time talking about STP preventing switching loops, and to leave the timers alone, and now you want to turn a couple of them *off?*"

Well, yeah, but only in a specific situation. If you have a host that has trouble getting an IP address via DHCP, configuring Portfast on that host's switchport is the way to go. The STP learning and listening stages can interfere with your host's DHCP address acquisition process. The chances of a switching loop on a single port with a single host connected are very small, so Portfast allows us to cheat just a bit in order to get that host up and running.

Enable portfast on a per-port level with *spanning-tree portfast*. Enabling this feature results in one long warning and an additional message.

```
SW2(config)#int fast 0/3
SW2(config-if)#spanning-tree ?
  bpdufilter    Don't send or receive BPDUs on this interface
  bpduguard     Don't accept BPDUs on this interface
  cost          Change an interface's spanning tree port path cost
  guard         Change an interface's spanning tree guard mode
  link-type     Specify a link type for spanning tree protocol use
```

```
   mst              Multiple spanning tree
   port-priority    Change an interface's spanning tree port priority
   portfast         Enable an interface to move directly to forwarding on link
   stack-port       Enable stack port
   vlan             VLAN Switch Spanning Tree

SW2(config-if)#spanning-tree portfast ?
   Disable   Disable portfast for this interface
   Trunk     Enable portfast on the interface even in trunk mode
   <cr>

SW2(config-if)#spanning-tree portfast
%Warning: portfast should only be enabled on ports connected to a single host.
   Connecting hubs, concentrators, switches, bridges, etc... to this interface
   when portfast is enabled, can cause temporary bridging loops. Use with
   CAUTION


%Portfast has been configured on FastEthernet0/3 but will only have effect
   when the interface is in a non-trunking mode.
```

The switch has given us a warning about the proper and improper use of Portfast, and has also let us know that trunking must be disabled in order for Portfast to be enabled. We *do* have the option of enabling Portfast on a trunk port, and after doing so, well, we'll be warned about it again!

```
SW2(config-if)#spanning-tree portfast trunk
%Warning: portfast should only be enabled on ports connected to a single host.
   Connecting hubs, concentrators, switches, bridges, etc... to this interface
   when portfast is enabled, can cause temporary bridging loops. Use with
   CAUTION
```

Enable Portfast globally with *spanning portfast default*. After doing so, a slightly different message appears. Using this command enables Portfast on all access ports.

```
SW2(config)#spanning portfast ?
   Bpdufilter   Enable portfast bpdu filter on this switch
   Bpduguard    Enable portfast bpdu guard on this switch
   Default      Enable portfast by default on all access ports

SW2(config)#spanning portfast default
%Warning: this command enables portfast by default on all interfaces. You
   should now disable portfast explicitly on switched ports leading to hubs,
   switches and bridges as they may create temporary bridging loops.
```

Verify with *show spanning interface portfast*. As IOS Help is so helpful to let us know, there's no "show spanning portfast" command.

```
SW2#show spanning portfast
                     ^
% Invalid input detected at '^' marker.

SW2#show spanning int fast 0/10 portfast
VLAN0001            disabled
VLAN0010            disabled
VLAN0020            disabled
VLAN0030            disabled
```

UplinkFast

When a port goes through the blocking-to-forwarding transition, we're looking at a 50-second delay before that port can actually begin forwarding frames. That almost-minute feels like almost-hours at times. Configuring a port with Portfast is one way to avoid part of that delay, but we're advised over and over by Cisco not to use Portfast unless it's on a port where a single host device is found. What if the device off that port is another switch?

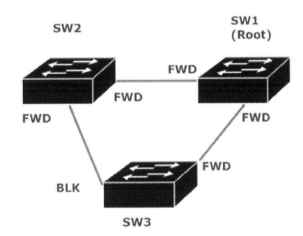

SW3 has two paths to the root, and assuming all port speeds are the same, the direct physical path will be the path SW3 uses to reach the root. STP blocks one of our six ports in order to prevent switching loops, which is *good*. If the open path between SW1 and SW3 goes down, there will be approximately a 50-second delay before that blocked port is open, and that's *bad*.

With Uplinkfast in use, the ports SW3 could potentially use to reach the root switch are collectively referred to as an *uplink group*. The uplink group includes ports in blocking and forwarding mode. If the forwarding port in the uplink group senses that the primary link is down, another port in the uplink group will be transitioned immediately (almost) from blocking to forwarding.

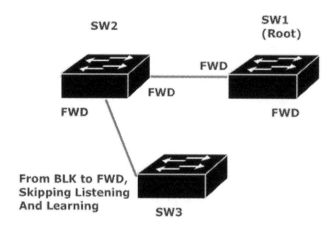

By "almost immediately", I mean 1 – 3 seconds, although some Cisco documentation makes it sound like there's no delay at all.

Frankly, Uplinkfast is Portfast for wiring closets. Cisco strongly recommends Uplinkfast not be used on distribution- and core-layer switches.

Uplinkfast is enabled globally and for all VLANs residing on the switch. It's all or nothing with this feature – you can't run it on a per-port or per-VLAN basis.

The original root port on the Uplinkfast-enabled switch will become the root port again when it detects that the original primary path to the root is available once more. This doesn't take place immediately. By default, the switch will wait *(2 x Forward Delay) + 5 seconds* before the primary root port enters forwarding state.

Uplinkfast does have two immediate actions you should be aware of, and they both occur when Uplinkfast is first enabled. The first is setting the switch priority to 49,152. This effectively prevents this switch from becoming the root unless all other switches go down, in which case you have much bigger problems to deal with!

```
SW2(config)#spanning uplinkfast ?
  max-update-rate Rate at which station address updates are sent
  <cr>

SW2#show spanning vlan 1

VLAN0001
  Spanning tree enabled protocol ieee
  Root ID    Priority    32769
             Address     000f.90e2.2540
             Cost        3019
             Port        14 (FastEthernet0/12)
             Hello Time  2 sec  Max Age 20 sec   Forward Delay 15 sec
```

```
Bridge ID  Priority      49153 (priority 49152 sys-id-ext 1)
           Address       0017.9466.f780
           Hello Time   2 sec  Max Age 20 sec   Forward Delay 15 sec
           Aging Time   300 sec
Uplinkfast enabled

Interface          Role Sts  Cost
------------------ ---- ---
Fa0/12             Root FWD  3019
```

The STP port cost is increased by 3000, making it unlikely that this switch will be used to reach the root switch by any downstream switches.

UplinkFast works really well, and on occasion it works a little too well. Actually, a little too fast! Let's revisit the original network and add two hosts.

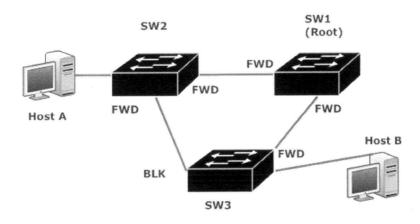

Frames from Host A will currently go through SW2, then SW1, then SW3. When the link between SW3 and SW1 goes down, that path is no longer valid, but the now-invalid entry to send frames to Host B via SW1 will still be in SW2's table.

That's where our single Uplinkfast option comes into play:

```
SW3(config)#spanning uplinkfast ?
  max-update-rate Rate at which station address updates are sent
  <cr>
```

The cutover to the backup path is so fast that the MAC address tables of other switches in the network may be out of date for a few seconds after the cutover. To avoid that, SW3 sends "dummy" multicast frames to SW2. The destination address is 0100.0ccd.cdcd, and the source address – well, that's the rub. We're going to send these frames for every single MAC address entry in SW3's table, which might be small or might be very large!

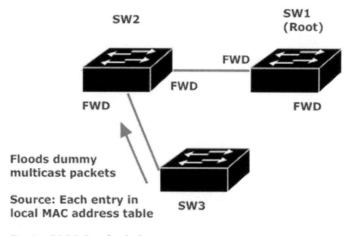

That flooding quickly updates SW2's MAC address table. If SW3's MAC address table is particularly large, you may want to adjust the maximum update rate, which by default is 150 packets per second. You can disable the sending of those dummy frames by setting this value to zero.

```
SW3(config)#spanning uplinkfast max-update-rate ?
  <0-32000> Maximum number of update packets per second
```

Verify your Uplinkfast settings with show spanning uplinkfast.

```
SW3#show spanning uplinkfast
UplinkFast is enabled

Station update rate set to 150 packets/sec.

UplinkFast statistics

Number of transitions via uplinkFast (all VLANs)         : 0
Number of proxy multicast addresses transmitted (all VLANs)  : 0
```

BackboneFast

The Cisco-proprietary feature BackboneFast helps our network recover from indirect link failures. The key word is *indirect*. If a switch detects an indirect link failure (a failure of a link not directly connected to the switch in question), BackboneFast goes into action. An indirect link failure is detected when an inferior BPDU is received, as we'll see in the upcoming walkthrough. Let's take a look at a three-switch setup where all links are working (currently!), and STP is running as expected. All links are running at the same speed.

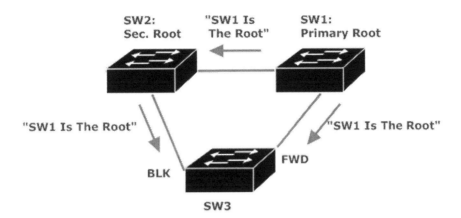

SW1 has been elected root, and it sends Configuration BPDUs to SW2 and SW3 every two seconds reminding them of that. In turn, SW2 takes the BPDU it's receiving from SW1 and relays it to SW3. All is well until SW2 loses its connection to SW1, which means SW2 will start announcing itself as the root. SW3 will receive two separate BPDUs from two claimants to the root bridge role.

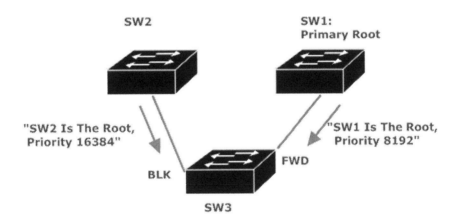

SW3 compares the priority in each BPDU and sees SW2 has a higher BID, making the BPDU from SW2 an *inferior BPDU*. As a result, SW3 ignores that BPDU. Once SW3's MaxAge timer on the port leading to SW2 hits zero, that port will transition to the listening state and start relaying the information contained in the BPDU coming from SW1 – the *superior BPDU*.

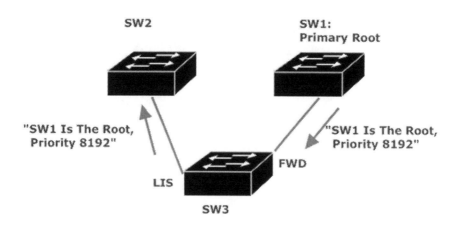

Backbonefast speeds up the overall process by skipping the MaxAge stage. This doesn't eliminate the delay, but it does cut the overall delay from 50 to 30 seconds (the overall duration of the listening and learning states).

When an indirect link outage is detected, the *Root Link Query* goes into action in the form of *requests* and *responses*. These message types act as a sort of echo and echo reply combo. The request is sent to ensure connectivity to the root, is sent via a port receiving BPDUs, and is sent by the switch detecting the indirect link outage.

The request names the switch believed by the sender to be the root. The *recipient* forwards that RLQ request out its own root port, and after a short period of time (hopefully), the request comes back with the name of the root that can be reached via that port. If they match, all is well!

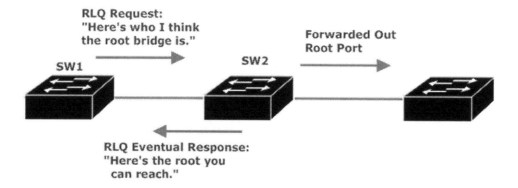

There are two circumstances under which the recipient will respond immediately, one good and one bad. The bad one: The recipient has a different root bridge listed.

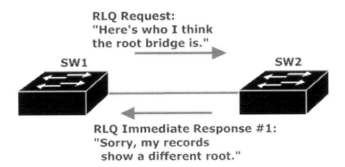

The good one: The recipient IS the root bridge.

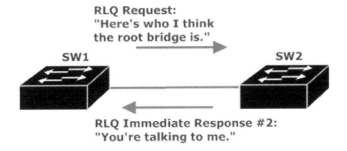

All switches in the network have to be able to send, relay, and respond to RLQ requests. Since RLQ is enabled by enabling BackboneFast, you should run this feature on every switch in the network. The easiest part of BackboneFast is enabling it. This command is a true Cisco rarity in that there are no options. Just enable it, and verify with *show spanning backbonefast*.

```
SW3(config)#spanning backbonefast ?
  <cr>

SW3#show spanning backbonefast
BackboneFast is enabled
```

Root Guard

The root we're guarding, of course, is the root switch!

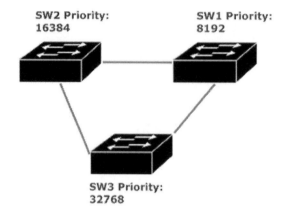

SW1 is entrenched as the root – until SW4 arrives!

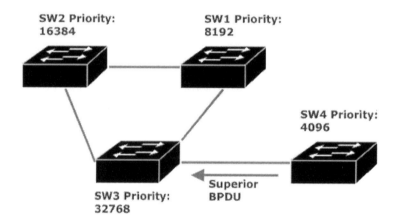

SW4 will take over as the root due to its lower BID, and depending on your network design and the switches' capabilities, you might not want that. SW4 could also be a rogue switch! If we go to the trouble of deciding which switch should be the root, we should likely go to a little bit of trouble in protecting that switch's role. That's where Root Guard comes in.

Root Guard is configured at the port level, and disqualifies any switch downstream from that port from becoming the primary or secondary root. To prevent SW4 from taking over either of those roles, configure Root Guard on SW3's port leading to SW4.

When a superior BPDU is received on a port running Root Guard, that BPDU is discarded and the port put into *root-inconsistent state*. That's verified by *show spanning vlan* and *show spanning inconsistent-ports* as well as this console message I received once SW4 came online and started sending those superior BPDUs to SW3.

```
%SPANTREE-2-ROOTGUARD _ BLOCK: Root guard blocking port Fast
```

Ethernet0/4 on VLAN0001.

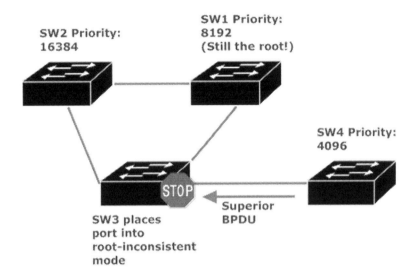

```
SW3#show spanning vlan 1

VLAN0001
  Spanning tree enabled protocol ieee
  Root ID    Priority    8193 (SW1 is still the root!)
             Address     000f.90e2.2540
             Cost        19
             Port        14 (FastEthernet0/12)
             Hello Time   2 sec  Max Age 20 sec   Forward Delay 15 sec

  Bridge ID  Priority    32769 (priority 32768 sys-id-ext 1)
             Address     001c.0fbf.2f00
             Hello Time   2 sec  Max Age 20 sec   Forward Delay 15 sec
             Aging Time  300 sec

Interface          Role Sts  Cost     Prio Nbr  Type
----------------   --- ----  -------  --------  --------------------
Fa0/4              Desg BKN  19       128.6     P2p*ROOT _ Inc
Fa0/11             Altn BLK  19       128.13 P2p
Fa0/12             Root FWD  19       128.14 P2p
```

The interface receiving the superior BPDU isn't totally shut down by Root Guard. It's still listening for BPDUs, and once those superior BPDUs stop coming, that port will transition normally through the STP port states and will come out of root-inconsistent state on its own. To illustrate, I'll set SW4's priority back to the default.

```
SW4(config)#no spanning vlan 1 priority 4096
```

SW4 quickly recognizes SW1 as the root...

```
SW4#show spanning vlan 1


VLAN0001
   Spanning tree enabled protocol ieee
   Root ID    Priority    8193
              Address     000f.90e2.2540
```

... and SW3's 0/4 port is no longer root-inconsistent.

```
%SPANTREE-2-ROOTGUARD _ UNBLOCK: Root guard unblocking port
FastEthernet0/4 on VLAN0001.


SW3#show spanning inc


Name                  Interface                 Inconsistency
------------------    --------------------      --------------


Number of inconsistent ports (segments) in the system : 0
```

What if we didn't want *any* BPDUs coming in on SW3's 0/4 port, you ask? Well...

BPDU Guard

Hey, remember that Portfast warning? Of course you do!

```
SW3(config)#int fast 0/2
SW3(config-if)#spanning portfast
%Warning: portfast should only be enabled on ports connected to a single host.
  Connecting hubs, concentrators, switches, bridges, etc... to this interface
  when portfast is enabled, can cause temporary bridging loops. Use with
  CAUTION
```

You would think that might discourage anyone thinking of connecting a switch to a Portfast-enabled port, but someone just might try it, and doing so creates the possibility of a switching loop.

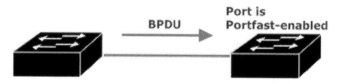

Recipe for a switching loop

Enabling *BPDU Guard* on a port will result in that port going into *error disabled state* ("err-disabled state") when *any* BPDU is received, superior or inferior. We'll use the topology from the Root Guard section to illustrate.

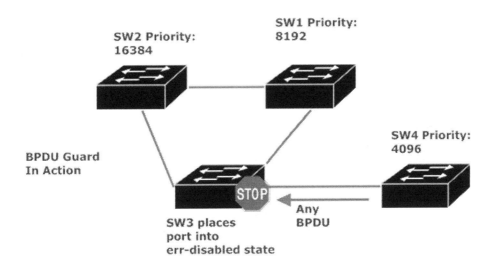

Enabling BPDU Guard on SW3's 0/4 port will block BPDUs coming in from SW4 and shut the port down. I'll open that port after enabling BPDU Guard. Note that the command requires you to specify "enable" or "disable" – "spanning bpduguard" is not a legal command on its own.

```
SW3(config)#int fast 0/4
SW3(config-if)#spanning ?
  bpdufilter     Don't send or receive BPDUs on this interface
  bpduguard      Don't accept BPDUs on this interface
  cost           Change an interface's spanning tree port path cost
  guard          Change an interface's spanning tree guard mode
  link-type      Specify a link type for spanning tree protocol use
  mst            Multiple spanning tree
  port-priority  Change an interface's spanning tree port priority
  portfast       Enable an interface to move directly to forwarding on link
                 up
  stack-port     Enable stack port
  vlan           VLAN Switch Spanning Tree

SW3(config-if)#spanning bpduguard ?
  Disable        Disable BPDU guard for this interface
  Enable         Enable BPDU guard for this interface

SW3(config-if)#spanning bpduguard enable
SW3(config-if)#no shut

%LINK-3-UPDOWN: Interface FastEthernet0/4, changed state to up
```

```
%LINEPROTO-5-UPDOWN:Line protocol on Int FastEthernet0/4,changedstate to up

%SPANTREE-2-BLOCK_BPDUGUARD: Received BPDU on port Fa0/4 with BPDU Guard
enabled. Disabling port.

%PM-4-ERR_DISABLE: bpduguard error detected on Fa0/4, putting Fa0/4 in err-
disable state

%LINEPROTO-5-UPDOWN: Line protocol on Int FastEthernet0/4, changed state to
down

%LINK-3-UPDOWN: Interface FastEthernet0/4, changed state to down
```

The interface came up physically and logically, but the first BPDU that came in resulted in the port being disabled by BPDU Guard.

```
SW3#show int fast 0/4
FastEthernet0/4 is down, line protocol is down (err-disabled)
```

An error-disabled port must be cleared manually. Once those BPDUs stop coming, you'll need to do a *shut/no shut* to reset the port.

You're not required to run BPDU Guard on a Portfast-enabled port, but it's a good idea! It's such a good idea that you can globally enable BPDU Guard on all Portfast-enabled ports via *spanning portfast bpduguard default*.

```
SW3(config)#spanning portfast bpduguard ?
  default Enable bpdu guard by default on all portfast ports
```

If you're not using that method of enabling BPDU Guard, remember that it's off by default and is enabled / disabled with *spanning-tree bpduguard* at the interface level.

BPDU Filtering

We have a similar but not identical service at our disposal to stop unwanted BPDUs. BPDU Filtering stops all BPDUs from leaving or being accepted on a Portfast-enabled port. To enable this feature globally on all your Portfast-enabled ports:

```
SW3(config)#spanning-tree portfast ?
  Bpdufilter  Enable portfast bpdu filter on this switch
  Bpduguard   Enable portfast bpdu guard on this switch
  Default     Enable portfast by default on all access ports
```

```
SW3(config)#spanning-tree portfast bpdufilter ?
   Default     Enable bpdu filter by default on all portfast ports

   SW3(config)#spanning-tree portfast bpdufilter default
```

To enable and disable this feature at the port level, regardless of Portfast:

```
SW3(config)#int fast 0/4
SW3(config-if)#spanning bpdufilter ?
   Disable  Disable BPDU filtering for this interface
   enable   Enable BPDU filtering for this interface
```

To verify this and several other features we've seen (and will see!), run *show spanning summary*.

```
SW3#show spanning summary
Switch is in pvst mode
Root bridge for: none
Extended system ID          is enabled
Portfast Default            is disabled
PortFast BPDU Guard Default is enabled
Portfast BPDU Filter Default is enabled
Loopguard Default           is disabled
EtherChannel misconfig guard is enabled
UplinkFast                  is disabled
BackboneFast                is enabled
```

You can also verify a port's individual BPDU Filter settings, along with gathering other important info, with *show spanning interface detail*.

```
SW1#show spanning int fast 0/3 detail
  Port 3 (FastEthernet0/3) of VLAN0003 is forwarding
    Port path cost 100, Port priority 128, Port Identifier 128.3
    Designated root has priority 32771, address 000f.90e2.2540
    Designated bridge has priority 32771, address 000f.90e2.2540
    Designated port id is 128.3, designated path cost 0
    Timers: message age 0, forward delay 0, hold 0
    Number of transitions to forwarding state: 1
    The port is in the portfast mode
    Link type is shared by default
    Bpdu filter is enabled
    BPDU: sent 23, received 0
```

With all this talk of blocking BPDUs, we better ensure we get the ones we need!

Loop Guard

With our three-switch network back at its defaults, we know SW1 is originating Config BPDUs and sending them to both SW2 and SW3, and the non-root switches are forwarding BPDUs to each other (hence the two-headed arrow).

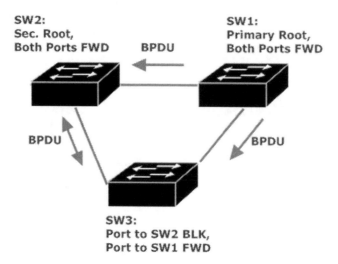

If the direct link between SW2 and SW3 goes unidirectional, we have a problem. What if SW3 can send BPDUs to SW2, but not vice versa? SW3 will wait the duration of the MaxAge timer and then begin to transition the port on that link from blocking to forwarding. When all six ports hit forwarding mode, we have a switching loop.

Loop Guard doesn't allow that port on SW3 to go from blocking to forwarding. Instead, the port no longer receiving the BPDUs will go from blocking to *loop-inconsistent*, which acts a lot like blocking mode. A switching loop is prevented, and once the cable is repaired and the BPDUs begin flowing from SW2 to SW3 again, the port will come back up on its own.

To enable Loop Guard globally, run *spanning-tree loopguard default*.

```
SW1(config)#spanning-tree loopguard ?
  Default   Enable loopguard by default on all ports

SW1(config)#spanning-tree loopguard default
```

To enable Loop Guard on a per-port basis, run *spanning-tree guard loop*.

```
SW1(config)#int fast 0/2
SW1(config-if)#spanning-tree guard ?
  Loop      Set guard mode to loop guard on interface
  none      Set guard mode to none
  root      Set guard mode to root guard on interface

SW1(config-if)#spanning-tree guard loop
```

To disable Loop Guard at the port level, run *no spanning-tree guard loop*.

```
SW1(config-if)#no spanning-tree guard loop
```

Dept. Of Oddities: Loop Guard is enabled globally or on a per-port basis, but it operates on a per-VLAN basis. If a trunk is carrying traffic for VLANs 10, 20, and 30, and BPDUs stop coming in for VLAN 10, the port will go port-inconsistent for VLAN 10 only. The port will continue to operate normally for VLANs 20 and 30.

Detecting Unidirectional Links With UDLD

BPDUs may not arrive at their destination due to a unidirectional link where SW1 can send to SW2, but SW2 can't send a BPDU back over the same connection.

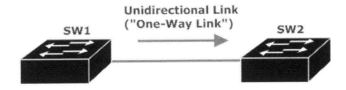

UDLD's basic operation is simple. A UDLD-enabled port sends a UDLD frame across the link every 15 seconds. If something comes back, we have a bidirectional link and all is well. If nothing comes back, we have a unidirectional link.

The sent UDLD message lets the recipient know which port sent the message, and then the recipient sends it right back with info on the port that received the message.

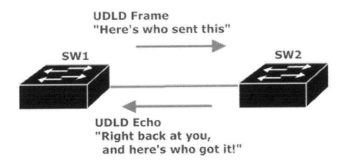

When UDLD runs in Normal mode, it gives us a syslog message to let us know about the problem. Run UDLD in aggressive mode, and the results are much more... aggressive! The port will be put into err-disabled state after eight sent UDLD messages result in zero UDLD frames from the remote switch.

We call this mode "aggressive" for two reasons. First, the port is shut down after eight missed messages, as opposed to Normal mode, which doesn't shut the port down under any circumstances. Second, a UDLD message is sent every second once a possible unidirectional link is detected.

UDLD can be enabled and disabled on a global and per-port basis. For global enabling and disabling, use udld followed by the mode you want.

```
SW1(config)#udld ?
  Aggressive  Enable UDLD protocol in aggressive mode on fiber ports except
              where locally configured
  enable      Enable UDLD protocol on fiber ports except where locally
              configured
  message     Set UDLD message parameters
```

Use the same command at the interface level. If you don't specify aggressive mode, the port defaults to normal mode.

```
SW2(config-if)#udld ?
  port        Enable UDLD protocol on this interface despite global UDLD
              setting

SW2(config-if)#udld port ?
  aggressive  Enable UDLD protocol in aggressive mode on this interface
              despite global UDLD setting
  disable     Disable UDLD protocol on this interface despite global UDLD
              setting
  <cr>
```

For UDLD to be effective, it must be enabled on both endpoints. Problem is, if aggressive mode shuts a port down after failing to receive an echo reply to eight consecutive UDLD frames going out once per second, won't the second port you configure always shut down before you finish the config?

Actually, no. When UDLD's aggressive mode is configured on the first endpoint, that port will indeed start sending UDLD frames every 15 seconds. The absence of a UDLD echo from the remote endpoint doesn't trigger the aggressive 8-second countdown to shutting the port down. Before that can happen, the remote switch has to answer back with a UDLD echo, letting the local switch know that the remote switch is indeed running UDLD.

"I haven't heard anything back,
so the remote switch must not be
running UDLD. No need to start
the countdown."

SW1   SW2

SW1 has   SW2 has no
UDLD config   UDLD config

Once SW1 has received an echo reply from SW2, the eight-second countdown will begin if SW1 stops getting UDLD replies from SW2.

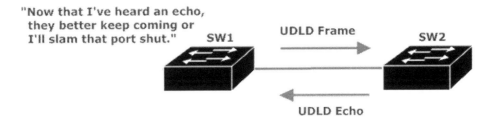

"Now that I've heard an echo,
they better keep coming or   UDLD Frame
I'll slam that port shut."   SW1   SW2

                                           UDLD Echo

Rapid Spanning-Tree Protocol

STP is fantastic at what it does – we'd just like it to get done a little faster, and that's why the Rapid Spanning Tree Protocol (RSTP) was developed! RSTP is defined by IEEE 802.1w, and it's considered an extension of 802.1d.

The overall 30-second delay built into STP convergence via the listening and learning states was once considered an acceptable delay, and still is in many networks. However, RSTP makes things just a bit more... rapid. The overall concept of the root bridge is still present in RSTP, but the port roles themselves are different. Let's take a look at the RSTP roles in this network, where SW1 is the root. Note SW3 has multiple connections to the Ethernet segment. Root and designated ports have already been selected.

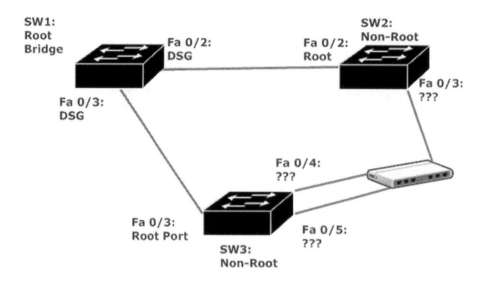

The root port concept stays the same as we move from STP to RSTP. Non-root switches select a root port, that port being the one with the lowest root path cost. SW2 and SW3 have both selected their root ports. As with STP, RSTP-enabled root bridges will not have root ports, but rather designated ports.

As with our STP example, a designated port must be elected on the segment connecting SW2 and SW3. As you'd expect, the DP will be the port with the lowest root path cost of all the ports on that segment, and we'll assume that to be one of the two ports SW3 has connected to that segment.

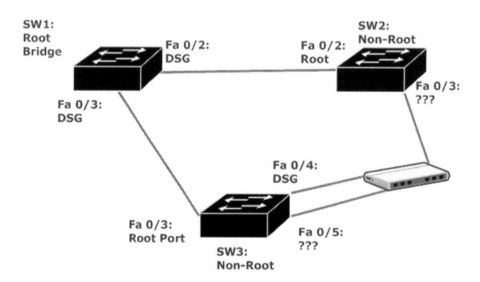

Here come the differences! RSTP has *alternate ports* rather than blocked ports. The "alternate" refers to the port having an alternate path to the root switch than the actual root port does.

SW2's port on the shared segment is an alternate port (ALT) – but what of the remaining port on SW3? That port becomes the *backup port* for that segment. This port gives SW3 a redundant path on that segment without guaranteeing that the root switch will still be accessible.

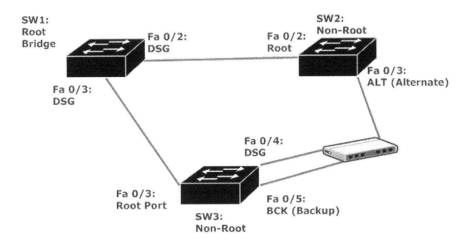

There are slight and important differences between STP and RSTP port states as well. The STP ports *disabled, blocking,* and *listening* are combined into the RSTP state *discarding,* the initial RSTP port state.

RSTP ports transition from discarding to learning, where incoming frames are discarded but the MAC addresses are being learned by the switch. Finally, the RSTP port transitions to the forwarding state, the equivalent of STP's forwarding state. A quick comparison:

STP: disabled > blocking > listening > learning > forwarding

RSTP: discarding > learning > forwarding

In addition to the familiar root port concept, RSTP brings with it two unique port types, *edge ports* and *point-to-point ports.* A point-to-point port is any port running in full-duplex mode. (Any ports running half-duplex are considered shared ports and must run STP rather than RSTP.)

An edge port is simply a port on the edge of the network, likely connected to a single host such as an end user's PC. To configure a port as an RSTP edge port, just run the familiar *spanning-tree portfast* command.

RSTP edge ports are simply PortFast-enabled ports, so they can go straight from discarding to forwarding. If a BPDU comes in on an RSTP edge port, it's "demoted" to a regular RSTP port and then generates a TCN BPDU. (More on that very soon.)

Edge ports play a huge part in RSTP's determination of when a topology change has taken place. Well, actually, they don't play a role, since RSTP considers a topology change to have taken place when a port moves into forwarding mode – unless that port is an edge port. RSTP does not consider that a change in the network, since only a single host will be connected to that particular port. That's hardly an earth-shattering change to our network, so RSTP doesn't bother alerting the rest of the network about it.

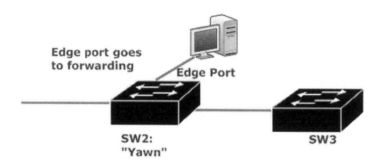

When a *non*-edge port moves into forwarding mode, that's when RSTP *does* bother letting the rest of the network know! RSTP does so by sending BPDUs out all non-edge designated ports, and naturally the TC bit is set on those BPDUs.

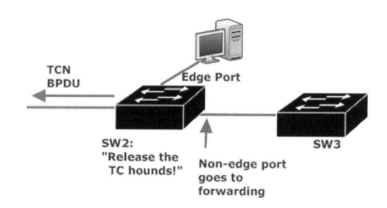

Switches that receive those BPDUs will remove all entries from their MAC tables except for the port the BPDU rode in on, and as we'd expect, *those* switches send BPDUs with the TC bit set out their non-edge DPs, and that continues until the entire network's been notified of the change – a "ripple effect", if you will.

Another major difference between STP and RSTP is the way BPDUs are generated. With STP, the root bridge generates and transmits BPDUs every two seconds, and the nonroot bridges read 'em and relay 'em. RSTP-enabled switches generate a BPDU every two seconds, regardless of whether they've received a BPDU from the root in that period of time. (This *hello time* interval is the same in both STP and RSTP.)

This slight change in operation from STP to RSTP allows all switches to have a role in detecting link failures, and the discovery of those failures is faster. Every switch expects to see a BPDU from its neighbor every two seconds, and if three BPDUs are missed, the link is considered down. The switch then immediately ages out all information concerning the port that was receiving the BPDUs.

This change cuts the error detection process from 20 seconds in STP to 6 seconds in RSTP. How? When a switch running STP misses a BPDU, the MaxAge timer kicks in. That timer dictates how long the switch will retain the contents of the last superior BPDU it received before it ages out and the STP recalculation process begins. We know the MaxAge default – 20 seconds! Compare that to the RSTP process, where the superior BPDU is aged out when three Hello Time intervals pass without it being refreshed!

RSTP Synchronization

The RSTP synch process is a simple series of handshakes between switches, carried out until all switches in the network are – wait for it – *synchronized*! Let's walk through the process with this three-switch network.

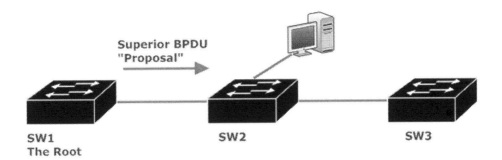

SW2 realizes SW1 is the root, and would like to agree to the proposal. But not so fast, my friend! First, SW2 has to synch itself, and in order for SW2 to consider itself synched, all ports on SW2 must either be discarding or an edge port. We see a PC off one of SW2's ports, so that's an edge port; now SW2 must place the port leading to SW3 into discarding mode.

SW2 will of course move its root port into forwarding. At that point, SW2 will reply to the proposal with an agreement and will send a proposal of its own out any non-edge port that was just placed into discarding state. There's a lot going on here – and it goes on quickly!

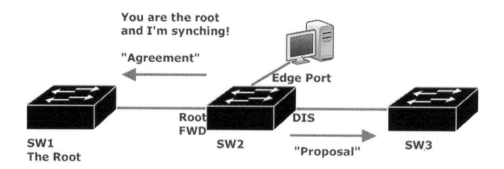

The *ripple effect* is powerful in RSTP synchronization. SW2 is agreeing with SW1 while almost simultaneously sending a proposal to SW3 (and any other downstream switches it's connected to). In turn, SW3 goes through the same process we saw SW2 go through – SW3 would accept that proposal from SW2 while sending proposals of its own. This ripple effect fans throughout the entire network until all switches are synched.

The Question Haunting Networks Everywhere

Does RSTP play well with STP? Pretty well, actually! If a switch is running RSTP and needs to communicate with switches using both STP and RSTP, it's the version number in the BPDU that tells the switch how to handle things. In our lab, SW3 is running RSTP after being configured with the *spanning-tree mode rapid-pvst* command, verified with *show spanning vlan*.

```
SW3(config)#spanning mode ?
   mst          Multiple spanning tree mode
   pvst         Per-Vlan spanning tree mode
   rapid-pvst   Per-Vlan rapid spanning tree mode

SW3(config)#spanning mode rapid-pvst ?
   <cr>

SW3(config)#spanning mode rapid-pvst
SW3#show spanning vlan 1

VLAN0001
   Spanning tree enabled protocol rstp
   Root ID     Priority    4097
               Address     000f.90eb.d480
               Cost        19
               Port        6 (FastEthernet0/4)
               Hello Time   2 sec  Max Age 20 sec   Forward Delay 15 sec
```

```
Bridge ID Priority      32769 (priority 32768 sys-id-ext 1)
            Address     001c.0fbf.2f00
            Hello Time   2 sec  Max Age 20 sec   Forward Delay 15 sec
            Aging Time  300 sec


Interface          Role Sts Cost      Prio.Nbr  Type
----------------   ---- --  --------- -------
Fa0/4              Root FWD 19        128.6     P2p
Fa0/11             Desg FWD 19        128.13    P2p Peer(STP)
Fa0/12             Desg FWD 19        128.14    P2p Peer(STP)
```

Note the output under "Type". The link via Fast0/4 is to SW4, a switch running RSTP. This is a full-duplex point-to-point link, and when there's no additional info after "P2p", the link is to an RSTP-enabled switch. When you see "Peer (STP)" as we do for the Fast0/11 and Fast0/12 links, you know those connections are to switches running STP.

It's a rare occasion indeed when you need to manually change the link type on an interface, but if you do, just use *spanning link-type*.

```
SW3(config-if)#spanning-tree link-type ?
  point-to-point   Consider the interface as point-to-point
  shared           Consider the interface as shared
```

Per-VLAN Spanning Tree Versions (PVST and PVST+)

The ultimate "the name is the recipe" protocol, the Cisco-proprietary PVST runs a separate instance of STP for each VLAN.

The Good: PVST does allow for much better fine-tuning of spanning tree performance than regular ol' STP does.

The Bad: Running PVST does mean extra work for your CPU and memory.

The Ugly: PVST requires ISL trunking.

PVST doesn't play well with Common Spanning Tree (more on that in a moment), so Cisco came up with PVST+, which has the same functionality as PVST while having the capability to run over ISL or dot1q trunks. And speaking of CST...

Common Spanning Tree and Multiple Spanning Tree

When our pal IEEE 802.1q ("dot1q") is the trunking protocol, the trunk is using a common instance of STP for all VLANs – hence the name, "Common Spanning Tree". More on that in just a minute.

Defined by IEEE 802.1s, MST earns its name from a scheme that allows multiple VLANs to be mapped to a single instance of STP, rather than having an instance for every VLAN. MST serves as a middle ground between CST (one STP instance) and PVST (one STP instance per VLAN). MST allows us to reduce the number of STP instances without knocking it all the way back to one.

MST was designed with enterprise networks in mind. While it can be useful in the right environment, it's not for every network. MST configs can become quite complex and a great deal of planning is recommended before you even start a config. No matter the size of the network, the purpose of MST is to map multiple VLANs to a lesser number of STP instances.

Let's say we have traffic for 750 VLANs coming in, and three switches that can handle some or all of that traffic.

With CST's one STP instance, one switch ends up handling all the traffic. We can't perform any per-VLAN load balancing, since that requires multiple instances of STP!

With PVST+, we can configure per-VLAN load balancing as we did in an earlier lab, so we could spread the workload around a bit. As we know though, everything we do on a Cisco switch has a cost in terms of CPU and/or time. With PVST+, if we have 750 VLANs, we have 750 instances of STP running.

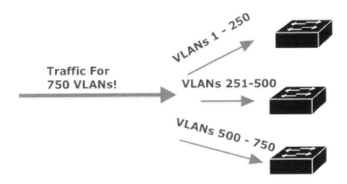

MST gives us a great middle ground, where we can map VLANs to instances of STP.

MST configuration involves logically dividing the switches into *regions*, and the switches in any given region must agree on the MST config name, the MST-instance / VLAN-mapping table, and the MST configuration revision number. Switches that disagree on any of these values are in different regions, and MST BPDUs are used to exchange values between switches. The MST BPDUs contain the MST config name, the config revision number, and a digest value derived from the mapping table.

A good way to get a mental picture of MST – CST interoperability is that CST will cover the entire network, and MST is a "subset" of the network. CST is going to maintain a loop-free network only with the links connecting the MST network subsets. MST's job is to keep a loop-free topology in the MST region itself. CST doesn't know what's going on inside the regions, nor does it want to know.

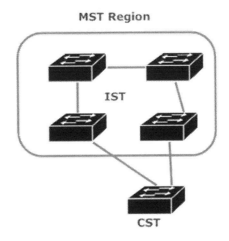

The "IST" in each region stands for Internal Spanning Tree, and it's the IST instance that is responsible for keeping communications in the MST regions loop-free.

Up to 16 MST instances (MSTIs) can exist in a region, numbered 0 – 15. MSTI Zero is reserved for the IST instance, and only the IST is going to send MST BPDUs. On occasion, you'll see the first ten MST instances referred to as "00" – "09"; those are decimal values, not hexadecimal values.

Enable MST on the switch with *spanning-tree mode mst*, and follow by dropping into MST configuration mode and naming the region and revision number.

```
SW3(config)#spanning-tree mode ?
  mst            Multiple spanning tree mode
  pvst           Per-Vlan spanning tree mode
  rapid-pvst     Per-Vlan rapid spanning tree mode

SW3(config)#spanning-tree mode mst
```

In MST configuration mode, *abort* exits the mode while not saving the changes; *exit* exits the mode and does save your changes.

```
SW3(config-mst)#?
  abort         Exit region configuration mode, aborting changes
  exit          Exit region configuration mode, applying changes
  instance      Map vlans to an MST instance
  name          Set configuration name
  no            Negate a command or set its defaults
  private-vlan  Set private-vlan synchronization
  revision      Set configuration revision number
  show          Display region configurations

SW3(config)#spanning-tree mst configuration
SW3(config-mst)#name CCNP
SW3(config-mst)#revision ?
  <0-65535> Configuration revision number

SW3(config-mst)#revision 1
SW3(config-mst)#instance ?
  <0-4094> MST instance id

SW3(config-mst)#instance 1 ?
  vlan Range of vlans to add to the instance mapping

SW3(config-mst)#instance 1 vlan ?
  LINE vlan range ex: 1-65, 72, 300 -200

SW3(config-mst)#instance 1 vlan 1 - 250
```

Verify with *show pending*. This is an MST configuration mode command. VLANs not manually assigned to an instance are mapped to Instance Zero.

```
SW3(config-mst)#show pending
Pending MST configuration
Name      [CCNP]
Revision  1     Instances configured 2

Instance Vlans mapped
--------
0         251-4094
1         1-250
```

Time to go from spanning to channeling!

Chapter 7:

ETHERCHANNELS

An Etherchannel is a logical bundling of two to eight parallel trunks running between two switches. This bundling of Fast Ethernet, Gig Ethernet, or even 10 Gig Ethernet ports is *aggregation*, and we love aggregation! We use more of our available bandwidth and we avoid some of that 50-second delay that comes with the MaxAge and Forward Delay timers. What's not to love?

(To avoid *aggravation*, though, ports placed inside an EC should be running at the same speed and have the same duplex settings.)

STP considers an Etherchannel to be a single link, regardless of how many physical links actually make up the Etherchannel. If one or more of the physical links in the Etherchannel go down, STP will give the link a higher cost due to the lost bandwidth, but the link is still considered up. That prevents the delay of bringing another link up!

In our lab, there are four FastEthernet trunks between SW2 and SW3. By default, STP allows us to use only one of the trunks.

Four physical links, but STP allows us to use only one.

SW2   SW3

```
SW2#show spanning vlan 1

Interface          Role Sts Cost
-----------------  ---- --- 
Fa0/21             Desg FWD 19
```

```
Fa0/22                    Desg FWD 19
Fa0/23                    Desg FWD 19
Fa0/24                    Desg FWD 19

SW3#show spanning vlan 1

Interface         Role Sts Cost
-----------------  ---- --
Fa0/21            Root FWD 19
Fa0/22            Altn BLK 19
Fa0/23            Altn BLK 19
Fa0/24            Altn BLK 19
```

As it stands, if 0/21 goes down on SW3, 0/22 will begin the transition from blocking to forwarding. In the meantime, communication between the two switches is lost. This temporary lack of a forwarding port can be avoided with an Etherchannel. By combining the physical ports into a single logical link, not only is the bandwidth of the links combined, but the failure of a link inside an Etherchannel will not force STP to start bringing another port from blocking to forwarding.

Let's put 0/21, 0/22, and 0/23 on both switches into an Etherchannel with the *channel-group* command. We'll leave 0/24 alone for now. (The channel group number does not have to match between switches.) I'll use *interface range* to make things a little quicker.

```
SW2(config-if-range)#channel-group 1 ?
  Mode   Etherchannel Mode of the interface

SW2(config-if-range)#channel-group 1 mode ?
  active     Enable LACP unconditionally
  auto       Enable PAgP only if a PAgP device is detected
  desirable  Enable PAgP unconditionally
  on         Enable Etherchannel only
  passive    Enable LACP only if a LACP device is detected

SW2(config-if-range)#channel-group 1 mode on

%LINK-3-UPDOWN: Interface Port-channel1, changed state to up

SW3(config)#int range fast 0/21 - 23
SW3(config-if-range)#channel-group 5 mode on

%LINEPROTO-5-UPDOWN: Line protocol on Interface Port-channel5, changed state
to up
```

The interfaces mentioned in the console messages, *port-channel1* and *port-channel5* are the logical representations of the Etherchannels on the respective switches.

Let's check out STP on SW3.

```
SW3#show spanning vlan 1

Interface           Role Sts Cost
-----------------   ---- --
Fa0/24              Altn BLK 19
Po5                 Root FWD 9
```

You can have 2 - 8 links
in an Etherchannel, and
STP sees only one.

SW2   SW3

Things have changed! The Etherchannel (Po5, short for *port-channel 5*) is now the connection in use, and with good reason. The path cost for that port is 9, less than half that of a single FastEthernet port! SW2 shows the same path cost result.

```
SW2#show spanning vlan 1

Interface           Role Sts Cost
-----------------   ---- --
Fa0/24              Desg FWD 19
Po1                 Desg FWD 9
```

Let's see what happens when one of the links inside the Etherchannel fails. We'll shut down 0/21 on R3 and then verify the changes, if any, to the STP costs and ports.

```
SW3(config)#int fast 0/21
SW3(config-if)#shut

SW3#show spanning vlan 1

Interface           Role Sts Cost
-----------------   ---- --
Fa0/24              Altn BLK 19
Po5                 Root FWD 12

SW2#show spanning vlan 1

Interface           Role Sts Cost
-----------------   ---- --
Fa0/24              Desg FWD 19
Po1                 Desg FWD 12
```

Thanks to our Etherchannel, STP didn't have to go to the trouble of opening 0/24. The down link in the Etherchannel was detected by STP, and the port's path cost increased, but the Etherchannel remained in forwarding mode and 0/24 stays blocked!

Negotiating An Etherchannel

The industry standard EC negotiation protocol is the *Link Aggregation Control Protocol* (LACP) and the Cisco-proprietary EC negotiation protocol is the *Port Aggregation Protocol* (PAgP).

I hate typing "PAgP", but I love how the protocol dynamically changes all of the other ports in an EC when you change a property of one of them statically (speed, duplex, etc.).

Defined in 802.3ad (the IEEE standard, not the year), LACP assigns a priority value to each port with Etherchannel capability. You can assign up to 16 ports to an LACP-negotiated Etherchannel, but only the eight ports with the lowest port priority will actually be part of the EC. The remaining ports will be bundled only if one or more of the already-bundled ports fails.

PAgP and LACP use different terminology to express the same modes. (Surprise!) We actually saw those in the *channel-group* command:

```
SW3(config)#int fast 0/24
SW3(config-if)#channel-group 5 mode ?
  active      Enable LACP unconditionally
  auto        Enable PAgP only if a PAgP device is detected
  desirable   Enable PAgP unconditionally
  on          Enable Etherchannel only
  passive     Enable LACP only if a LACP device is detected
```

With PAgP, a port in desirable mode will initiate bundling with a remote port, while a port in auto mode waits for the port on the other end of the trunk to start the process. If the ports at each endpoint are in auto, you know you'll be waiting a long time. (Forever.)

With LACP, a port in active mode initiates bundling and passive ports are just that! If the ports at each endpoint are passive, an EC will never form.

After re-opening 0/21 on SW3, I'll put all available trunks into a PAgP Etherchannel, verifying with *show pagp neighbor*.

```
SW2(config)#int range fast 0/21 - 24
SW2(config-if-range)#channel-group 1 mode ?
  active      Enable LACP unconditionally
  auto        Enable PAgP only if a PAgP device is detected
  desirable   Enable PAgP unconditionally
  on          Enable Etherchannel only
  passive     Enable LACP only if a LACP device is detected
```

```
SW2(config-if-range)#channel-group 1 mode desir

SW3(config)#int range fast 0/21 - 24
SW3(config-if-range)#channel-group 5 mode desir



SW3#show pagp neighbor
Flags:    S - Device is sending Slow hello.      C- Device  is  in  Consistent
                                                     state.

          A - Device is in Auto mode.            P- Device  learns  on  physical
                                                     port.


Channel group 5 neighbors
          Partner               Partner            Partner          Partner  Group
Port   Name               Device ID          Port             Age Flags Cap.
Fa0/21 SW2                0017.9466.f780     Fa0/21           14s SC    10001
Fa0/22 SW2                0017.9466.f780     Fa0/22           2s  SC    10001
Fa0/23 SW2                0017.9466.f780     Fa0/23           5s  SC    10001
Fa0/24 SW2                0017.9466.f780     Fa0/24           11s SC    10001
```

We're not going to get into every field of this output, but I'm sure you can see that having a command that gives you the name, device ID, and port of the partner in the group can be *very* helpful for verification and/or troubleshooting.

After removing the PAgP EC, I created one with LACP, verified with *show lacp neighbor*.

```
SW2(config)#int range fast 0/21 - 24
SW2(config-if-range)#channel-group 1 mode ?
    active      Enable LACP unconditionally
    auto        Enable PAgP only if a PAgP device is detected
    desirable   Enable PAgP unconditionally
    on          Enable Etherchannel only
    passive     Enable LACP only if a LACP device is detected

SW2(config-if-range)#channel-group 1 mode active

SW3(config)#int range fast 0/21 - 24
SW3(config-if-range)#channel-group 5 mode active

SW3#show lacp neighbor
Flags: S - Device is requesting Slow LACPDUs
        F - Device is requesting Fast LACPDUs
        A - Device is in Active mode
        P - Device is in Passive mode


Channel group 5 neighbors
```

```
  Partner's information:

Port    Flags  LACP port  Dev ID    Age    Admin  Oper Key  Port Number  Port State
               Priority                    key

Fa0/21  SA     32768      0017.9466. 20s    0x0    0x1       0x118        0x3D
                          f780

Fa0/22  SA     32768      0017.9466. 19s    0x0    0x1       0x119        0x3D
                          f780

Fa0/23  SA     32768      0017.9466. 21s    0x0    0x1       0x11A        0x3D
                          f780

Fa0/24  SA     32768      0017.9466. 23s    0x0    0x1       0x11B        0x3D
                          f780
```

The output is different, but matching up the Device ID and port information can be very helpful in troubleshooting. I've also used *show etherchannel brief* in troubleshooting, but last time I tried...

```
SW3#show etherchannel brief
% Command accepted but obsolete, unreleased or unsupported; see documentation.
              Channel-group listing:


Group: 5

Group state = L2
Ports: 4 Maxports = 16
Port-channels: 1 Max Port-channels = 16
Protocol: LACP
Minimum Links: 0
```

How about *show etherchannel summary*?

```
SW3#show etherchannel summary
Flags: D - down          P - bundled in port-channel
       I - stand-alone  s - suspended
       H - Hot-standby (LACP only)
       R - Layer3        S - Layer2
       U - in use        f - failed to allocate aggregator

       M - not in use, minimum links not met
       u - unsuitable for bundling
       w - waiting to be aggregated
       d - default port
```

```
Number of channel-groups in use:  1
Number of aggregators:            1

Group Port-channel Protocol Ports
----- ------------ ----------
5     Po5(SU)      LACP       Fa0/21(P)    Fa0/22(P)    Fa0/23(P)
                              Fa0/24(P)
```

That's more like it! All four ports are marked with the "P" flag, meaning they're part of a port-channel, and that's just what we wanted to see. Note the flags next to Po5, "SU". The "U" indicates the channel is in use (good) and the "S" means it's a Layer 2 EC (hmmm, more on that later!).

How The Link Is Chosen For A Particular Traffic Flow

Etherchannels give us load balancing, but not *pure* load balancing. In our lab, we have four parallel links in the EC, but that doesn't mean each link is carrying 25% of the load. Basically, a Cisco-proprietary hash algorithm is run that will deliver a value of 0 – 7, and those values are assigned to links in the EC. It's these values that are used to determine which link will handle which traffic flow. (We're dealing with *per-flow* balancing here, not per-packet or per-frame.) That algorithm can use any of the following:

Source IP address

Destination IP address

Both source and destination IP address

Both source and destination MAC address

TCP / UDP port numbers

The switch may use the hash of the last low-order bits to choose the link that will carry the traffic flow, or it may get the exclusive-OR operation ("XOR") involved. The only time the XOR operation is used is when one of the combination load-balancing methods is used – the source *and* destination IP address, source *and* destination port number, or the source *and* destination MAC address. (You get the point.) For every method involving only one value, the hash of the bits reveals the port that will handle traffic for that particular flow.

The XOR operation's name might look scary, but it's one of the easiest math operations you'll ever carry out. It's a bit-by-bit comparison, with only two possible answers:

If the compared bits are the same, the result is 0.

If the compared bits are different, the result is 1.

That's it! The number of bits needed for the XOR depends on how many links we have in the EC:

Number of links in EC	# of lowest-order bits to XOR	Possible results
2	1	0,1
4	2	0,1,2,3
8	3	0,1,2,3,4,5,6,7

Using our four-link EC, let's figure out which link traffic sourced from 179.38.47.11 and destined for 210.49.39.22 would use. If you want to break down the entire address for practice (ahem), that's a great idea, but with a 4-link EC we only need the last two bits. The last octet of each address, with the two lowest-order bits highlighted:

11 = 0000101**1**

22 = 0001011**0**

We perform the XOR on a bit-by-bit basis, from left to right, so we'll first XOR the 7th bit of each octet, 1 and 1. That gives us a "0" for the first bit of the XOR result. When we XOR the 8th bit of each octet, "1" and "0", the return is a "1" for the XOR's second and final bit. "01" converts to the decimal 1, so the switch will use the port assigned value "01" to send the data.

Let's walk through another example, using a source IP address of 179.38.47.11 and a destination of 190.49.39.15. With our four-path EC, we need the last two bits of each address for our XOR.

11 = 0000101**1**

15 = 0000111**1**

Since both bits in the 7th position and both bits in the 8th position match up, we know our XOR return is "00", resulting in the link assigned value 0 as the winner!

To change the load-balancing method for your switch, use *port-channel load-balance* and verify with *show etherchannel load-balance*. This is a global command – you can't change the load balancing method on a per-port or per-EC basis.

```
SW3(config)#port-channel load-balance ?
  dst-ip        Dst IP Addr
  dst-mac       Dst Mac Addr
  src-dst-ip    Src XOR Dst IP Addr
  src-dst-mac   Src XOR Dst Mac Addr
  src-ip        Src IP Addr
  src-mac       Src Mac Addr
```

The "XOR" choices balance on source and destination IP or source and destination MAC. Verify with *show etherchannel load-balance*.

```
SW3#show etherchannel load-balance
EtherChannel Load-Balancing Configuration:
        dst-ip

EtherChannel Load-Balancing Addresses Used Per-Protocol:
Non-IP:  Destination MAC address
  IPv4:  Destination IP address
  IPv6:  Destination IP address
```

And finally....

Hey, Remember This?

```
SW2(config)#spanning ?
   backbonefast  Enable BackboneFast Feature
   etherchannel  Spanning tree etherchannel specific configuration
   extend        Spanning Tree 802.1t extensions
   logging       Enable Spanning tree logging
   loopguard     Spanning tree loopguard options
   mode          Spanning tree operating mode
   mst           Multiple spanning tree configuration
   pathcost      Spanning tree pathcost options
   portfast      Spanning tree portfast options
   transmit      STP transmit parameters
   uplinkfast    Enable UplinkFast Feature
   vlan          VLAN Switch Spanning Tree
```

In the midst of all the loop guarding and MSTing and BackboneFasting we did earlier was a little something about ECs. Let's use IOS Help to flesh this out.

```
SW2(config)#spanning etherchannel ?
   Guard     Configure guard features for etherchannel

SW2(config)#spanning etherchannel guard ?
   Misconfig  Enable guard to protect against etherchannel misconfiguration

SW2(config)#spanning etherchannel guard misconfig ?
   <cr>
```

If you use one of the EC negotiation protocols, you really shouldn't run into an issue with a misconfigured EC, since the EC won't be created in the first place if there's a problem. The *channel-group* "on" option sidesteps negotiation, and you could run into trouble if one side of your links is set up for an EC and the other isn't (I speak from experience).

To prevent the creation of a switching loop due to EC misconfiguration, run *spanning ether-channel guard misconfig*. As a result, ports will be placed into err-disabled state if a condition exists that might result in a switching loop.

EC Troubleshooting Tips

Ports configured for dynamic VLAN assignment from a VMPS cannot become part of an EC, nor can such a port remain part of an EC if that change occurs after the port is already part of an EC.

The allowed range of VLANs on the ports in the EC must match that of the port-channel. Here's what happened after I changed the range of allowed VLANs on all ports in SW3's EC without doing so on the port-channel:

```
SW3(config-if-range)#switchport trunk allowed vlan 100,20

%EC-5-CANNOT _ BUNDLE2: Fa0/22 is not compatible with Po5 and will be suspended
(vlan mask is different)
%EC-5-CANNOT _ BUNDLE2: Fa0/23 is not compatible with Po5 and will be suspended
(vlan mask is different)
%EC-5-CANNOT _ BUNDLE2: Fa0/24 is not compatible with Po5 and will be suspended
(vlan mask is different)
%EC-5-CANNOT _ BUNDLE2: Fa0/23 is not compatible with Po5 and will be suspended
(vlan mask is different)
```

Not good! However, once I went to SW2 and ran the same command, the EC came back up.

```
SW2(config)#int range fast 0/21 - 24
SW2(config-if-range)#switchport trunk allowed vlan 100,20

SW2#show etherchannel summary
(Flags removed)
Number of channel-groups in use: 1
Number of aggregators:           1

Group   Port-channel   Protocol    Ports
------  -------------  ----------- 
1       Po1(SU)        LACP        Fa0/21(P)  Fa0/22(P)  Fa0/23(P)  Fa0/24(P)
```

Individual ports inside the EC must agree on this value as well. When I changed the allowed VLAN setting for SW2's 0/21, that port immediately unbundled.

```
SW2(config)#int fast 0/21
SW2(config-if)#switchport trunk allowed vlan 200,300
```

```
SW2(config-if)#^Z
SW2#
*Mar 1 01:18:39.472: %EC-5-CANNOT _ BUNDLE2: Fa0/21 is not compatible with Fa0/22
and will be suspended (vlan mask is different)
*Mar 1 01:18:39.472: %EC-5-CANNOT _ BUNDLE2: Fa0/21 is not compatible with Fa0/22
and will be suspended (vlan mask is different)
```

This is really true of any port attribute, including speed, duplex, and native VLAN. If you change one of those and the EC comes down, you know what to do – change it back!

A few more notes that can save you CCNP exam points and troubleshooting time...

A SPAN source port can be part of an Etherchannel, but not a SPAN destination port.

Ports in an EC cannot be configured with port security.

Ports in an EC should have the same native VLAN set.

If one end of the EC is running in *on* mode, the other end one has to as well.

Know your LACP and PAgP modes! The mode doesn't have to match, but you do have to have LACP or PAgP modes on each side. You can't have LACP negotiating one side and PAgP negotiating the other, or you'll never have an EC!

While keeping in mind that EC load-balancing methods do not have to match between switches, be sure to choose the load-balancing method that fits your situation. If you have multiple source IP addresses and one destination IP address, there's not much use in using destination IP addresses in your load-balancing methods!

With our trunks neatly bundled, it's time to do a little multilayer switching and work with our First Hop Redundancy Protocols (FHRPs). Let's get started!

Chapter 8:

MULTILAYER SWITCHING AND HIGH AVAILABILITY PROTOCOLS

One of the first things you get hit over the head with in your CCNA studies is that a switch runs at Layer 2, a router runs at Layer 3, and never the two shall meet.

Let me take this time to "un-hit" you while introducing you to *Layer 3 Switches*, also known as multilayer switches. Multilayer switches are devices that switch and route packets in the switch hardware itself. If two hosts in separate VLANs are connected to the same multilayer switch, the correct configuration will allow that communication without the data ever leaving the switch.

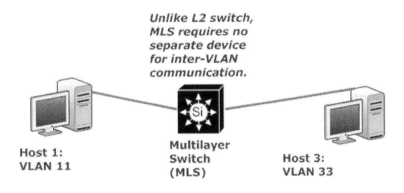

Unlike L2 switch, MLS requires no separate device for inter-VLAN communication.

Host 1:
VLAN 11

Multilayer
Switch
(MLS)

Host 3:
VLAN 33

When it comes to Cisco Catalyst switches, this hardware switching is performed by a router processor (or "L3 engine"). This processor must download routing information to the hardware itself. To make this hardware-based packet processing happen, the switch will run the legacy Multilayer Switching (MLS) or the newer Cisco Express Forwarding (CEF).

Application-Specific Integrated Circuits (ASICs) will perform the L2 rewriting operation of these packets. From your CCNA studies, you know that the IP source and destination addresses of a packet do not change as the packet travels the network, but the MAC addresses just might and probably will. With multilayer switching, it's the ASICs that perform this L2 address overwriting.

The CAM And TCAM Tables

The CAM table, also known as the *bridging table*, the *MAC address table*, and on occasion the *switching table*, is still present in a multilayer switch. The table operates just as an L2 switch's CAM table does. Thing is, we have a lot more going on with our L3 switches, including routing, ACLs, and QoS.

A simple CAM table can't handle all of this, so we also have the TCAM table – *Ternary Content Addressable Memory*. Basically, the TCAM table stores everything the CAM table can't, including info regarding ACLs and QoS.

Multilayer Switching Methods

The first MLS method is *route caching*. Route caching devices have both a routing processor and a switching engine. The routing processor routes a flow's first packet, the switching engine snoops in on that packet and the destination, and then the switching engine takes over and forwards the rest of the packets in that flow. A *flow* is a unidirectional stream of packets from a given source to a given destination, and such packets sent by a given protocol will be part of a single flow. If a source is sending both WWW and TFTP packets to the same destination, we have two flows of traffic. The MLS cache entries support such unidirectional flows.

Route caching can be effective, but there's one slight drawback: the first packet in any flow will be switched by software. Even though all other packets in the flow will be hardware-switched, it is more effective to have *all* of the packets switched by hardware. That's where CEF comes in.

Primarily designed for backbone switches, this topology-based switching method requires special hardware, so it's not available on all L3 switches. CEF is highly scalable and is also easier on a switch's CPU than route caching.

The two major components of CEF are the Forwarding Information Base (FIB) and the Adjacency Table (AT). The FIB contains the usual routing information we need – destination networks, masks, next-hop IP addresses, etc. – and CEF will use the FIB to make L3 prefix-based decisions. The FIB's contents will mirror that of the IP routing table, since the FIB is really just the IP routing table in another format.

The FIB takes care of us at L3, but what of L2? That's where the AT comes in. As adjacent hosts are discovered via ARP, that next-hop L2 information is kept in the table for CEF switching. (A host is considered adjacent to another if they're just one hop apart.)

Should either the TCAM or AT hit capacity, there is a wildcard entry that redirects traffic to the routing engine.

Summing it up, the FIB contains L3 information and is created via the IP routing table, and the AT contains L2 information and is created via the ARP table.

At this point, the multilayer switch is just about ready to forward the packet. The switch will make the same changes to the packet that a router would, and that includes changing the L2 destination MAC address to the next-hop MAC address. The L2 source address will be the MAC address of the switch interface transmitting the packet.

Enabling CEF is EZ. CEF is on by default on any and all CEF-enabled switches, and you can't turn it off! Since CEF is hardware-based rather than software-based, this is not a situation where running "no cef" at the CLI will disable CEF. There's no such command! *IP routing must be on for CEF to run.*

With these important nuts and bolts out of the way, let's configure an L3 switch, starting with a Switched Virtual Interface!

Inter-VLAN Routing With An SVI

Multilayer switches allow us to create a logical interface, the Switched Virtual Interface (SVI), representing a VLAN. The VLAN 1 interface present by default on all L2 switches is an SVI, and it's the only default SVI.

```
interface Vlan1
   no ip address
```

We can create an SVI for any VLAN, and creating one is just like creating a loopback interface. Just go into config mode, create the interface, give it an IP address, and you're done. In this lab, we'll create SVIs that will allow hosts in different IP subnets and different VLANs to communicate without a separate L3 device. I'll send pings between the two now, even though we know *darn* well they can't have a chat... yet.

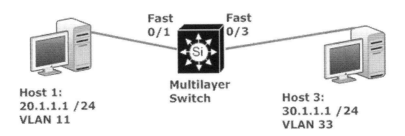

```
R1#ping 30.1.1.1
.....
Success rate is 0 percent (0/5)


R3#ping 20.1.1.1
.....
Success rate is 0 percent (0/5)
```

The ports have already been placed into their respective VLANs and the ports are access ports. We'll now create two SVIs on the switch, one representing VLAN 11 and the other VLAN 33. Both SVIs show as up/up immediately after creation on our multilayer switch, SW3.

```
SW3(config)#int vlan 11
%LINEPROTO-5-UPDOWN: Line protocol on Interface Vlan11, changed state to up
SW3(config-if)#ip address 20.1.1.11 255.255.255.0

SW3(config-if)#int vlan 33
SW3(config-if)#ip address
%LINEPROTO-5-UPDOWN: Line protocol on Interface Vlan33, changed state to up
SW3(config-if)#ip address 30.1.1.11 255.255.255.0
```

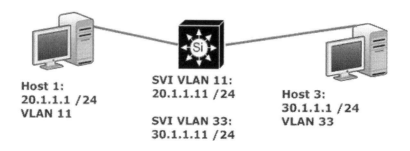

Host 1:
20.1.1.1 /24
VLAN 11

SVI VLAN 11:
20.1.1.11 /24

SVI VLAN 33:
30.1.1.11 /24

Host 3:
30.1.1.1 /24
VLAN 33

We'll verify the status on both with this clipped output from *show interface vlan*. Note that the hardware is listed as "EtherSVI".

```
SW3#show int vlan11
Vlan11 is up, line protocol is up
   Hardware is EtherSVI, address is 001c.0fbf.2f41 (bia 001c.0fbf.2f41)
   Internet address is 20.1.1.11/24

SW3#show int vlan 33
Vlan33 is up, line protocol is up
   Hardware is EtherSVI, address is 001c.0fbf.2f42 (bia 001c.0fbf.2f42)
   Internet address is 30.1.1.11/24
```

Looks good! Let's check those routing tables!

```
SW3#show ip route
Default gateway is not set

Host              Gateway          Last Use    Total Uses    Interface
ICMP redirect cache is empty
```

Doesn't look good! Let's enable IP routing, which is *disabled on a multilayer switch by default*!

```
SW3(config)#ip routing

SW3#show ip route
Codes:  L - local, C - connected, S - static, R - RIP, M - mobile, B - BGP
        D - EIGRP, EX - EIGRP external, O - OSPF, IA - OSPF inter area
        N1- OSPF NSSA external type 1, N2 - OSPF NSSA external type 2
        E1- OSPF external type 1, E2 - OSPF external type 2
        I - IS-IS, su - IS-IS summary, L1 - IS-IS level-1, L2 - IS-IS level-2
        ia- IS-IS inter area, * - candidate default, U - per-user static route
        o - ODR, P - periodic downloaded static route, H - NHRP, l - LISP
        + - replicated route, % - next hop override

Gateway of last resort is not set

        20.0.0.0/8 is variably subnetted, 2 subnets, 2 masks
C          20.1.1.0/24 is directly connected, Vlan11
L          20.1.1.11/32 is directly connected, Vlan11
        30.0.0.0/8 is variably subnetted, 2 subnets, 2 masks
C          30.1.1.0/24 is directly connected, Vlan33
L          30.1.1.11/32 is directly connected, Vlan33
```

That looks just a bit more like our routing table!

When SVIs are in use, the default gateway on the hosts must be the IP address assigned to the SVI that represents that host's VLAN. With that default gateway set correctly, the hosts can communicate, and no routing protocol is required in this case. Since we're using Cisco routers for hosts, we'll use *ip route* to set the default gateway.

```
HOST1(config)#ip route 0.0.0.0 0.0.0.0 20.1.1.11

HOST3(config)#ip route 0.0.0.0 0.0.0.0 30.1.1.11
```

Can they ping? Yes, they can!

```
HOST1#ping 30.1.1.1
!!!!!
Success rate is 100 percent (5/5), round-trip min/avg/max = 4/5/8 ms
```

```
HOST3#ping 20.1.1.1
Type escape sequence to abort.
!!!!!
Success rate is 100 percent (5/5), round-trip min/avg/max = 4/5/8 ms
```

SVI Success Tips:

1. Have active ports in the VLAN *before* you create an SVI for that same VLAN. If you create the SVI before doing that, you end up with a sad SVI.

    ```
    SW3(config)#int vlan 66
    SW3(config-if)#
    *Mar  1  03:14:32.831:  %LINEPROTO-5-UPDOWN:  Line  protocol  on  Interface
    Vlan66, changed state to down
    SW3(config-if)#ip address 66.1.1.1 255.255.255.0

    SW3#show int vlan 66
    Vlan66 is down, line protocol is down
    ```

2. One SVI per VLAN and one VLAN per SVI.

3. The hosts must have their default gateway set to the IP address on the SVI representing their VLAN. If you don't get the ping results you expect *and* your SVIs are up, I can almost guarantee that the hosts have an incorrect default gateway set.

4. The only default SVI on the switch is the one for VLAN 1.

Routed Ports (Layer 3 Ports)

On L3 switches, we also have the option of configuring a physical port as a *routed port*. You assign an IP address to a routed port in the same way you would an SVI, but routed ports are physical interfaces and SVIs are logical interfaces. Routed ports do not represent a particular VLAN as an SVI does.

Let's add a router to our network that leads our hosts to the Internet.

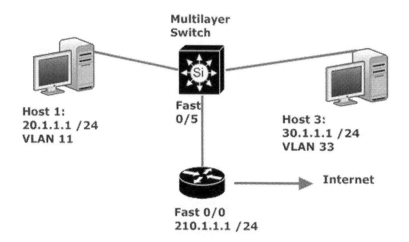

144

Even though IP routing is enabled, the ports on our multilayer switch are still in L2 mode (that's the default for many Cisco multilayer switches). To configure a routed port, use *no switchport* followed by the desired IP address. In the following config, the line protocol on the switch port goes down, but comes back up in a few seconds. That's the normal and expected behavior.

```
SW3(config-if)#no switchport
%LINEPROTO-5-UPDOWN: Line protocol on Interface FastEthernet0/5, changed state
to down
%LINEPROTO-5-UPDOWN: Line protocol on Interface Vlan1, changed state to down
%LINK-3-UPDOWN: Interface FastEthernet0/5, changed state to up
%LINEPROTO-5-UPDOWN: Line protocol on Interface FastEthernet0/5, changed state
to up
SW3(config-if)#ip address 210.1.1.11 255.255.255.0
```

Verify addressing and status with *show interface fast 0/5* and verify L3 status with *show interface switchport.*

```
SW3#show int fast 0/5
FastEthernet0/5 is up, line protocol is up (connected)
   Hardware is Fast Ethernet, address is 001c.0fbf.2f44 (bia 001c.0fbf.2f44)
   Internet address is 210.1.1.11/24

SW3#show int fast 0/5 switchport
Name: Fa0/5
Switchport: Disabled (Note: If this is disabled, the port is running at L3.)
```

The switch can now ping 210.1.1.1, the downstream router. Always a good sign!

```
SW3#ping 210.1.1.1
!!!!!
Success rate is 100 percent (5/5), round-trip min/avg/max = 1/2/8 ms
```

Right now, each host can ping 210.1.1.11, the switch's interface in that subnet. However, they can't ping 210.1.1.1, the router's interface.

```
HOST1#ping 210.1.1.11
!!!!!
Success rate is 100 percent (5/5), round-trip min/avg/max = 4/5/8 ms

HOST1#ping 210.1.1.1
.....
Success rate is 0 percent (0/5)

HOST3#ping 210.1.1.11
!!!!!
Success rate is 100 percent (5/5), round-trip min/avg/max = 4/4/4 ms
```

```
HOST3#ping 210.1.1.1
.....
Success rate is 0 percent (0/5)
```

The pings can't find their way back to the hosts because the router has no path to either 20.1.1.0 /24 or 30.1.1.0 /24.

```
R1#show ip route
(code table removed for clarity)
Gateway of last resort is not set

      210.1.1.0/24 is variably subnetted, 2 subnets, 2 masks
C        210.1.1.0/24 is directly connected, FastEthernet0/0
```

To remedy that, we'll configure EIGRP between the multilayer switch and the router. The adjacency comes up very quickly:

```
SW3(config)#router eigrp 100
SW3(config-router)#no auto
SW3(config-router)#network 210.1.1.0 0.0.0.255
%DUAL-5-NBRCHANGE: EIGRP-IPv4 100: Neighbor 210.1.1.1 (FastEthernet0/5) is up:
new adjacency
SW3(config-router)#network 20.1.1.0 0.0.0.255
SW3(config-router)#network 30.1.1.0 0.0.0.255
```

The router now has the VLAN subnets in its routing table...

```
R1#show ip route
Gateway of last resort is not set
      20.0.0.0/24 is subnetted, 1 subnets
D        20.1.1.0 [90/28416] via 210.1.1.11, 00:01:07, FastEthernet0/0
      30.0.0.0/24 is subnetted, 1 subnets
D        30.1.1.0 [90/28416] via 210.1.1.11, 00:01:00, FastEthernet0/0
      210.1.1.0/24 is variably subnetted, 2 subnets, 2 masks
C        210.1.1.0/24 is directly connected, FastEthernet0/0
L        210.1.1.1/32 is directly connected, FastEthernet0/0
```

... and the hosts now have two-way connectivity with R1's at 210.1.1.1.

```
HOST1#ping 210.1.1.1
!!!!!
Success rate is 100 percent (5/5), round-trip min/avg/max = 1/3/4 ms


HOST3#ping 210.1.1.1
!!!!!
Success rate is 100 percent (5/5), round-trip min/avg/max = 1/3/4 ms
```

Routed Port Success Checklist (Short, but important)

1. Be sure to enable IP routing with the global *ip routing* command. It's off by default.

2. Be just as sure to enable your routed port's L3 capabilities with the interface-level *no switchport* command, and verify with *show interface switchport*. Need to turn the port's L2 capabilities back on? Just use *switchport* and you're gold!

We'll wrap this section up with a look at the FIB, now that we have some routes and other info in there! Here's a segment of the FIB from the multilayer switch in our lab.

```
SW3#show ip cef
Prefix              Next Hop           Interface
0.0.0.0/0           receive
20.1.1.0/24         attached           Vlan11
20.1.1.0/32         receive            Vlan11
20.1.1.1/32         attached           Vlan11
20.1.1.11/32        receive            Vlan11
20.1.1.255/32       receive            Vlan11
```

Under "Next Hop", *receive* indicates packets that will be handled by the L3 engine. Those include the broadcasts for the 20.1.1.0 /24 segment ("20.1.1.255/32"). The *attached* entries include directly connected addresses and subnets.

High Availability Schemes And Redundancy Protocols

Before we hit our First Hop Redundancy Protocols (FHRPs), we're going to take a brief and important look at two redundancy tactics that don't involve a particular protocol.

The Virtual Switching System

With VSS, we're representing a pair of physical switches (the "VSS Pair") as a single logical switch. One switch is the active switch, the other the standby switch. The active switch handles the workload, with the standby ready to step in if the active switch becomes unavailable. The physical switches in a VSS pair communicate via the virtual switch link (VSL).

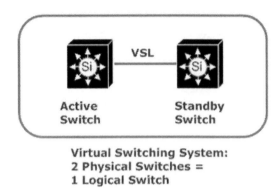

Virtual Switching System:
2 Physical Switches =
1 Logical Switch

The VSL is actually an Etherchannel, and we have the ability to create MultiChassis Etherchannels where ports on the physical switches in the VSS can be bundled.

Our redundancy comes in the form of Stateful SwitchOver (SSO) and NonStop Forwarding (NSF). With SSO, the backup supervisor is fully booted, fully initialized, and ready to step in as the active router at a moment's notice – literally!

NSF is all about keeping the overall downtime to a minimum by preventing link flapping ("route flapping") during the cutover. Between SSO and NSF, the speed of the cutover to the new active switch and the continued forwarding of packets during that cutover make the transition as smooth as the proverbial baby's butt. Even better, SSO and NSF are enabled by default in a VSS config.

Side note: There are other redundancy modes available to us on Cat switches, including Router Processor Redundancy (RPR) and Router Processor Redundancy Plus (RPR+). RPR allows the backup supervisor to boot partially, while RPR+ allows the backup supervisor to boot fully and initialize its routing engine. SSO is faster than RPR+, and RPR+ is faster than RPR.

Now back to our story!

How does the standby switch know when it needs to take over as the active switch? The two switches regularly exchange control info over the VSL, and should the backup switch detect via the VSL that the active switch has failed, the standby switch takes it upon itself to become the active switch.

When the previous switch is back online, it will not take over its original role as the active router. Instead, that switch now becomes the active switch.

All well and good, but what if the VSL itself goes down? How could the standby switch know whether the active switch is still active?

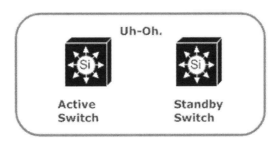

In this situation, both switches will be active, and we have a dual-active situation. This sounds great, but if it was all that great, this would be the default and we wouldn't have a standby! Dual-active is not desirable, since the two switches will now be using a lot of the same information, including the same IP address. At this point, VSS goes into dual-active recovery. For the network to recover, one of these switches needs to take itself out of the picture – but which one?

It's the first active switch that drinks the virtual hemlock in the form of putting every single one of its non-VSL interfaces into err-disabled mode. It'll stay that way until the VSL is back up.

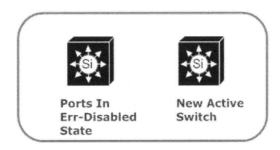

The remaining active switch will forward traffic normally. When the VSL is repaired, the switch with the err-disabled ports will come back online and assume the standby role.

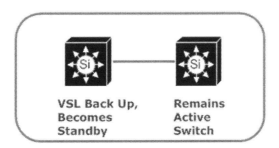

Most Cisco white papers on VSS will mention that VSS eliminates the need for an FHRP. That may be true of production networks, but not of your CCNP Switch and Tshoot exams. Those exams will be covered with FHRP questions, and we'll hit FHRPs hard right after this word to the (stack)wise!

StackWise

We're about to *stack* cables in a *wise* manner. (Get it?) StackWise lets us physically link up to nine switches to create a switch unit or switch stack. When we're done connecting our switches with some very special stack interconnect cables, we end up with a fully functioning two-way path. Each path supports up to 16 Gbps in each direction. The entire stack is given one IP address and one config file, a copy of which is sent to every switch in the stack.

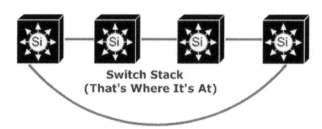

Switch Stack
(That's Where It's At)

One of these switches has to be a "boss switch", and that's the aptly named master switch. That switch is chosen via a master switch election:

1. The network admin can select a particular switch to be the master.

2. If none are selected in that manner, the switch with the best feature set wins.

3. If that's a tie, a preconfigured switch wins over a non-preconfigured switch.

4. If that's a tie, the switch that's been up the longest wins.

5. If that's somehow a tie, the switch with the lowest MAC is selected as master.

That master switch has quite the workload, including downloading forwarding tables, ACL info, and QoS info to the non-masters. The master switch is also responsible for letting non-masters know of additions and removals of switches in the stack. The master switch keeps a master MAC address table, a copy of which is sent to non-masters. The master switch also has to handle ping requests and remote connection requests.

You and I, the network admins, can not only add and remove switches without interrupting service, but we don't even have to configure the new switch. StackWise will take care of that for us! The master switch will autoconfig the new arrival with the stack's IOS image.

There is no single point of failure in a switch stack, but there is a single point of pain. If one of our cables breaks, we lose 50% of our capacity immediately. That's quite a cap hit, and thankfully it's a very temporary hit. The failover takes microseconds. Our new pal NonStop Forwarding (NSF) is supported in StackWise, which helps the packets flowing when there's the slightest break in service.

NSF works with RPR+ to keep things rolling when we're cutting over from one master to another. RPR+ has those non-master switches fully initialized and ready to step in when needed.

StackWise requires every switch in the stack to run the same IOS. When we add a new switch to the stack, the master will ask the newcomer if it's running the same IOS image as the master. If so, the master sends the config to the new switch and all is well.

If the new switch does not have the same IOS image, all is *not* well, but we'll make it well with this process:

1. The master will download the Cisco IOS image from its own Flash to the new switch, then send the config to the new switch, and the new switch joins the stack.

2. We can configure a TFTP server for that IOS download. With that option, the master switch will grab the IOS image from the TFTP server, send it to the new switch, then send the config over. The new switch can then join the stack.

3. The first two possibilities assume that the new switch's hardware can handle the necessary IOS image. If not, the master will put the new switch into suspension, let us know about the problem, and then wait for us to do something about it! Namely, the master expects to be supplied with an IOS image that supports the master's hardware and the new switch's hardware. Once that happens, the master will then upgrade every switch that was already part of the stack to that IOS, along with the new switch, and the entire stack then goes live.

Whew! With all that said, let's hope our hardware is compatible!

This is enough to get you started with StackWise. There's a lot more to StackWise; frankly, Cisco could probably have a certification based just on VSS and StackWise. If your network uses it or you want to learn more about it, head to Cisco's website and grab some PDFs. Right now, we're moving on to FHRPs!

The Hot Standby Routing Protocol

In this section, I'm going to refer to routers rather than L3 switches, since the HSRP terminology refers to "active routers" and "standby routers". The theory and commands of HSRP run the same on an L3 switch as on a router. Also, the icon I'm using for multilayer switches is slightly different than the one you saw earlier – there's no "Si" in the middle. I wanted to make sure you saw both versions.

Defined in RFC 2281, HSRP is a Cisco-proprietary router redundancy protocol in which routers are placed into an HSRP router group. One of the routers in the group is selected as the *active router,* while others in the group are *standby routers*. It won't surprise you to learn that the active router handles the actual workload while the standby routers do just that – stand by! HSRP ensures a high network uptime, since it routes IP traffic without reliance on a single router.

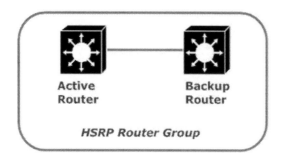

Active
Router

Backup
Router

HSRP Router Group

The terms *active* and *standby* do not refer to the actual operational status of the routers, just to their status in their HSRP group.

The actual IP and MAC addresses of the physical routers in the group are unknown to downstream devices. Those devices are actually communicating with a *pseudo-router*, a *virtual router* created by the HSRP configuration. This virtual router will have a MAC and IP address of its own, and downstream devices send data to *those* addresses.

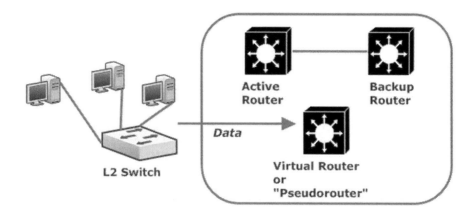

Active
Router

Backup
Router

Data

Virtual Router
or
"Pseudorouter"

L2 Switch

In our first lab, MLS_1 (int VLAN 100, 172.16.23.1 /24) and MLS_2 (int VLAN 100, 172.16.23.2 /24) are the routers in the HSRP group. The configuration will create a virtual router with the IP address 172.16.23.12 /24, and it's *that* address that should be used by all hosts in VLAN 100 as their default gateway.

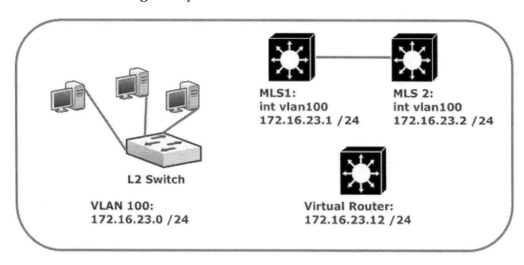

MLS1:
int vlan100
172.16.23.1 /24

MLS 2:
int vlan100
172.16.23.2 /24

L2 Switch

VLAN 100:
172.16.23.0 /24

Virtual Router:
172.16.23.12 /24

After verifying the SVI for VLAN 100 on each router, we're off!

```
MLS_1#show int vlan 100
Vlan100 is up, line protocol is up
   Hardware is EtherSVI, address is 0017.9466.f7c1 (bia 0017.9466.f7c1)
   Internet address is 172.16.23.1/24

MLS_2#show int vlan 100
Vlan100 is up, line protocol is up
   Hardware is EtherSVI, address is 001c.0fbf.2f41 (bia 001c.0fbf.2f41)
   Internet address is 172.16.23.2/24
```

We'll put both SVIs in HSRP group 5 and let 'em fight it out over the active router role to see what happens. I'll use IOS Help on MLS_1 to show our HSRP options. The *ip* command is the only required command for HSRP.

```
MLS_1(config)#int vlan 100
MLS_1(config-if)#standby ?
  <0-255>         group number
  Authentication  Authentication
  Delay           HSRP initialisation delay
  Follow          Name of HSRP group to follow
  Ip              Enable HSRP IPv4 and set the virtual IP address
  mac-refresh     Refresh MAC cache on switch by periodically sending packe
                  from virtual mac address
  name            Redundancy name string
  preempt         Overthrow lower priority Active routers
  priority        Priority level
  redirect        Configure sending of ICMP Redirect messages with an HSRP
                  virtual IP address as the gateway IP address
  timers          Hello and hold timers
  track           Priority tracking
  version         HSRP version

MLS_1(config-if)#standby 5 ?
  authentication  Authentication
  follow          Name of HSRP group to follow
  ip              Enable HSRP IPv4 and set the virtual IP address
  name            Redundancy name string
  preempt         Overthrow lower priority Active routers
  priority        Priority level
  timers          Hello and hold timers
  track           Priority tracking

MLS_1(config-if)#standby 5 ip ?
  A.B.C.D Virtual IP address
  <cr>
```

```
MLS _ 1(config-if)#standby 5 ip 172.16.23.1 ?
  secondary Make this IP address a secondary virtual IP address
  <cr>


MLS _ 1(config-if)#standby 5 ip 172.16.23.1
% address cannot equal interface IP address (so don't try it!)
MLS _ 1(config-if)#standby 5 ip 172.16.23.12
```

You can't assign an IP address from the MLS as the IP address for the virtual router.

Let's finish the config on MLS_2.

```
MLS _ 2(config)#int vlan 100
MLS _ 2(config-if)#standby 5 ip 172.16.23.12
```

Let's verify our config on MLS_2 with *show standby*, your #1 friend when it comes to verifying and troubleshooting HSRP.

```
MLS _ 2#show standby
Vlan100 - Group 5
  State is Active
    2 state changes, last state change 00:01:19
  Virtual IP address is 172.16.23.12
  Active virtual MAC address is 0000.0c07.ac05
    Local virtual MAC address is 0000.0c07.ac05 (v1 default)
  Hello time 3 sec, hold time 10 sec
    Next hello sent in 2.368 secs
  Preemption disabled
  Active router is local
  Standby router is 172.16.23.1, priority 100 (expires in 10.272 sec)
  Priority 100 (default 100)
  Group name is "hsrp-Vl100-5" (default)
```

There's a treasure trove of HSRP info here! From the top down, we see...

Interface VLAN100 is in HSRP Group 5

This router is in the Active state, there have been 2 state changes, and the last one was 1 minute and 19 seconds ago

The virtual router's IP address and MAC address

This router sends HSRP Hellos every 3 seconds

"Preemption" is disabled – more on that very soon!

This is the Active router ("local")

The standby router is at 172.16.23.1 and that router's priority is 100

The local HSRP priority is 100, and finally, the HSRP group name is displayed.

Let's look at the same command's output on MLS_1.

```
MLS_1#show standby
Vlan100 - Group 5
  State is Standby
    3 state changes, last state change 00:01:45
  Virtual IP address is 172.16.23.12
  Active virtual MAC address is 0000.0c07.ac05
    Local virtual MAC address is 0000.0c07.ac05 (v1 default)
  Hello time 3 sec, hold time 10 sec
    Next hello sent in 1.936 secs
  Preemption disabled
  Active router is 172.16.23.2, priority 100 (expires in 9.920 sec)
  Standby router is local
  Priority 100 (default 100)
  Group name is "hsrp-Vl100-5" (default)
```

That output verifies everything we saw on MLS_2. Here's our HSRP group:

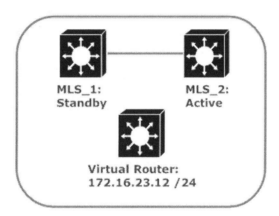

We know how the virtual router got its IP address; after all, we're the ones who configured it! However, we didn't enter any info regarding a MAC address. Where the heck did that come from?

```
Active virtual MAC address is 0000.0c07.ac05
```

Most of that address was predetermined. The MAC address 00-00-0c-07-ac-xx is HSRP's well-known virtual MAC address, and the "xx" is the HSRP group number in *hexadecimal*. Had we gone with HSRP group 10, the address would have been 00-00-0c-07-ac-0a. Brush up on your hex before you take the SWITCH exam!

Now that we have the MAC address source down, let's talk about that election.

The HSRP Active Router Election

The HSRP priority is the first value considered in the election. The priority is 100 by default, as we saw on both routers. Should there be a tie – and there always will be if the routers are left at their defaults – theory holds that the router with the highest IP address wins the election. MLS_2 won the election in our first lab, so the theory holds true.

(Real world note: Always, always, *always* verify your Active router.)

Let's make MLS_1 the Active router by raising its priority. We'll go double or nothing...

```
MLS _ 1(config)#int vlan 100
MLS _ 1(config-if)#standby 5 priority 200
```

... and we get nothing! Let's verify the priority change:

```
MLS _ 1#show standby
Vlan100 - Group 5
  State is Standby
    1 state change, last state change 00:17:26
  Virtual IP address is 172.16.23.12
  Active virtual MAC address is 0000.0c07.ac05
    Local virtual MAC address is 0000.0c07.ac05 (v1 default)
  Hello time 3 sec, hold time 10 sec
    Next hello sent in 1.376 secs
  Preemption disabled
  Active router is 172.16.23.2, priority 100 (expires in 10.368 sec)
  Standby router is local
  Priority 200 (configured 200)
  Group name is "hsrp-Vl100-5" (default)
```

Just raising the priority on MLS_1 isn't enough to get the job done here. Either we have to reload MLS_2 so MLS_1 can take over as Active in its absence, or MLS_1 must have preemption enabled. We'd like to avoid reloads here, so let's do the latter.

```
MLS _ 1(config)#int vlan 100
MLS _ 1(config-if)#standby 5 ?
  Authentication  Authentication
  Follow          Name of HSRP group to follow
  Ip              Enable HSRP IPv4 and set the virtual IP address
  Name            Redundancy name string
  Preempt         Overthrow lower priority Active routers
  Priority        Priority level
  Timers          Hello and hold timers
  Track           Priority tracking

MLS _ 1(config-if)#standby 5 preempt
```

Just a few seconds after enabling preemption on MLS_1...

```
%HSRP-5-STATECHANGE: Vlan100 Grp 5 state Standby -> Active
```

... MLS_1 takes over as the Active router. This state change and the enabling of preemption are verified by *show standby*.

```
MLS_1#show standby
Vlan100 - Group 5
  State is Active
    2 state changes, last state change 00:00:51
  Virtual IP address is 172.16.23.12
  Active virtual MAC address is 0000.0c07.ac05
    Local virtual MAC address is 0000.0c07.ac05 (v1 default)
  Hello time 3 sec, hold time 10 sec
    Next hello sent in 0.976 secs
  Preemption enabled
  Active router is local
  Standby router is 172.16.23.2, priority 100 (expires in 10.896 sec)
  Priority 200 (configured 200)
  Group name is "hsrp-Vl100-5" (default)
```

Had I wanted to delay any takeover by MLS_1, I could have set *delay* on the preemption. You can also delay a takeover until after the next reload.

```
MLS_1(config-if)#standby 5 preempt ?
  delay Wait before preempting
  <cr>

MLS_1(config-if)#standby 5 preempt delay ?
  minimum Delay at least this long
  reload Delay after reload
  sync Wait for IP redundancy clients

MLS_1(config-if)#standby 5 preempt delay minimum ?
  <0-3600> Number of seconds for minimum delay
```

We've seen a few of the HSRP states, but for t-shooting and exam prep, let's see them in order along with a quick description of each.

Disabled: Similar to the disabled STP port state, in that you won't see this state actually mentioned, but it is the official first HSRP port state.

Initial (INIT): The interface enters this state when HSRP is first enabled. HSRP isn't actually running at this point.

Listen: The router knows the virtual router's IP address, but is not the primary or standby router. It's listening for Hello packets from those routers.

Speak: The router is now sending Hello messages and participating in the election of the primary and standby routers.

Standby: The router is now a candidate to become the active router and continues to send hello packets.

Active: The router is now forwarding packets sent to the group's virtual IP address.

Load Balancing With HSRP

This redundancy is all well and good, but there's one thing driving me crazy. (A short drive, I admit.) I've reset the priority for both routers in Group 5 to 100, and MLS_2 is again the Active router. As a result, MLS_2 is doing all the work of handling traffic from 60 hosts, and MLS_1 is just sitting there.

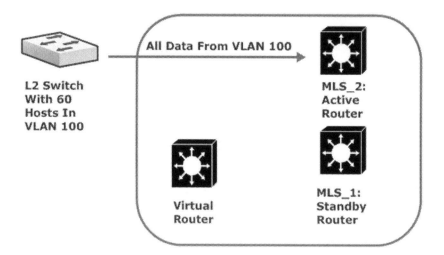

We're going to put MLS_1 to work via HSRP load balancing. Unlike the load balancing techniques we've used to this point, this one requires a little help from those 60 hosts. HSRP Group 5 has MLS_2 as the Active router, and that group is using 172.16.23.12 to represent its virtual router. We're going to create Group 10 with the same two routers, making sure that MLS_1 is the Active, and that group will use the address 172.16.23.21 for its virtual router.

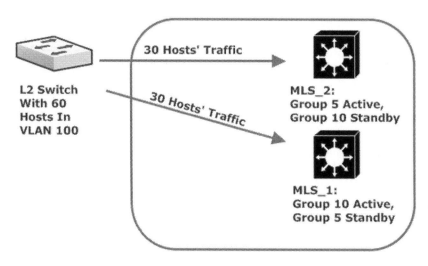

```
MLS _ 1(config)#int vlan 100
MLS _ 1(config-if)#standby 10 ip 172.16.23.21
MLS _ 1(config-if)#standby 10 priority 200

MLS _ 2(config)#int vlan 100
MLS _ 2(config-if)#standby 10 ip 172.16.23.21
MLS _ 2(config-if)#standby 10 priority 100 (hardcoding the default)
```

Verify with *show standby*. I'll show only the info related to the election.

```
MLS _ 1#show standby
Vlan100 - Group 5
   Preemption disabled
   Active router is 172.16.23.2, priority 200 (expires in 8.704 sec)
   Standby router is local
   Priority 100 (default 100)

Vlan100 - Group 10
   Preemption enabled
   Active router is local
   Standby router is 172.16.23.2, priority 100 (expires in 9.792 sec)
   Priority 201 (configured 201)

MLS _ 2#show standby
Vlan100 - Group 5
   Preemption enabled
   Active router is local
   Standby router is 172.16.23.1, priority 100 (expires in 10.384 sec)
   Priority 200 (configured 200)

Vlan100 - Group 10
   Preemption disabled
   Active router is 172.16.23.1, priority 201 (expires in 9.808 sec)
   Standby router is local
   Priority 100 (default 100)
   Group name is "hsrp-Vl100-10" (default)
```

MLS_1 is the Active router for Group 10, and MLS_2 is the Active router for Group 5, just as we wanted. To finish the load balancing, half of the hosts would be configured with 172.16.23.12 as their default gateway, and the other half with 172.16.23.21. To test this, I've configured a different default gateway on Host 2 and Host 3, and we'll send pings from each.

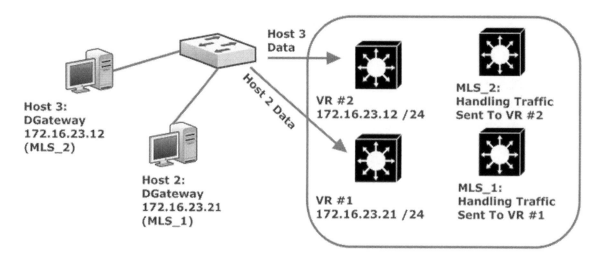

```
HOST2#ping 172.16.23.21
!!!!!
Success rate is 100 percent (5/5), round-trip min/avg/max = 1/3/4 ms

HOST3#ping 172.16.23.12
!!!!!
Success rate is 100 percent (5/5), round-trip min/avg/max = 4/4/4 ms
```

Both hosts are pinging their default gateways, and the load is now shared!

HSRP Interface Tracking

This great feature enables the HSRP process to monitor a particular interface, and the status of this interface will dynamically change the HSRP priority for a specified router – for better or for worse!

When that tracked interface's line protocol is down, the HSRP priority of the router is decremented. This can lead to another HSRP router in the group becoming the Active router, but that other router must have preemption enabled.

In our next lab, MLS_2 has a priority of 105 and is the Active router. MLS_1 is the standby and has the default priority of 100. As a result, MLS_2 will handle all the traffic sent to the server behind MLS_2 and MLS_1. That's all well and good, but there is a single point of failure – and we *hate* those. (IP addresses shown for the multilayer switches in the next lab are for their SVI, interface VLAN100.)

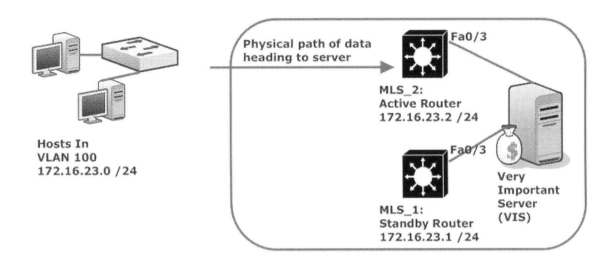

If Fast 0/3 on MLS_2 fails, the hosts in VLAN 100 can't reach the ecommerce server. We can and will configure HSRP to drop MLS_2's priority if the line protocol of Fast 0/3 on that server goes down. HSRP's default decrement with interface tracking is 10, so as long as MLS_1 has preemption enabled, the current priority would be fine for our purposes.

```
MLS _ 2(config-if)#standby 1 ip 172.16.23.12
MLS _ 2(config-if)#standby 1 priority 105

MLS _ 1(config)#int vlan 100
MLS _ 1(config-if)#standby 1 ip 172.16.23.12
MLS _ 1(config-if)#standby 1 preempt
```

Verify with *show standby*. I'm showing you only the info relating to the election.

```
MLS _ 2#show standby
Vlan100 - Group 1
  State is Active
  Preemption disabled
  Active router is local
  Standby router is 172.16.23.1, priority 100 (expires in 8.656 sec)
  Priority 105 (configured 105)

MLS _ 1#show standby
Vlan100 - Group 1
  State is Standby
  Preemption enabled
  Active router is 172.16.23.2, priority 105 (expires in 10.464 sec)
  Standby router is local
  Priority 100 (default 100)
```

Before configuring HSRP interface tracking, *be sure the interface you're tracking is up!*

```
MLS _ 2#show int fast 0/3
FastEthernet0/3 is up, line protocol is up (connected)
```

We'll add tracking to MLS_2's HSRP config and verify with *show standby.*

```
MLS _ 2(config)#int vlan 100
MLS _ 2(config-if)#standby 1 track fastethernet 0/3
```

```
MLS _ 2#show standby
Vlan100 - Group 1
  State is Active
    5 state changes, last state change 00:00:17
  Virtual IP address is 172.16.23.12
  Active virtual MAC address is 0000.0c07.ac01
    Local virtual MAC address is 0000.0c07.ac01 (v1 default)
  Hello time 3 sec, hold time 10 sec
    Next hello sent in 1.920 secs
  Preemption disabled
  Active router is local
  Standby router is 172.16.23.1, priority 100 (expires in 11.184 sec)
  Priority 105 (configured 105)
    Track interface FastEthernet0/3 state Up decrement 10
  Group name is "hsrp-Vl100-1" (default)
```

The default HSRP interface tracking decrement of 10 is shown to us here. I would not count on your CCNP SWITCH and TSHOOT exams being so kind, so know it by heart.

According to theory, if Fast0/3's line protocol goes down, MLS_2's priority should go down to 95. In turn, since MLS_1's priority is the default of 100 and that router is configured for preemption, MLS_1 should then take over as the Active. Let's shut Fast 0/3 down and see what happens!

```
MLS _ 2(config)#int fast 0/3
MLS _ 2(config-if)#shut
%TRACKING-5-STATE: 1 interface Fa0/3 line-protocol Up->Down
%HSRP-5-STATECHANGE: Vlan100 Grp 1 state Active -> Speak

%LINK-5-CHANGED:Interface FastEthernet0/3, changed state to administratively down
%LINEPROTO-5-UPDOWN: Line protocol on Interface FastEthernet0/3, changed state
to down
%HSRP-5-STATECHANGE: Vlan100 Grp 1 state Speak -> Standby
```

I removed the timestamps for clarity, so let me throw this in – all of that happened in less than 10 seconds. Let's check *show standby* for verification.

```
MLS _ 2#show standby
Vlan100 - Group 1
  State is Standby
    7 state changes, last state change 00:00:10
  Virtual IP address is 172.16.23.12
  Active virtual MAC address is 0000.0c07.ac01
    Local virtual MAC address is 0000.0c07.ac01 (v1 default)
  Hello time 3 sec, hold time 10 sec
    Next hello sent in 0.608 secs
  Preemption disabled
  Active router is 172.16.23.1, priority 100 (expires in 10.688 sec)
  Standby router is local
  Priority 95 (configured 105)
    Track interface FastEthernet0/3 state Down decrement 10
  Group name is "hsrp-Vl100-1" (default)
```

MLS_2 is indeed the standby as a result of that decrement.

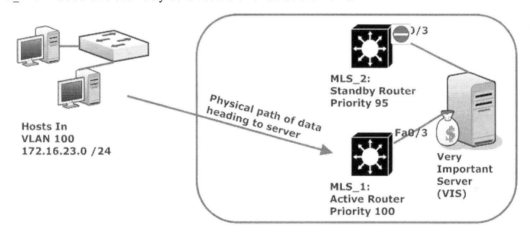

When Fast 0/3 on MLS_2 is back up, the priority will go back to 105, but MLS_2 will *not* become the Active router again unless we enable preemption. Let's do that and then re-open Fast 0/3.

```
MLS _ 2(config)#int vlan 100
MLS _ 2(config-if)#standby 1 preempt
MLS _ 2(config-if)#int fast 0/3
MLS _ 2(config-if)#no shut

%TRACKING-5-STATE: 1 interface Fa0/3 line-protocol Down->Up

%HSRP-5-STATECHANGE: Vlan100 Grp 1 state Standby -> Active

%LINK-3-UPDOWN: Interface FastEthernet0/3, changed state to up

%LINEPROTO-5-UPDOWN:Line protocolon Interface FastEthernet0/3,changed state to up
```

```
MLS _ 2#show standby
Vlan100 - Group 1
   State is Active
      8 state changes, last state change 00:02:58
   Virtual IP address is 172.16.23.12
   Active virtual MAC address is 0000.0c07.ac01
      Local virtual MAC address is 0000.0c07.ac01 (v1 default)
   Hello time 3 sec, hold time 10 sec
      Next hello sent in 1.136 secs
   Preemption enabled
   Active router is local
   Standby router is 172.16.23.1, priority 100 (expires in 10.000 sec)
   Priority 105 (configured 105)
      Track interface FastEthernet0/3 state Up decrement 10
   Group name is "hsrp-Vl100-1" (default)
```

And that's that!

On occasion, the default decrement might not be enough for the failover to take place. If MLS_2's priority is 150 and MLS_1's priority is 100, the default decrement of 10 wouldn't be enough for MLS_1 to take over as the Active should Fast 0/3 on MLS_2 go down. You can set a new decrement value at the very end of standby track; note that you never actually enter the word "decrement".

I'll set MLS_2's priority to 150 and then set a decrement of 51...

```
MLS _ 2(config)#int vlan 100
MLS _ 2(config-if)#standby 1 priority 150
MLS _ 2(config-if)#standby 1 track fastethernet 0/3 ?
   <1-255> Decrement value
   <cr>

MLS _ 2(config-if)#standby 1 track fastethernet 0/3 51
```

... shut down fast 0/3...

```
MLS _ 2(config-if)#int fast 0/3
MLS _ 2(config-if)#shut
```

... and verify any changes with *show standby*.

```
MLS _ 2#show standby
Vlan100 - Group 1
   State is Standby
      13 state changes, last state change 00:00:05
   Virtual IP address is 172.16.23.12
```

```
Active virtual MAC address is 0000.0c07.ac01
   Local virtual MAC address is 0000.0c07.ac01 (v1 default)
Hello time 3 sec, hold time 10 sec
   Next hello sent in 2.560 secs
Preemption enabled
Active router is 172.16.23.1, priority 100 (expires in 7.600 sec)
Standby router is local
Priority 99 (configured 150)
   Track interface FastEthernet0/3 state Down decrement 51
Group name is "hsrp-Vl100-1" (default)
```

The default decrement would not have been enough to get the cutover done, but setting the decrement to 51 and enabling MLS_1 for preemption (done in the previous lab) got the job done!

Changing This And That In HSRP

I don't like to call these "miscellaneous" commands, because they are important, but they're not everyday commands. You can leave most HSRP defaults as they are, but just in case you need to change a few things, here's how!

To change the HSRP hello and hold timers, use *standby timers*. You do have to enter a value for each timer, even if there's one you're not changing.

```
MLS _2(config-if)#standby 1 timers ?
  <1-254>    Hello interval in seconds
  msec       Specify hello interval in milliseconds

MLS _2(config-if)#standby 1 timers 6 ?
  <7-255>    Hold time in seconds

MLS _2(config-if)#standby 1 timers 6 15
```

Want to change the HSRP group name from that ugly default? Use standby name.

```
MLS _2(config-if)#standby 1 name CCNP

MLS _2#show standby (output edited, group name appears at very bottom of
output)
Vlan100 - Group 1
  Group name is "CCNP" (cfgd)
```

Want to set up authentication between your HSRP speakers? Use *standby authentication*. I'd tell you not to use plain text authentication, but I know you won't do that. It is an option, though. Choose "key string" to set a single word as the password.

```
MLS _ 2(config-if)#standby 1 authentication ?
  WORD   Plain text authentication string (8 chars max)
  md5    Use MD5 authentication
  text   Plain text authentication

MLS _ 2(config-if)#standby 1 authentication md5 ?
  key-chain    Set key chain
  key-string   Set key string

MLS _ 2(config-if)#standby 1 authentication md5 key-string CCNP

MLS _ 1(config)#int vlan 100
MLS _ 1(config-if)#standby 1 authentication md5 key-string CCNP
```

Using MD5 authentication means that a hash of the password is sent to other HSRP group neighbors, not that the password is hashed in the config. Check out MLS_2's config:

```
interface Vlan100
  ip address 172.16.23.2 255.255.255.0
  standby 1 ip 172.16.23.12
  standby 1 priority 150
  standby 1 preempt
  standby 1 authentication md5 key-string CCNP
  standby 1 name CCNP
  standby 1 track 1 decrement 51
```

To disguise that password in the config, use your old friend *service password-encryption.*

```
MLS _ 2(config)#service password-encryption
```

The result:

```
interface Vlan100
  ip address 172.16.23.2 255.255.255.0
  standby 1 ip 172.16.23.12
  standby 1 priority 150
  standby 1 preempt
  standby 1 authentication md5 key-string 7 0327782536
  standby 1 name CCNP
  standby 1 track 1 decrement 51
```

VRRP – The Virtual Router Redundancy Protocol

Defined in RFC 2338, VRRP is the open-standard equivalent of the Cisco-proprietary HSRP. VRRP works very much like HSRP, with one or two important differences (naturally!). They're so much alike that you pretty much learned VRRP during the last section, where you learned HSRP! Let's check out those differences, though...

VRRP's equivalent to HSRP's Active router is the Master router

VRRP's equivalent to HSRP's Standby router is the Backup router

Preemption is enabled by default in VRRP

VRRP's advertisements are multicast to 224.0.0.18, where HSRP ads are multicast to 224.0.0.2

The MAC address of VRRP routers is 00-00-5e-00-01-xx, and yes, the "xx" is the VRRP group number in hex

Let's have a look at VRRP in action, using the same two multilayer switches and the same IP addresses as we used in the HSRP section.

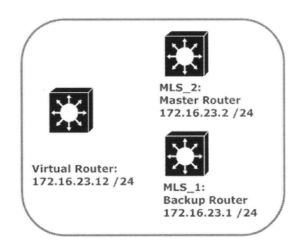

These options should look familiar...

```
MLS _2(config)#int vlan 100
MLS _2(config-if)#vrrp ?
  <1-255>   Group number

MLS _2(config-if)#vrrp 1 ?
  authentication  Authentication string
  description     Group specific description
  ip              Enable Virtual Router Redundancy Protocol (VRRP) for IP
  preempt         Enable preemption of lower priority Master
  priority        Priority of this VRRP group
  timers          Set the VRRP timers
  track           Event Tracking

MLS _2(config-if)#vrrp 1 ip 172.16.23.12

MLS _1(config)#int vlan 100
MLS _1(config-if)#vrrp 1 ip 172.16.23.12
```

Let's verify!

```
MLS_2#show vrrp
Vlan100 - Group 1
  State is Master
  Virtual IP address is 172.16.23.12
  Virtual MAC address is 0000.5e00.0101
  Advertisement interval is 1.000 sec
  Preemption enabled
  Priority is 100
  Master Router is 172.16.23.2 (local), priority is 100
  Master Advertisement interval is 1.000 sec
  Master Down interval is 3.609 sec

MLS_1#show vrrp
Vlan100 - Group 1
  State is Backup
  Virtual IP address is 172.16.23.12
  Virtual MAC address is 0000.5e00.0101
  Advertisement interval is 1.000 sec
  Preemption enabled
  Priority is 100
  Master Router is 172.16.23.2, priority is 100
  Master Advertisement interval is 1.000 sec
  Master Down interval is 3.609 sec (expires in 3.458 sec)
```

With preemption enabled by default, MLS_1 should take over as The Master Router if its priority is raised, correct?

```
MLS_1(config)#int vlan 100
MLS_1(config-if)#vrrp 1 priority 200

07:53:32: %VRRP-6-STATECHANGE: Vl100 Grp 1 state Backup -> Master

MLS_1#show vrrp
Vlan100 - Group 1
  State is Master
  Virtual IP address is 172.16.23.12
  Virtual MAC address is 0000.5e00.0101
  Advertisement interval is 1.000 sec
  Preemption enabled
  Priority is 200
  Master Router is 172.16.23.1 (local), priority is 200
  Master Advertisement interval is 1.000 sec
  Master Down interval is 3.218 sec
```

Correct!

While we're at it, let's do a little interface tracking after making MLS_2 the Master again.

```
MLS _ 2(config)#int vlan 100
MLS _ 2(config-if)#vrrp 1 priority 250
07:55:53: %VRRP-6-STATECHANGE: Vl100 Grp 1 state Backup -> Master
```

The overall concept of tracking is the same in VRRP as it is in HSRP, but the process is a little bit different. MLS_2 is the Master router, and we want MLS_1 to take that role should the line protocol on MLS_2's Fast 0/3 interface go down. Here's where we stand:

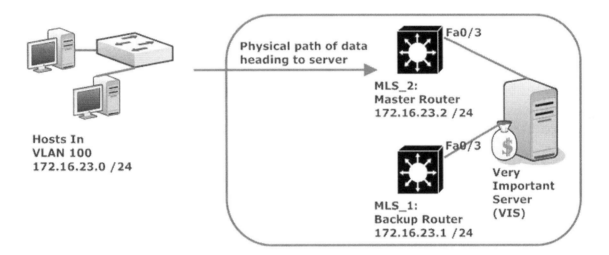

Check the interface before you start tracking:

```
MLS _ 2#show int fast 0/3
FastEthernet0/3 is up, line protocol is up (connected)
```

With VRRP, we need to define the interface as an object before moving forward with the actual *vrrp track* command. Sounds complicated, but it isn't. (I've always remembered this by saying "*track, then vrrp track*". Feel free to steal it.) We're not limited to using the line protocol as the tracked object, but that's the easiest and most effective track to use for an interface IMHO.

```
MLS _ 2(config)#track ?
  <1-1000>        Tracked object
  resolution      Tracking resolution parameters
  timer           Polling interval timers

MLS _ 2(config)#track 1 ?
  interface       Select an interface to track
  ip              IP protocol
  list            Group objects in a list
  <cr>
```

```
MLS _ 2(config)#track 1 interface fast 0/3 ?
  ip             IP parameters
  line-protocol  Track interface line-protocol

MLS _ 2(config)#track 1 interface fast 0/3 line-protocol ?
  <cr>

MLS _ 2(config)#track 1 interface fast 0/3 line-protocol
```

The object number referred to in the *track* command must be the same one used in the *vrrp track* command.

```
MLS _ 2(config)#int vlan 100
MLS _ 2(config-if)#vrrp 1 ?
  authentication  Authentication string
  description     Group specific description
  ip              Enable Virtual Router Redundancy Protocol (VRRP) for IP
  preempt         Enable preemption of lower priority Master
  priority        Priority of this VRRP group
  timers          Set the VRRP timers
  track           Event Tracking
```

```
MLS _ 2(config-if)#vrrp 1 track ?
  <1-1000> Tracked object

MLS _ 2(config-if)#vrrp 1 track 1 ?
  decrement Priority decrement
  <cr>

MLS _ 2(config-if)#vrrp 1 track 1
```

We accepted the VRRP default priority decrement (10). Verify the config:

```
MLS _ 2#show vrrp
Vlan100 - Group 1
  State is Master
  Virtual IP address is 172.16.23.12
  Virtual MAC address is 0000.5e00.0101
  Advertisement interval is 1.000 sec
  Preemption enabled
  Priority is 250
    Track object 1 state Up decrement 10
  Master Router is 172.16.23.2 (local), priority is 250
  Master Advertisement interval is 1.000 sec
  Master Down interval is 3.023 sec
```

Now we'll shut down fast 0/3 and see what happens.

```
MLS _ 2(config)#int fast 0/3
MLS _ 2(config-if)#shut
%TRACKING-5-STATE: 1 interface Fa0/3 line-protocol Up->Down

%LINK-5-CHANGED: Interface FastEthernet0/3, changed state to administr
atively down

%LINEPROTO-5-UPDOWN: Line protocol on Interface FastEthernet0/3, changed state
to down

MLS _ 2#show vrrp
Vlan100 - Group 1
   State is Master
   Virtual IP address is 172.16.23.12
   Virtual MAC address is 0000.5e00.0101
   Advertisement interval is 1.000 sec
   Preemption enabled
   Priority is 240 (cfgd 250)
     Track object 1 state Down decrement 10
   Master Router is 172.16.23.2 (local), priority is 240
   Master Advertisement interval is 1.000 sec
   Master Down interval is 3.023 sec
```

The tracking is working, but since we changed the default priority a couple of times early on, the decrement isn't large enough to make MLS_1 the Master router. Let's change that decrement to 51.

```
MLS _ 2(config)#int vlan 100
MLS _ 2(config-if)#vrrp 1 track 1 ?
   decrement Priority decrement
   <cr>

MLS _ 2(config-if)#vrrp 1 track 1 decrement 51

08:14:20: %VRRP-6-STATECHANGE: Vl100 Grp 1 state Master -> Backup

MLS _ 2#show vrrp
Vlan100 - Group 1
   State is Backup
   Virtual IP address is 172.16.23.12
   Virtual MAC address is 0000.5e00.0101
   Advertisement interval is 1.000 sec
   Preemption enabled
   Priority is 199 (cfgd 250)
     Track object 1 state Down decrement 51
```

171

```
Master Router is 172.16.23.1, priority is 200
Master Advertisement interval is 1.000 sec
Master Down interval is 3.023 sec (expires in 2.100 sec)
```

Ta da!

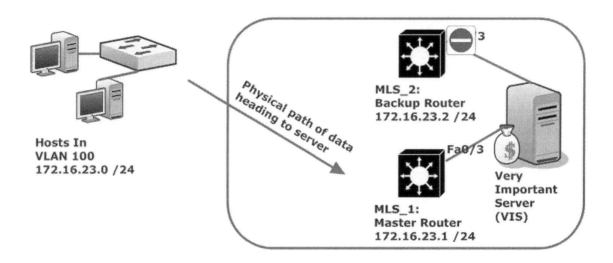

It's all about the decrement – and in this case, knowing how to create a VRRP tracked object!

Since VRRP wasn't exactly developed with load balancing in mind, we're going to use much the same technique as we did with HSRP. Before proceeding, I'll unblock fast0/3 on MLS_2 and we'll watch MLS_2 take over as Master.

```
MLS _ 2(config)#int fast 0/3
MLS _ 2(config-if)#no shut
%SYS-5-CONFIG _ I: Configured from console by console
%LINK-3-UPDOWN: Interface FastEthernet0/3, changed state to down
%TRACKING-5-STATE: 1 interface Fa0/3 line-protocol Down->Up
%LINK-3-UPDOWN: Interface FastEthernet0/3, changed state to up
%LINEPROTO-5-UPDOWN: Line protocol on Interface FastEthernet0/3,
Changed state to up
08:34:58: %VRRP-6-STATECHANGE: Vl100 Grp 1 state Backup -> Master

MLS _ 2#show vrrp
Vlan100 - Group 1
  State is Master
  Virtual IP address is 172.16.23.12
  Virtual MAC address is 0000.5e00.0101
  Advertisement interval is 1.000 sec
  Preemption enabled
  Priority is 250
    Track object 1 state Up decrement 51
  Master Router is 172.16.23.2 (local), priority is 250
```

For VRRP load balancing, we need to create another VRRP virtual router, which means creating a separate VRRP group. Half of the hosts will use VR #1 as their default gateway, and the other half will use VR #2.

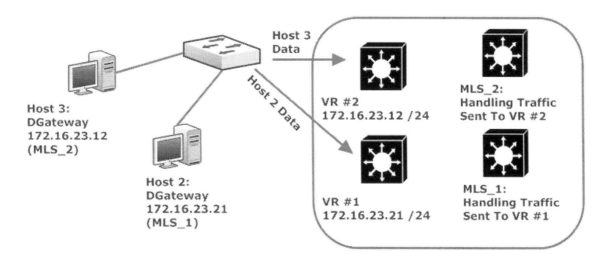

Let's create another VRRP group with a new IP address for the virtual router, using *vrrp priority* to ensure MLS_1 becomes the Master for the new group.

```
MLS _ 2(config)#int vlan 100
MLS _ 2(config-if)#vrrp 55 ip 172.16.23.21

MLS _ 1(config)#int vlan 100
MLS _ 1(config-if)#vrrp 55 ip 172.16.23.21
%VRRP-6-STATECHANGE: Vl100 Grp 55 state Init -> Backup

MLS _ 1(config)#int vlan 100
MLS _ 1(config-if)#vrrp 55 priority 200
%VRRP-6-STATECHANGE: Vl100 Grp 55 state Backup -> Master
```

MLS_1 went to Backup for our new VRRP group first, but then went to Master after having its priority for VRRP group 55 raised to 200. After verifying that MLS_1 is the Master for VRRP group 55 and MLS_2 is the Master for group 1, we just need to configure half the hosts in VLAN 100 to use 172.16.23.12 as their default gateway, and the other half 172.16.23.21.

```
MLS _ 1#show vrrp
Vlan100 - Group 1
   State is Backup
   Virtual IP address is 172.16.23.12

Vlan100 - Group 55
   State is Master
   Virtual IP address is 172.16.23.21
```

```
MLS _ 2#show vrrp
Vlan100 - Group 1
   State is Master
   Virtual IP address is 172.16.23.12


Vlan100 - Group 55
   State is Backup
   Virtual IP address is 172.16.23.21
```

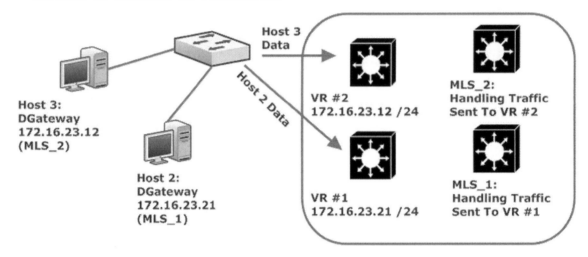

Let's finish our look at FHRPs with a protocol that was actually built with load balancing in mind!

The Gateway Load Balancing Protocol (GLBP)

HSRP and VRRP have some great features, but as we've seen, load balancing with these protocols is more of a workaround than a native behavior. The primary purpose of the Gateway Load Balancing Protocol is, well, load balancing! It's also suitable for use only on Cisco routers and switches, because GLBP is Cisco-proprietary.

As with HSRP and VRRP, GLBP routers will be placed into a router group. By default, GLBP allows every router in the group to handle some of the load in a round-robin manner, rather than having a primary router handle the entire load while the standby routers remain idle. With GLBP, the hosts think they're sending all of their data to a single gateway, but actually multiple gateways are in use at one time. For this reason, GLBP allows us to configure a single default gateway on all of our hosts.

This is a major step forward over HSRP and VRRP load balancing, both of which are inexact sciences at best and a pain in the buttocks at worst.

In the following illustration, three hosts send an ARP request for the MAC of the virtual router.

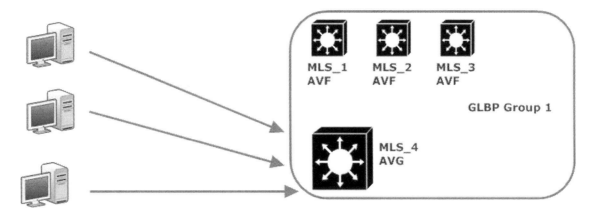

ARP Requests Sent To AVG (Active Virtual Gateway)

The router with the highest GLBP priority is chosen as the Active Virtual Gateway, and it's that router that will respond with ARP responses that contain virtual MAC addresses assigned to the physical routers in the group. The routers receiving and forwarding traffic received on these virtual MAC addresses are Active Virtual Forwarders (AVFs).

The AVG is also in charge of assigning the virtual MAC addresses, and the virtual MAC follows this format:

00-07-b4-00-xx-yy

"XX" is the GLBP group number, "YY" is the AVF number.

If all routers have the same GLBP priority, the router with the highest IP address becomes the AVG.

In the following illustration, MLS_4 is the AVG in GLBP group 1. It has assigned a virtual MAC address of 00-07-b4-00-01-01 to MLS_1, 00-07-b4-00-01-04 to itself, 00-07-b4-00-01-02 to MLS_2, and 00-07-b4-00-01-03 to MLS_3, putting us at the limit of four AVFs in a GLBP group. The routers receiving and forwarding traffic received on these virtual MAC addresses are Active Virtual Forwarders (AVFs).

The AVG answers incoming ARP requests with ARP responses containing the virtual MAC of one of the routers in the group. Our GLBP deployment in this illustration is using the default GLBP load balancing technique of round-robin, so the first ARP response contains the virtual MAC of MLS_1, the next the virtual MAC of MLS_2, and the third the virtual MAC of MLS_3. The next response, naturally, would contain the virtual MAC of MLS_4.

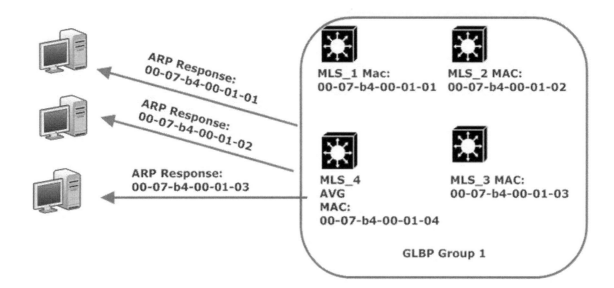

Should the AVG fail, the router serving as the standby AVG will take over. (That's the router with the next-highest GLBP priority in the group; if that's a tie, the router with the next-highest IP address takes that role.) If any of the AVFs fail, another router will handle the load destined for a MAC assigned to the down router. GLBP routers use Hellos multicast to 224.0.0.102 to detect the availability of other GLBP-speaking routers.

By default, GLBP will load-balance in a round-robin fashion, where a host that sends an ARP request will receive a response from the next MAC address in line. We can also use *weighted assignments*, where the higher the assigned weight, the more often a particular router's virtual MAC will be sent to a requesting host. If a host needs the same MAC gateway address every time it sends an ARP request, *host-dependent load balancing* is the way to go.

Our lab is going to be a bit different than the previous HSRP and VRRP labs, and here's the topology. Since GLBP doesn't run on all Cisco switch platforms, we're going to use Cisco routers in this lab. This will also illustrate that GLBP runs the same on multilayer switches and routers. With that in mind, I'm going to use the same multilayer switch icon and names as used in the previous FHRP labs. Each physical device is running the IP address shown on its FastEthernet 0/0 interface.

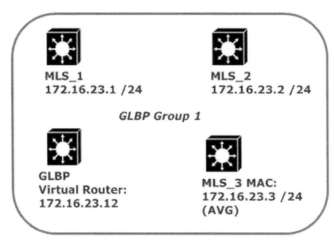

The beginning configuration, along with some IOS Help on the first one:

```
MLS_3(config)#int fast 0/0
MLS_3(config-if)#glbp 1 ?
   authentication  Authentication method
   client-cache    Client cache
   forwarder       Forwarder configuration
   ip              Enable group and set virtual IP address
   ipv6            Enable group for IPv6 and set the virtual IPv6 address
   load-balancing  Load balancing method
   name            Redundancy name
   preempt         Overthrow lower priority designated routers
   priority        Priority level
   timers          Adjust GLBP timers
   weighting       Gateway weighting and tracking

MLS_3(config-if)#glbp 1 ip ?
   A.B.C.D Virtual IP address
   <cr>

MLS_3(config-if)#glbp 1 ip 172.16.23.12
MLS_3(config-if)#glbp 1 preempt

MLS_2(config-if)#glbp 1 ip 172.16.23.12
MLS_2(config-if)#glbp 1 preempt

MLS_1(config-if)#glbp 1 ip 172.16.23.12
MLS_1(config-if)#glbp 1 preempt
```

show glbp is an incredibly important GLBP command; it's also incredibly verbose. The first half of the output deals with the Active Virtual Gateway selection, and the second half with the Active Virtual Forwarders. We're going to examine the output of this command on the current AVG, MLS_3, starting with the first half.

```
MLS_3#show glbp
FastEthernet0/0 - Group 1
   State is Active
      1 state change, last state change 00:11:40
   Virtual IP address is 172.16.23.12
   Hello time 3 sec, hold time 10 sec
      Next hello sent in 2.272 secs
   Redirect time 600 sec, forwarder timeout 14400 sec
   Preemption enabled, min delay 0 sec
   Active is local
   Standby is 172.16.23.2, priority 100 (expires in 9.888 sec)
   Priority 100 (default)
   Weighting 100 (default 100), thresholds: lower 1, upper 100
```

```
Load balancing: round-robin
Group members:
   0017.59e2.474a (172.16.23.3) local
   001b.d4c2.0990 (172.16.23.2)
   001f.ca96.2754 (172.16.23.1)
```

Great info here! From top to bottom, we see the interface and group number, followed by the state of Active, which means we're on the AVG. After the state change info, hello and hold time, and some timers new to us ("redirect" and "forwarder"), we see that preemption is enabled. Following "Active is local", we're given the IP address and priority of the standby AVG. Much like beauty pageants, should MLS_3 be unable to fulfill its duties, the AVG title is given to the runner-up, MLS_2.

Continuing down the output, we see the Priority and Weighting values are set to 100, the default for each. These values are often confused, but after the labs later in this section, you'll be clear – crystal clear – on the usage of each, along with "thresholds".

We then see the load balancing method in use is round-robin, also a GLBP default, followed by the *actual* MAC and IP addresses of the GLBP group members. These are not the virtual MAC addresses that are sent by the AVG in response to ARP requests.

Let's have a look at the second half of the *show glbp* output, which deals with the AVF status of each member. This is also from MLS_3.

```
There are 3 forwarders (1 active)
  Forwarder 1
    State is Active
      1 state change, last state change 00:11:29
    MAC address is 0007.b400.0101 (default)
    Owner ID is 0017.59e2.474a
    Redirection enabled
    Preemption enabled, min delay 30 sec
    Active is local, weighting 100
  Forwarder 2
    State is Listen
    MAC address is 0007.b400.0102 (learnt)
    Owner ID is 001b.d4c2.0990
    Redirection enabled, 599.904 sec remaining (maximum 600 sec)
    Time to live: 14399.904 sec (maximum 14400 sec)
    Preemption enabled, min delay 30 sec
    Active is 172.16.23.2 (primary), weighting 100 (expires in 10.816 sec)
  Forwarder 3
    State is Listen
    MAC address is 0007.b400.0103 (learnt)
    Owner ID is 001f.ca96.2754
    Redirection enabled, 599.392 sec remaining (maximum 600 sec)
    Time to live: 14399.392 sec (maximum 14400 sec)
```

```
Preemption enabled, min delay 30 sec
Active is 172.16.23.1 (primary), weighting 100 (expires in 10.656 sec)
```

The local forwarder (Forwarder 3) is shown as "State is Active", and the other two forwarders are shown as "State is Listen". This means that the other two AVFs are listening for Hellos from the local forwarder, and should those hellos stop coming, one of the other AVFs would step in and handle traffic destined for that down AVF's virtual MAC address. You'll see an example of this in an upcoming lab.

The virtual MAC address for each router is shown in this output as well.

Each physical router in our group is an AVF, and they'll each show their forwarder as "Active" while the other two are in "Listen". Here's that same info from MLS_2:

```
There are 3 forwarders (1 active)
Forwarder 1
   State is Listen
   MAC address is 0007.b400.0101 (learnt)
   Owner ID is 0017.59e2.474a
   Time to live: 14399.360 sec (maximum 14400 sec)
   Preemption enabled, min delay 30 sec
   Active is 172.16.23.3 (primary), weighting 100 (expires in 10.912 sec
Forwarder 2
   State is Active
      1 state change, last state change 00:28:09
   MAC address is 0007.b400.0102 (default)
   Owner ID is 001b.d4c2.0990
   Preemption enabled, min delay 30 sec
   Active is local, weighting 100
Forwarder 3
   State is Listen
   MAC address is 0007.b400.0103 (learnt)
   Owner ID is 001f.ca96.2754
   Time to live: 14397.440 sec (maximum 14400 sec)
   Preemption enabled, min delay 30 sec
   Active is 172.16.23.1 (primary), weighting 100 (expires in 7.936 sec)
```

That same command's output on MLS_1, showing the local forwarder as Active and other two as listening:

```
There are 3 forwarders (1 active)
  Forwarder 1
   State is Listen
   MAC address is 0007.b400.0101 (learnt)
   Owner ID is 0017.59e2.474a
   Time to live: 14399.136 sec (maximum 14400 sec)
   Preemption enabled, min delay 30 sec
```

```
    Active is 172.16.23.3 (primary), weighting 100 (expires in 10.112 sec)
  Forwarder 2
    State is Listen
    MAC address is 0007.b400.0102 (learnt)
    Owner ID is 001b.d4c2.0990
    Time to live: 14398.784 sec (maximum 14400 sec)
    Preemption enabled, min delay 30 sec
    Active is 172.16.23.2 (primary), weighting 100 (expires in 10.560 sec)
  Forwarder 3
    State is Active
      1 state change, last state change 00:29:10
    MAC address is 0007.b400.0103 (default)
    Owner ID is 001f.ca96.2754
    Preemption enabled, min delay 30 sec
    Active is local, weighting 100
```

That differing info on your AVFs can throw you at first, but just remember that the local AVF will always be seen as Active and the others will be listening in!

You'll be happy to know there is a *brief* option for this command, and while it doesn't give the details the full command gives, it's a great place to get started with t-shooting.

```
MLS_3#show glbp brief

Interface  Grp  Fwd  Pri  State   Address         Active router   Standby router

Fa0/0      1    -    100  Active  172.16.23.12    local           172.16.23.2

Fa0/0      1    1    -    Active  0007.b400.0101  local           -

Fa0/0      1    2    -    Listen  0007.b400.0102  172.16.23.2     -

Fa0/0      1    3    -    Listen  0007.b400.0103  172.16.23.1     -
```

When you see a dash under "Fwd" and "Active" under "State", you're on the AVG. The devices with a number under "Fwd" are your AVFs, and it's commonplace for a router to serve as both an AVG and an AVF.

According to that output, MLS_2 should take over as the AVG if MLS_3 is unavailable. Let's test that by making MLS_3 unavailable and then running *show glbp brief* on MLS_2.

```
MLS_3(config)#int fast 0/0
MLS_3(config-if)#shut

%GLBP-6-STATECHANGE: FastEthernet0/0 Grp 1 state Standby -> Active
%GLBP-6-FWDSTATECHANGE: FastEthernet0/0 Grp 1 Fwd 1 state Listen -> Active

MLS_2#show glbp brief
```

Interface	Grp	Fwd	Pri	State	Address	Active router	Standby router
Fa0/0	1	–	100	Active	172.16.23.12	local	172.16.23.1
Fa0/0	1	1	–	Active	0007.b400.0101	local	–
Fa0/0	1	2	–	Active	0007.b400.0102	local	–
Fa0/0	1	3	–	Listen	0007.b400.0103	172.16.23.1	–

Take careful note of both GLBP console messages. We expected MLS_2 to take over as the AVG, and that's verified by *show glbp brief.* What you might not have expected is that MLS_2 is now the Active router for the MAC address previously handled by MLS_3 (0007.b400.0101), and it's handling traffic sent to that MAC address as well as its own assigned address, 0007.b400.0102.

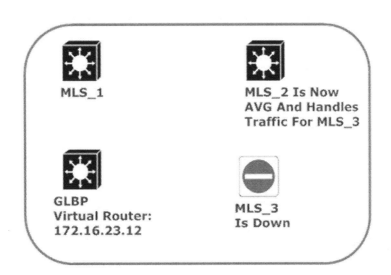

Once MLS_3 comes back online, it reclaims the role of AVG and begins acting as an AVF for its original virtual MAC address.

```
MLS _ 3#show glbp brief
```

Interface	Grp	Fwd	Pri	State	Address	Active router	Standby router
Fa0/0	1	–	100	Active	172.16.23.12	local	172.16.23.2
Fa0/0	1	1	–	Active	**0007.b400.0101**	**local**	–
Fa0/0	1	2	–	Listen	0007.b400.0102	172.16.23.2	–
Fa0/0	1	3	–	Listen	0007.b400.0103	172.16.23.1	–

Watch The Timers

Two of the GLBP timers are just the same as those found in HSRP; they even have the same default. There are two others that can be a tad confusing at first. Let's clear up any confusion on these right now.

```
MLS_3#show glbp
FastEthernet0/0 - Group 1
  State is Active
    3 state changes, last state change 00:15:34
  Virtual IP address is 172.16.23.12
  Hello time 3 sec, hold time 10 sec
    Next hello sent in 0.192 secs
  Redirect time 600 sec, forwarder timeout 14400 se
```

The hello and hold times operate the same here as they do in HSRP – it's the redirect and forwarder timeout values we need to examine closely.

In the previous lab, MLS_2 began accepting frames with the destination 0007.b400.0101, which had been MLS_3's virtual MAC address. That's mighty kind of MLS_2, but that kindness will not last forever.

When the redirect time expires, the AVG will no longer use the virtual MAC address in question as a response to ARP replies.

Then, when the forwarder timeout timer expires, the now-disappeared VRF and its virtual MAC address disappear from every GLBP router in the group.

Use *glbp timers redirect* to change either timer, and watch your syntax! The redirect timer is the first timer in this command, and the timeout interval is the second. They both have to be set even if you're just changing one, and should you set the forwarder timeout too low...

```
MLS_3(config-if)#glbp 1 timers ?
  <1-60>    Hello interval in seconds
  msec      Specify hello interval in milliseconds
  redirect  Specify timeout values for failed forwarders

MLS_3(config-if)#glbp 1 timers redirect ?
  <0-3600>  Interval in seconds to redirect to failed forwarders

MLS_3(config-if)#glbp 1 timers redirect 1800 ?
  <2400-64800>  Timeout interval in seconds for failed forwarders

MLS_3(config-if)#glbp 1 timers redirect 1800 3600 ?
  <cr>
```

```
MLS_3(config-if)#glbp 1 timers redirect 1800 3600
% Forwarder timeout is less than the default ARP cache timeout (4 hours)
```

... well, if you've ever watched *Shark Tank*, you've heard Barbara Corcoran say "I'm going to give you a minute to rethink that." That's pretty much what the router is telling us here. The timer change does take effect, but I *did* go back to the defaults after seeing that message. Change these timers with care!

```
MLS_3(config)#int fast 0/0
MLS_3(config-if)#no glbp 1 timers redirect 1800 3600
```

Selecting The AVG And Backup AVG

Selecting another router to serve as the AVG is no problem. In these labs, MLS_3 was selected because of its higher IP address – but perhaps we want MLS_2 to be the AVG instead. Since we enabled preemption on all three routers at the beginning of the lab, all we need to do is raise the GLBP priority on MLS_2.

```
MLS_2(config)#int fast 0/0
MLS_2(config-if)#glbp 1 priority 150


01:24:57: %GLBP-6-STATECHANGE: FastEthernet0/0 Grp 1 state Standby -> Active


MLS_2#show glbp brief
Interface  Grp  Fwd  Pri  State    Address         Active router  Standby router

Fa0/0      1    -    150  Active   172.16.23.12    local          172.16.23.3

Fa0/0      1    1    -    Listen   0007.b400.0101  172.16.23.3    -

Fa0/0      1    2    -    Active   0007.b400.0102  local          -

Fa0/0      1    3    -    Listen   0007.b400.0103  172.16.23.1    -
```

MLS_2 has taken over as the AVG, and MLS_3 is the standby AVG since it has a higher IP address than MLS_1. To make MLS_1 the standby AVG, assign it a priority higher than that of MLS_3 (100) and less than that of MLS_2 (150). After changing the priority on MLS_1 to 125, *show glbp brief* verifies that MLS_1 is indeed the standby AVG while MLS_2 remains the AVG.

```
MLS_1(config)#int fast 0/0
MLS_1(config-if)#glbp 1 priority 125


MLS_1#show glbp brief
```

Interface	Grp	Fwd	Pri	State	Address	Active router	Standby router
Fa0/0	**1**	**-**	**125**	**Standby**	**172.16.23.12**	**172.16.23.2**	**local**
Fa0/0	1	1	-	Listen	0007.b400.0101	172.16.23.3	-
Fa0/0	1	2	-	Listen	0007.b400.0102	172.16.23.2	-
Fa0/0	1	3	-	Active	0007.b400.0103	local	-

Now, about those weights...

Using Weights And Tracking

Slight warning: This is one of those things that sounds complicated when you hear or read about it, but when you see it in action, you'll wonder what the fuss was. Hang in there during this quick explanation and then you'll see it all in action.

Before proceeding with this lab, I raised MLS_3's priority to 160 and it is now the AVG for the group.

```
MLS_3(config)#int fast 0/0
MLS_3(config-if)#glbp 1 priority 160
```

```
MLS_3#show glbp brief
```

Interface	Grp	Fwd	Pri	State	Address	Active router	Standby router
Fa0/0	**1**	**-**	**160**	**Active**	**172.16.23.12**	**local**	**172.16.23.2**
Fa0/0	1	1	-	Active	0007.b400.0101	local	-
Fa0/0	1	2	-	Listen	0007.b400.0102	172.16.23.2	-
Fa0/0	1	3	-	Listen	0007.b400.0103	172.16.23.1	-

The default weight of a GLBP-enabled router is 100, and this is the value that determines whether a router can be a VRF. The weight has two default thresholds, *lower* and *upper*:

```
MLS_3#show glbp
FastEthernet0/0 - Group 1
  State is Active
    5 state changes, last state change 00:00:52
  Virtual IP address is 172.16.23.12
  Hello time 3 sec, hold time 10 sec
    Next hello sent in 0.992 secs
  Redirect time 600 sec, forwarder timeout 14400 sec
```

```
Preemption enabled, min delay 0 sec
Active is local
Standby is 172.16.23.2, priority 150 (expires in 8.000 sec)
Priority 160 (configured)
Weighting 100 (default 100), thresholds: lower 1, upper 100
Load balancing: round-robin
```

We can use interface tracking, GLBP weight, and those thresholds to determine whether the local router is eligible to be an AVF. In this lab, we'll configure MLS_3 to disqualify itself as an AVF if the line protocol on fast 0/1 goes down. *This does not in any way affect MLS_3's status as the AVG.*

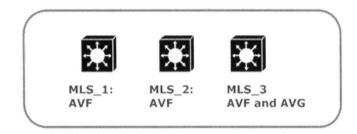

Before configuring interface tracking, what do we do? CHECK THAT INTERFACE!

```
MLS_3#show int fast 0/1
FastEthernet0/1 is up, line protocol is up
```

Huzzah! Now to set up tracking with the *track* command, which is a globally configured command rather than an interface-level command.

```
MLS_3(config)#track ?
  <1-500>      Tracked object
  rcsolution   Tracking resolution parameters
  timer        Polling interval timers

MLS_3(config)#track 1 ?
  application  Application
  interface    Select an interface to track
  ip           IP protocol
  list         Group objects in a list
  stub-object  Stub tracking object
<cr>

MLS_3(config)#track 1 interface fastethernet0/1 ?
  ip              IP parameters
  line-protocol Track interface line-protocol

MLS_3(config)#track 1 interface fastethernet0/1 line-protocol ?
  <cr>
```

```
MLS_3(config)#track 1 interface fastethernet0/1 line-protocol
```

Now we'll head back to the GLBP configuration. First, we have to set up the value for weighting along with the high and low thresholds. When the router's weight drops below the *low* threshold, it can no longer act as a VRF. Once that weight meets or rises above the *high* threshold, that router can go right back to work as a VRF. We'll keep the default weight of 100 while setting a low threshold of 95 and a high of 100.

```
MLS_3(config)#int fast 0/0
MLS_3(config-if)#glbp 1 weighting ?
  <1-254>    Weighting maximum value
  track      Interface tracking

MLS_3(config-if)#glbp 1 weighting 100 ?
  lower      Weighting lower threshold
  upper      Weighting upper threshold
  <cr>

MLS_3(config-if)#glbp 1 weighting 100 lower ?
  <1-99>     Weighting lower threshold value

MLS_3(config-if)#glbp 1 weighting 100 lower 95 ?
  upper      Weighting upper threshold
  <cr>

MLS_3(config-if)#glbp 1 weighting 100 lower 95 upper ?
  <95-100>   Weighting upper threshold value

MLS_3(config-if)#glbp 1 weighting 100 lower 95 upper 100 ?
  <cr>


MLS_3(config-if)#glbp 1 weighting 100 lower 95 upper 100
```

The second command needed here is the one specifying the interface to be tracked and the decrement, which by default is 10. We're accepting that default here by not entering a value for the decrement.

```
MLS_3(config-if)#glbp 1 weighting ?
  <1-254>     Weighting maximum value
  track       Interface tracking

MLS_3(config-if)#glbp 1 weighting track ?
  <1-500>     Tracked object

MLS_3(config-if)#glbp 1 weighting track 1 ?
  decrement   Weighting decrement
  <cr>
```

```
MLS _ 3(config-if)#glbp 1 weighting track 1
```

Verify with *show glbp.*

```
MLS _ 3#show glbp
FastEthernet0/0 - Group 1
   State is Active
13 state changes, last state change 00:43:17
   Virtual IP address is 172.16.23.12
   Hello time 3 sec, hold time 10 sec
Next hello sent in 1.344 secs
   Redirect time 600 sec, forwarder timeout 14400 sec
   Preemption enabled, min delay 0 sec
   Active is local
   Standby is 172.16.23.2, priority 150 (expires in 8.000 sec)
   Priority 160 (configured)
   Weighting 100 (configured 100), thresholds: lower 95, upper 100
   Track object 1 state Up decrement 10
```

With this configuration, MLS_3 should be disqualified from consideration as a VRF if that weight drops below 95. Let's shut down fast 0/1 on that router and watch the fun!

show glbp tells us that the weight has indeed dropped to 90.

```
Weighting 90, low (configured 100), thresholds: lower 95, upper 100
   Track object 1 state Down decrement 10
```

show glbp brief verifies that while MLS_3 is still the AVG, it's no longer an AVF. MLS_2 is now handling traffic with a destination MAC of 0007.b400.0101, which was formerly handled by MLS_3.

```
MLS _ 3#show glbp brief
```

Interface	Grp	Fwd	Pri	State	Address	Active router	Standby router
Fa0/0	1	–	160	Active	172.16.23.12	local	172.16.23.2
Fa0/0	1	1	–	Listen	0007.b400.0101	172.16.23.2	–
Fa0/0	1	2	–	Listen	0007.b400.0102	172.16.23.2	–
Fa0/0	1	3	–	Listen	0007.b400.0103	172.16.23.1	–

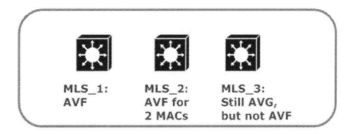

MLS_1:
AVF

MLS_2:
AVF for
2 MACs

MLS_3:
Still AVG,
but not AVF

I'll now bring MLS_3's fast0/1 interface back online, and shortly after we see the GLBP syslog message shown here, MLS_3 will resume its VRF duties.

```
*Apr 3 19:09:49: %GLBP-6-FWDSTATECHANGE: FastEthernet0/0 Grp 1 Fwd 1 state
Listen -> Active

MLS_3#show glbp brief
Interface Grp  Fwd  Pri  State   Address         Active router   Standby router

Fa0/0     1    -    160  Active  172.16.23.12    local           172.16.23.2

Fa0/0     1    1    -    Active  0007.b400.0101  local           -

Fa0/0     1    2    -    Listen  0007.b400.0102  172.16.23.2     -

Fa0/0     1    3    -    Listen  0007.b400.0103  172.16.23.1     -
```

The reason I ran this lab on our AVG is to emphasize that the AVG election and a router's ability to serve as an AVF are two separate operations.

In short:

Use *priority* to affect the choice of your primary and backup AVGs, and use *weighting* to affect a router's ability to serve as an AVF, perhaps in tandem with interface tracking.

Let's shift our focus to securing our switches!

Chapter 9:

SECURING THE SWITCHES

When some people think of network security, they immediately think of protecting their network from attacks originating on the outside of the network. We're not "some people", though, and we can't afford to think like that. Many successful network attacks are inside jobs, and originate from seemingly innocent sources like DHCP, ARP, CDP, Telnet, and even from other hosts on the same VLAN.

While it's certainly wise to protect the perimeter of our network, we have to be vigilant against attacks from the interior too. We've got important work to do, so let's get to it!

Port Security

A basic Cisco switch security feature that's often overlooked, port security uses the source MAC address of incoming frames as a password. A port enabled with port security will expect frames sourced from a particular MAC address or group of addresses ("secure MAC addresses"), and if frames with non-secure source MAC addresses come in on that port, the port takes action ranging from shutting down to "just" letting you and I know about it.

In a nutshell, port security entails having the switch look at the source MAC address of an incoming frame and asking itself, "Do I trust the source of this frame?"

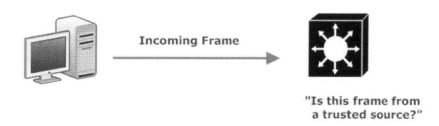

Incoming Frame

"Is this frame from a trusted source?"

Port security is enabled with the *switchport port-security* command, and before we can consider any options...

```
MLS _ 1(config-if)#switchport port-security
Command rejected: FastEthernet0/1 is a dynamic port.
```

... we need to make the port a non-trunking port. Port security can't be configured on a port that even has a *possibility* of becoming a trunk. This switch has no trunks...

```
MLS _ 1#show int trunk

< crickets chirping >

MLS _ 1#
```

... but we still can't secure that port until it's an access port. Let's make that happen and put it into VLAN 11.

```
MLS _ 1(config)#int fast 0/11
MLS _ 1(config-if)#switchport mode access
MLS _ 1(config-if)#switchport access vlan 11
% Access VLAN does not exist. Creating vlan 11
MLS _ 1(config-if)#switchport port-security
```

We'll verify with *show port-security* and then view our *switchport port-security* options.

```
MLS _ 1#show port-security

Secure Port    MaxSecureAddr   CurrentAddr   SecurityViolation   Security Action

               (Count)         (Count)       (Count)

-------------------------------------------------------------------------------------
Fa0/11         1               0             0                   Shutdown
-------------------------------------------------------------------------------------

Total Addresses in System (excluding one mac per port)     : 0
Max Addresses limit in System (excluding one mac per port) : 6144


MLS _ 1(config-if)#switchport port-security ?
  Aging        Port-security aging commands
  mac-address  Secure mac address
  maximum      Max secure addresses
  violation    Security violation mode
  <cr>
```

Let's tackle each of these important options, starting with *maximum*, which defines the number of secure MAC addresses the port can learn. The default is one, and the maximum you'll see on your switch depends on your switch! I've seen ranges from 132 to the whopping 6144 allowed on this port. (I would not recommend allowing 6,144 secure MAC addresses on any port.)

```
MLS_1(config-if)#switchport port-security maximum ?
  <1-6144> Maximum addresses
```

Use the *aging* options to define how long dynamically learned secure MAC addresses should be considered secure. You have the rarely used option of enabling aging for static entries.

```
MLS_1(config-if)#switchport port-security aging ?
  static       Enable aging for configured secure addresses
  time         Port-security aging time
  type         Port-security aging type

MLS_1(config-if)#switchport port-security aging type ?
  absolute     Absolute aging (default)
  inactivity   Aging based on inactivity time period

MLS_1(config-if)#switchport port-security aging time ?
  <1-1440>       Aging time in minutes. Enter a value between 1 and 1440

MLS_1(config-if)#switchport port-security aging static ?
  <cr>
```

We'll use the *mac-address* option to define secure MAC addresses for this port, as well as something called a "sticky address" (sounds gross, but it isn't).

```
MLS_1(config-if)#switchport port-security mac-address ?
  H.H.H        48 bit mac address
  sticky       Configure dynamic secure addresses as sticky

MLS_1(config-if)#switchport port-security mac-address
```

The *violation* option defines the action the port should take when a frame with a non-secure MAC address comes in.

```
MLS_1(config-if)#switchport port-security violation ?
  protect      Security violation protect mode
  restrict     Security violation restrict mode
  shutdown     Security violation shutdown mode
```

The default port security mode is *shutdown*, which does just that – the port is placed into error-disabled state ("err-disabled"), and manual intervention is needed to reopen the port. That means you or I have to fix the problem and then do a shut / no shut on the port. With shutdown mode, an SNMP trap message is also generated.

Protect mode simply drops the offending frames and no other action is taken.

Our middle-ground security mode is *restrict*. The non-secure frames are dropped, an SNMP trap notification and a syslog message are generated, and the port remains open.

Here's the network topology for the port-security labs. We're using the hosts primarily to send pings that will (or will not) trigger port security.

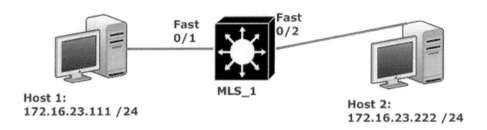

Let's see port security in action! I'll configure port security on port fast0/1 after shutting the interface, and then set the secure MAC address to aaaa-bbbb-cccc.

```
MLS _ 1(config)#int fast 0/1
MLS _ 1(config-if)#shut
MLS _ 1(config-if)#switchport port-security
MLS _ 1(config-if)#switchport port-security mac-address aaaa.bbbb.cccc
```

After reopening the port, I'll send some pings from R1 and then quickly head back over to the switch to see what happens.

```
R1#ping 172.16.23.222
```

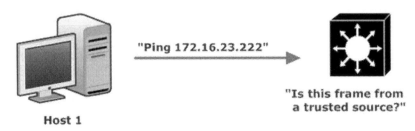

Back on the switch:

```
SECURITY-2-PSECURE _ VIOLATION: Security violation occurred, caused by MAC address
0017.59e2.474a on port FastEthernet0/1.

01:46:31: %LINEPROTO-5-UPDOWN: Line protocol on Interface FastEthernet0/1,
changed state to down
01:46:32: %LINK-3-UPDOWN: Interface FastEthernet0/1, changed state to down
```

Looks like the data was NOT from a trusted source, as both *show port-security* and *show int fast 0/1* verify the security violation.

```
MLS_1#show port-security

Secure Port   MaxSecureAddr   CurrentAddr   SecurityViolation   Security Action

              (Count)         (Count)       (Count)
--------------------------------------------------------------------------------
Fa0/1         1               1             1                   Shutdown
--------------------------------------------------------------------------------

  Total Addresses in System (excluding one mac per port)     : 0
  Max Addresses limit in System (excluding one mac per port) : 6144

MLS_1#show int fast 0/1
FastEthernet0/1 is down, line protocol is down (err-disabled)
```

"Ping 172.16.23.222"

Host 1

"That's not the secure MAC source address, so I'm shutting that port down."

Time for the network admins to step in! First, we resolve the problem by removing the currently defined secure MAC address on Fast0/1. When a secure MAC address is allowed on a port, but none is defined, the next dynamically learned source MAC address is considered the secure address. That's why I shut the port before configuring port security – just in case traffic came in on that port before I could finish.

```
MLS_1(config)#int fast 0/1
MLS_1(config-if)#no switchport port-security mac-address aaaa.bbbb.cccc
```

We'll do a *shut / no shut* on the interface and verify with *show int fast 0/1.*

```
MLS_1(config-if)#shut
MLS_1(config-if)#no shut
01:53:47: %LINEPROTO-5-UPDOWN: Line protocol on Interface FastEthernet0/1,
changed state to up
01:53:49: %LINK-3-UPDOWN: Interface FastEthernet0/1, changed state to up
```

To test the new config, we'll send some pings from R1 again and then head right back to the switch.

```
R1#ping 172.16.23.222
```

Back on the switch, there's no message about the port shutting down, so we'll verify that everything's beautiful with three separate *show port-security* commands, starting with the main one. We see there's one secure address allowed on Fast0/1 (the default), and that one current address is considered secure. Note carefully that you see the *Security Action* listed, but none has been taken as there are no *Security Violations*.

```
MLS _ 1#show port-security

Secure Port    MaxSecureAddr   CurrentAddr   SecurityViolation   Security Action

               (Count)         (Count)       (Count)

-------------------------------------------------------------------------------------
Fa0/1          1               1             0                   Shutdown
-------------------------------------------------------------------------------------
Total Addresses in System (excluding one mac per port) : 0
Max Addresses limit in System (excluding one mac per port) : 6144
```

show port-security address verifies the exact address that's been learned and considered secure, along with the VLAN, the port, and method used to learn the address. This one's marked as *SecureDynamic* since it is a secure address that was learned, well, dynamically (rather than statically, as with the aaaa.bbbb.cccc address configured earlier).

```
MLS _ 1#show port-security address ?
  vlan  Vlan limits
  |     Output modifiers
  <cr>


MLS _ 1#show port-security address
            Secure Mac Address Table


Vlan  Mac Address      Type            Ports        Remaining      Age
(mins)
-     ----------       ------------    -----
100   0017.59e2.474a   SecureDynamic   Fa0/1        -


Total Addresses in System (excluding one mac per port) : 0
Max Addresses limit in System (excluding one mac per port) : 6144
```

Finally, *show port-security interface fast 0/1* verifies port security is enabled, the port is secured and up, the violation mode is at the default, and provides other handy info including the last source address of incoming frames and the VLAN it belonged to.

```
    MLS _ 1#show port-security interface fast 0/1
Port Security              : Enabled
Port Status                : Secure-up
Violation Mode             : Shutdown
Aging Time                 : 0 mins
Aging Type                 : Absolute
SecureStatic Address Aging : Disabled
Maximum MAC Addresses      : 1
Total MAC Addresses        : 1
Configured MAC Addresses   : 0
```

```
Sticky MAC Addresses        : 0
Last Source Address:Vlan    : 0017.59e2.474a:100
Security Violation Count     : 0
```

The aging time of "0 minutes" means that secure MAC addresses will never age out on this port, not that they'll actually age out in 59 seconds.

I just *know* someone out there is wondering what happens if you allow multiple secure MAC addresses on a port, and you statically configure a few without hitting the maximum. Let's find out on port Fast0/2, where I'll allow 3 addresses to be considered secure while configuring 2 static secure addresses.

```
MLS _ 1(config)#int fast 0/2
MLS _ 1(config-if)#switchport port-security
MLS _ 1(config-if)#switchport port-security maximum 3
MLS _ 1(config-if)#switchport port-security mac-address aaaa.bbbb.aaaa
MLS _ 1(config-if)#switchport port-security mac-address aaaa.aaaa.aaaa
```

I'll then send pings from R2 and head quickly back over to the switch.

```
R2#ping 172.16.23.111
```

No messages on the switch regarding a shutdown. Let's run *show port-security interface fast0/2*.

```
MLS _ 1#show port-security int fast 0/2
Port Security               : Enabled
Port Status                 : Secure-up
Violation Mode              : Shutdown
Aging Time                  : 0 mins
Aging Type                  : Absolute
SecureStatic Address Aging  : Disabled
Maximum MAC Addresses       : 3
Total MAC Addresses         : 3
Configured MAC Addresses    : 2
Sticky MAC Addresses        : 0
Last Source Address:Vlan    : 001b.d4c2.0990:100
Security Violation Count     : 0
```

The port is secure and up, and note that there are now a total of 3 secure addresses and 2 configured addresses. If you allow a certain number of secure MAC addresses and don't statically configure all of them, the next dynamically learned MAC addresses will be considered secure until the limit is hit. Had we allowed four secure addresses and configured only two static ones, the next two source MAC addresses for incoming frames on that port would be considered secure.

Let's run *show port-security address* and *show port-security*.

```
MLS _ 1#show port-security address
          Secure Mac Address Table

   Vlan  Mac Address         Type                    Ports       Remaining      Age
(mins)
   -     ----------          -----------             -----
   100   0017.59e2.474a      SecureDynamic           Fa0/1       -
   100   001b.d4c2.0990      SecureDynamic           Fa0/2       -
   100   aaaa.aaaa.aaaa      SecureConfigured        Fa0/2       -
   100   aaaa.bbbb.aaaa      SecureConfigured        Fa0/2       -


Total Addresses in System (excluding one mac per port) : 2
Max Addresses limit in System (excluding one mac per port) : 6144


MLS _ 1#show port-security


Secure Port  MaxSecureAddr   CurrentAddr    SecurityViolation Security Action

             (Count)         (Count)        (Count)
----------------------------------------------------------------------------------
Fa0/1        1               1              0                 Shutdown

Fa0/2        3               3              0                 Shutdown
----------------------------------------------------------------------------------
    Total Addresses in System (excluding one mac per port)    : 2
    Max Addresses limit in System (excluding one mac per port) : 6144
```

There are three entries for Fa0/2, two of them statically configured and the other dynamically learned. While we're here, let's enable aging and set it to 300 seconds (the default aging time for our "regular" MAC address table). We'll accept the aging type default shown via IOS Help and then verify with show *port-security address*.

```
MLS _ 1(config)#int fast 0/2
MLS _ 1(config-if)#switchport port-security aging ?
   static  Enable.aging for configured secure addresses
   time    Port-security aging time
   type    Port-security aging type

MLS _ 1(config-if)#switchport port-security aging time ?
   <1-1440> Aging time in minutes. Enter a value between 1 and 1440

MLS _ 1(config-if)#switchport port-security aging time 300
MLS _ 1(config-if)#switchport port-security aging type ?
   absoluteAbsolute aging (default)
   inactivity   Aging based on inactivity time period

MLS _ 1#show port-security address
          Secure Mac Address Table
```

```
Vlan   Mac Address         Type                  Ports       Remaining Age (mins)
 -     ----------          -----------           -----
100    0017.59e2.474a      SecureDynamic         Fa0/1       -
100    001b.d4c2.0990      SecureDynamic         Fa0/2       299
100    aaaa.aaaa.aaaa      SecureConfigured      Fa0/2       -
100    aaaa.bbbb.aaaa      SecureConfigured      Fa0/2       -


Total Addresses in System (excluding one mac per port)     : 2
Max Addresses limit in System (excluding one mac per port) : 6144
```

So, did I get that right?

Nope. I got it wrong – and here's why I'm always telling you to check the unit of measure when you change anything on a Cisco router or switch. The command to change the aging time of our entire MAC address table uses *seconds*...

```
MLS _ 1(config)#mac address-table aging-time ?
  <0-0>           Enter 0 to disable aging
  <10-1000000>    Aging time in seconds
```

... but the command to change the aging time of the secure MAC address table uses *minutes*.

```
MLS _ 1(config)#int fast 0/2
MLS _ 1(config-if)#switchport port-security aging time ?
  <1-1440>        Aging time in minutes. Enter a value between 1 and 1440

MLS _ 1(config-if)#switchport port-security aging time 5

MLS _ 1#show port-security address
        Secure Mac Address Table

Vlan   Mac Address         Type                  Ports       Remaining Age (mins)
 -     ----------          -----------           -----
100    0017.59e2.474a      SecureDynamic         Fa0/1       -
100    001b.d4c2.0990      SecureDynamic         Fa0/2       4
100    aaaa.aaaa.aaaa      SecureConfigured      Fa0/2       -
100    aaaa.bbbb.aaaa      SecureConfigured      Fa0/2       -


Total Addresses in System (excluding one mac per port)     : 2
Max Addresses limit in System (excluding one mac per port) : 6144
```

Always use IOS Help to check the unit of time, data, when changing *anything*!

Making Secure Addresses Sticky

Right now, Fa0/1 has one secure MAC address, for which the default of "no aging" has not been changed. (The dynamically learned address for R2 has now aged out.)

```
MLS_1#show port-security address
          Secure Mac Address Table

Vlan   Mac Address       Type             Ports      Remaining Age (mins)
-      ----------        -----------      -----
100    0017.59e2.474a    SecureDynamic    Fa0/1      -
100    aaaa.aaaa.aaaa    SecureConfigured Fa0/2      -
100    aaaa.bbbb.aaaa    SecureConfigured Fa0/2      -
```

That dynamically learned address will be lost if the port is reset or the switch is reloaded. I'll do a *shut / no shut* on the port to illustrate.

```
MLS_1(config)#int fast 0/1
MLS_1(config-if)#shut
%LINEPROTO-5-UPDOWN: Line protocol on Interface Vlan100, changed state to down
%LINK-5-CHANGED: Interface FastEthernet0/1, changed state to administratively
down
%LINEPROTO-5-UPDOWN: Line protocol on Interface FastEthernet0/1, changed state
to down
MLS_1(config-if)#no shut


MLS_1#show port-security address
00:28:20: %LINK-3-UPDOWN: Interface FastEthernet0/1, changed state to up
00:28:21: %LINEPROTO-5-UPDOWN: Line protocol on Interface FastEthernet0/1,
changed state to up

MLS_1#show port-security address
          Secure Mac Address Table

Vlan   Mac Address       Type             Ports      Remaining Age (mins)
-      ----------        -----------      -----
100    aaaa.aaaa.aaaa    SecureConfigured Fa0/2      -
100    aaaa.bbbb.aaaa    SecureConfigured Fa0/2      -

Total Addresses in System (excluding one mac per port)       : 1
Max Addresses limit in System (excluding one mac per port)   : 6144
MLS_1#
```

The same thing would happen if I rebooted the switch. To have dynamically learned addresses retained in case of a port reset or reboot, enable sticky address learning on the port. These addresses are written to the running config, so be sure to save the changes! I'll do that here, then send pings from R1 and check the secure address table.

```
MLS_1(config)#int fast 0/1
MLS_1(config-if)#switchport port-security ?
  Aging         Port-security aging commands
  mac-address   Secure mac address
  maximum       Max secure addresses
  violation     Security violation mode
  <cr>

MLS_1(config-if)#switchport port-security mac-address ?
  H.H.H    48 bit mac address
  Sticky   Configure dynamic secure addresses as sticky

MLS_1(config-if)#switchport port-security mac-address sticky

R1#ping 172.16.23.222

MLS_1#show port-security address
        Secure Mac Address Table
```

Vlan	Mac Address	Type	Ports	Remaining Age (mins)
-	----------	-----------	-----	
100	0017.59e2.474a	SecureSticky	Fa0/1	-
100	aaaa.aaaa.aaaa	SecureConfigured	Fa0/2	-
100	aaaa.bbbb.aaaa	SecureConfigured	Fa0/2	-

```
Total Addresses in System (excluding one mac per port)    : 1
Max Addresses limit in System (excluding one mac per port) : 6144
```

The address is now shown in the secure MAC table as "SecureSticky". I'll shut the port and then take a look at this table again.

```
MLS_1(config)#int fast 0/1
MLS_1(config-if)#shut

MLS_1#show port-security address
        Secure Mac Address Table
```

Vlan	Mac Address	Type	Ports	Remaining Age (mins)
-	----------	-----------	-----	
100	0017.59e2.474a	SecureSticky	Fa0/1	-
100	aaaa.aaaa.aaaa	SecureConfigured	Fa0/2	-
100	aaaa.bbbb.aaaa	SecureConfigured	Fa0/2	-

```
Total Addresses in System (excluding one mac per port)    : 1
```

```
Max Addresses limit in System (excluding one mac per port) : 6144
```

The entry is still in the table! I did reload the switch at this point, and the address was still in the table after the reboot, along with the *SecureConfigured* addresses. Stickiness works!

Automatic Recovery From Err-Disabled Status

We know via first-hand experience that by default, a port that goes into err-disabled state must be manually reset – after resolving the condition that put the port in that state to begin with, of course!

To have err-disabled ports come out of that state dynamically after a certain period of time, use errdisable recovery. First, define what conditions should be allowed to have ports use this feature with errdisable recovery cause. Ports are shut down by port security due to a psecure-violation, so we'll enable this feature only for ports put into err-disabled state in that fashion. To have errdisable recovery apply to ports placed into err-disabled state for any reason, use the all option.

```
SW1(config)#errdisable recovery cause ?
  All                 Enable timer to recover from all causes
  Bpduguard           Enable timer to recover from BPDU Guard error disable
                      state
  channel-misconfig   Enable timer to recover from channel misconfig disable
                      state
  dhcp-rate-limit     Enable timer to recover from dhcp-rate-limit error
                      disable state
  dtp-flap            Enable timer to recover from dtp-flap error disable
                      stat
  gbic-invalid        Enable timer to recover from invalid GBIC error disable
                      state
  link-flap           Enable timer to recover from link-flap error disable
                      state
  loopback            Enable timer to recover from loopback detected disable
                      state
  pagp-flap           Enable timer to recover from pagp-flap error disable
                      state
  psecure-violation   Enable timer to recover from psecure violation disable
                      state
  security-violation  Enable timer to recover from 802.1x violation disable
                      state
  udld                Enable timer to recover from udld error disable state
```

```
unicast-flood          Enable timer to recover from unicast flood disable
                       state
vmps                   Enable timer to recover from vmps shutdown error
                       disable state
```

To change the interval from the default of 300 seconds, use *errdisable recovery interval*. I'll set it to 30 seconds for our lab.

```
SW1(config)#errdisable recovery cause psecure-violation
SW1(config)#erridsable recovery interval ?
% Unrecognized command
SW1(config)#erridsable recovery ?
% Unrecognized command
SW1(config)#errdisable recovery interval ?
  <30-86400> timer-interval(sec)

SW1(config)#errdisable recovery interval 30
```

At this point, I removed any previous port security config from Fa0/2, and reconfigured the port with the single secure MAC address aaaa.aaaa.aaaa. The first frames that came in from R2 shut the port down...

```
%PM-4-ERR_DISABLE: psecure-violation error detected on Fa0/2, putting Fa0/2
in err-disable state

%PORT_SECURITY-2-PSECURE_VIOLATION: Security violation occurred, caused by
MAC address 001b.d4c2.0990 on port FastEthernet0/2.
```

... and 30 seconds later, the port begins to come out of err-disabled state!

```
%PM-4-ERR_RECOVER: Attempting to recover from psecure-violation err-disable
state on Fa0/2
%LINK-3-UPDOWN: Interface FastEthernet0/2, changed state to up
%LINEPROTO-5-UPDOWN: Line protocol on Interface FastEthernet0/2, changed state
to up
```

I then configured Fa0/2 to consider the first source MAC address learned on that port to be the secure address, and all is well. You have to fix the problem or the port will bounce in and out of err-disabled state!

Dot1x Port-Based Authentication

We can take port-level security (cliché alert!) to the next level with dot1x port-based authentication. The name refers to IEEE 802.1x, the standard upon which this feature is based. It's a bit unusual in that the Cisco authentication server must be RADIUS-based; you can't use TACACS or TACACS+.

A major difference between this feature and port security is that both the host and switch-port must be configured for 802.1x EAPOL, the *Extensible Authentication Protocol over LANs.* That's a major departure from the switch features we've studied to date, since few (if any) of those require us configuring anything on the host. (The RADIUS version you'll use is technically RADIUS with EAP extensions.)

A typical dot1x port-based authentication deployment involves the dot1x-enabled PC (the *supplicant*), the dot1x-enabled switch (the *authenticator*), and a RADIUS server (the *authentication server*).

Dot1x-enabled PC   **Dot1x-enabled switch**   **RADIUS w/ EAP Extentions**
"Supplicant"   **"Authenticator"**   **"Authentication Server"**

Of course, the PC has a single physical port connected to the switch, but that physical port is logically divided into two ports by dot1x, the *controlled* and *uncontrolled* ports. Unlike typical subinterfaces, the network admins do not have to configure these logical ports. Dot1x handles that. We just need to configure the supplicant for dot1x!

Strange but true: If the switch is ready for dot1x authentication and the supplicant isn't, communications between the two will fail. (That's not the strange part.) If the supplicant is running dot1x but the switch isn't, the PC will not concern itself with dot1x and will communicate with the switch as it normally would.

The controlled port cannot transmit data until authentication actually takes place. The uncontrolled port can transmit without authentication, but on a limited basis, as only EAPOL, STP, and CDP can be transmitted at that time. By default, once the user authenticates, all traffic can be received and sent via the port.

To get started with dot1x, we first have to enable AAA with *aaa new-model*. We'll follow that by pointing the switch to our RADIUS server(s), and then enable dot1x to use those RADIUS servers for authentication.

```
MLS _ 1(config)#aaa new-model
```

The *radius-server* command literally has about 40 options; the only one we need to concern ourselves with right now is *host*, followed by the password for that server.

```
MLS _ 1(config)#radius-server host 172.16.23.55

MLS _ 1(config)#aaa authentication ?
  arap              Set authentication lists for arap.
```

```
  attempts          Set the maximum number of authentication att
  banner            Message to use when starting login/authentic
  dot1x             Set authentication lists for IEEE 802.1x.
  enable            Set authentication list for enable.
  eou               Set authentication lists for EAPoUDP
  fail-message      Message to use for failed login/authenticati
  login             Set authentication lists for logins.
  password-prompt   Text to use when prompting for a password
  ppp               Set authentication lists for ppp.
  Sgbp              Set authentication lists for sgbp.
  Suppress          Do not send access request for a specific ty
  username-prompt   Text to use when prompting for a username

MLS_1(config)#radius-server host 172.16.23.55 key CCNP

MLS_1(config)#aaa authentication dot1x ?
  WORD     Named authentication list (max 31 characters, longer rejected).
  Default  The default authentication list.

MLS_1(config)#aaa authentication dot1x default ?
  cache    Use Cached-group
  group    Use Server-group
  local    Use local username authentication.

MLS_1(config)#aaa authentication dot1x default group ?
  WORD     Server-group name
  ldap     Use list of all LDAP hosts.
  Radius   Use list of all Radius hosts.

MLS_1(config)#aaa authentication dot1x default group radius ?
```

Finally, we get to *enable* dot1x port-based authentication!

```
MLS_1(config)#dot1x ?
  Credentials          Configure 802.1X credentials profiles
  Critical             Set 802.1x Critical Authentication parameters
  guest-vlan           Configure Guest Vlan and 802.1x Supplicant behavior
  logging              Set logging parameters
  supplicant           802.1X supplicant configuration
  system-auth-control  Enable or Disable SysAuthControl
  test                 Configure dot1x test related parameters

MLS_1(config)#dot1x system-auth-control
```

And even more finally, we get to set the authentication type.

```
R1(config-if)#dot1x port-control ?
  auto                  PortState will be set to AUTO
  force-authorized      PortState set to Authorized
  force-unauthorized    PortState will be set to UnAuthorized
```

That's a lot of force! The first force-based option, *force-authorized*, tells the port to uncon-ditionally authorize the host, using no authentication. That's the default, and it's a default you may well want to change. *force-unauthorized* tells the port to never authorize the host, which seems a tad harsh. *auto* may be the way to go, as it allows a host to authorize via an exchange of dot1x messages.

Now that we've covered port security and dot1x port-based authentication, a natural question arises: "Can you run port security and dot1x authentication on the same port?" Surprisingly, the answer is yes! From Cisco's website: "When you enable port security and 802.1x on a port, 802.1x authenticates the port and port security manages the number of MAC addresses allowed on that port, including that of the client."

SPAN

We've securely secured our ports, but one day, we're likely to want to connect a network analyzer ("sniffer") to one of those ports. A common situation is illustrated here, where we want to analyze traffic sourced from the three PCs. To get the job done, the analyzer needs a copy of every frame the hosts are sending and/or receiving, and we'll use SPAN to capture that traffic.

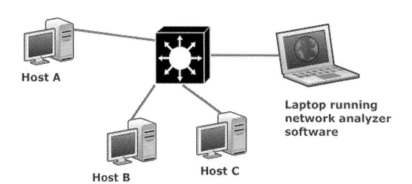

SPAN allows the switch to mirror traffic from source port(s) to destination port, and it's the destination port to which our network analyzer will be connected. In this example, we're running local SPAN, since the source and destination ports are on the same switch (or same switch stack). By default, both traffic destined for and sourced from the source ports are mirrored to the destination port.

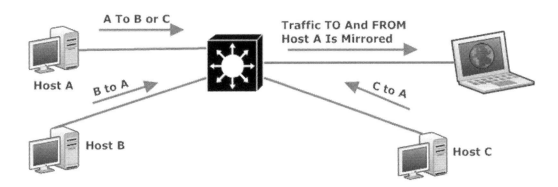

The command *monitor session* starts a SPAN session, along with defining the source and destination ports. Multiple SPAN sessions are totally separate operations, and the number of simultaneous SPAN sessions you can run differs between switch platforms. Cisco 2950s allow only two, while the ones we're on here allow just a *few* more.

```
MLS_1(config)#monitor session ?
  <1-66> SPAN session number
```

Let's set up a local SPAN session, using ports Fa0/3, 4, and 5 as the source ports and Fa0/10 as the destination and then verifying with *show monitor*. No need to run *show vlan brief* for VLAN info, since it doesn't matter to SPAN whether the source ports are all in the same VLAN or not. Note that possible sources include:

Individual ports

Entire VLANs (in which case you're running VLAN-based SPAN, or VSPAN)

Port-channels, representing an entire Etherchannel

```
MLS_1(config)#monitor session ?
  <1-66> SPAN session number

MLS_1(config)#monitor session 47 ?
  Destination      SPAN destination interface or VLAN
  Filter           SPAN filter VLAN
  Source           SPAN source interface, VLAN

MLS_1(config)#monitor session 47 source ?
  Interface        SPAN source interface
  Remote           SPAN source Remote
  Vlan             SPAN source VLAN

MLS_1(config)#monitor session 47 source interface ?
  FastEthernet     FastEthernet IEEE 802.3
  GigabitEthernet  GigabitEthernet IEEE 802.3z
  Port-channel     Ethernet Channel of interfaces
MLS_1(config)#monitor session 47 source interface fast0/3 - 5
```

```
MLS _ 1(config)#monitor session 47 destination ?
   Interface        SPAN destination interface
   Remote           SPAN destination Remote

MLS _ 1(config)#monitor session 47 destination interface fast 0/9

MLS _ 1#show monitor
Session 47

Type                     : Local Session
Source Ports             :
     Both                : Fa0/3-5
Destination Ports        : Fa0/9
     Encapsulation       : Native
             Ingress     : Disabled
```

Let me save you some seriously unnecessary troubleshooting time with this little tip! If you look at fast 0/9 right now, you'll see something that might make ya cuss:

```
MLS _ 1#show int fast 0/9
FastEthernet0/9 is down, line protocol is down (monitoring)
```

No need to sweat, just read all the way to the end of that line and you'll see **(monitoring)**. That means you're looking at a SPAN destination port, and this is the one time in which seeing that an interface is "down and down" is what you *should* see!

That's all well and good, but what if SPAN isn't all local? What if the traffic to be monitored is originating on one particular switch and the only vacant port available is on another switch?

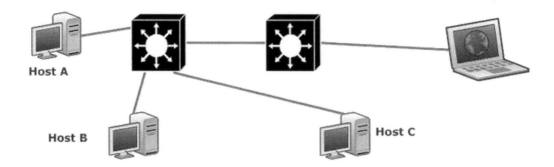

RSPAN to the rescue! Configuring *Remote SPAN* on *both* switches will allow mirrored frames to be sent over the trunk via a separate VLAN that will carry only those mirrored frames. This isn't a complex configuration, but we need to keep a few things in mind:

If there were intermediate switches between the two shown in the previous example, they would all need to be RSPAN-capable.

VTP treats the RSPAN VLAN like any other VLAN by propagating it throughout the VTP domain (if configured on a VTP server, natch!). Otherwise, that VLAN will have to be propagated manually on every switch along that path.

VTP pruning will prune the RSPAN VLAN under the same circumstances it would prune a normal VLAN.

MAC address learning is disabled for the RSPAN VLAN.

The source and destination ports must be defined on both the switch containing the source ports *and* the switch connected to the network analyzer, but the commands will *NOT* be the same, so don't cut and paste 'em!

Whew! After all that, the config is easy. Here's the setup for our RSPAN lab:

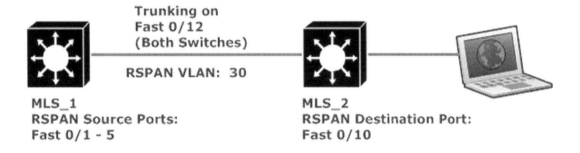

We'll create VLAN 30 and identify it as the RSPAN VLAN with *remote-span*.

```
MLS _ 1(config)#vlan 30
MLS _ 1(config-vlan)#remote-span
```

On MLS_1, we'll set up the SPAN session by naming the source ports and configuring the RSPAN VLAN as the destination.

```
MLS _ 1(config)#monitor session 1 source int fast 0/1 - 5
MLS _ 1(config)#monitor session 1 destination remote ?
   vlan Remote SPAN destination RSPAN VLAN

MLS _ 1(config)#monitor session 1 destination remote vlan ?
   <1006-4094>  Remote SPAN destination extended RSPAN VLAN number
   <2-1001>     Remote SPAN destination RSPAN VLAN number

MLS _ 1(config)#monitor session 1 destination remote vlan 30
MLS _ 1(config)#monitor session 1 destination remote vlan 30 ?
   <cr>
```

On MLS_2, we'll also define VLAN 30 as the RSPAN VLAN.

```
MLS _ 2(config)#vlan 30
```

```
MLS _ 2(config-vlan)#remote-span
```

The config on MLS_2 will name the source as the RSPAN VLAN and the destination as the port connected to the analyzer.

```
MLS _ 2(config)#monitor session 1 source remote vlan 30
MLS _ 2(config)#monitor session 1 destination int fast0/10
```

The toughest part of working with SPAN can be remembering the ports that are eligible and not eligible to be source or destination ports. Here are some tips for a successful SPAN configuration:

By default, traffic both from the source port and destined for the source port is mirrored to the destination port. To change this, use the *rx* and *tx* options at the end of monitor session.

```
SW2(config)#monitor session 47 source interface fast 0/1
    ,     Specify another range of interfaces
    -     Specify a range of interfaces
  both  Monitor received and transmitted traffic
  rx    Monitor received traffic only
  tx    Monitor transmitted traffic only
  <cr>
```

A source port can be monitored in multiple, simultaneous SPAN sessions.

A source port can be part of an Etherchannel, and you can use SPAN to monitor an entire EtherChannel by specifying that EC's port-channel interface as the source. Be aware that if a port that's in an EC is a source port, only the traffic going over that specific port will be mirrored. If you want all the traffic on an EC to be mirrored, you have to make the entire EC the source port.

A source port cannot also serve as a destination port.

VLAN membership doesn't matter; ports from different VLANs can serve as source ports for the same SPAN session.

Commonly referred to as VSPAN, an entire VLAN can be configured as a source port.

A trunk port can be a source port, but be aware that every single bit of traffic on any of the VLANs that are part of that trunk will be mirrored to the destination port.

The speed of the port doesn't affect a port's ability to be a source port, nor a destination port, but it's a good idea to have a destination port be equal or higher in speed than the source port(s).

Destination port notes:

A destination port can participate in only one SPAN session.

A destination port cannot be a source port, nor can a single port serve as the destination for multiple SPAN sessions.

While source ports can be part of an Etherchannel, a destination port cannot.

A destination SPAN port doesn't participate in STP, CDP, VTP, DTP, PaGP, or LACP.

Trunk ports can be configured as source and/or destination ports; the default behavior will result in the monitoring of all active VLANs on the trunk.

And just one more thing... remember the *remote-span* command we placed on both switches in our RSPAN config? If you have switches between the switch with source ports and the one with destination ports, you need that command on every intermediate switch.

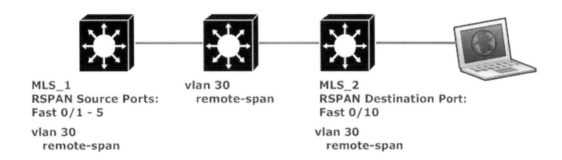

MLS_1
RSPAN Source Ports:
Fast 0/1 - 5

vlan 30
    remote-span

vlan 30
    remote-span

MLS_2
RSPAN Destination Port:
Fast 0/10

vlan 30
    remote-span

Storm Control

In your CCNA studies, you learned of the danger of broadcast storms, where the number of broadcasts and multicasts begin to overwhelm your switch. Whether accidentally or maliciously caused, these storms can also overwhelm your hosts with broadcasts and multicasts flooded by the switch, all the way to the point of non-operation.

Storm Control is specifically designed to proactively stop that flooding before our hosts are hit with a level of flooded traffic they just can't handle. It's enabled on a per-port basis:

```
SW1(config)#int fast 0/1
SW1(config-if)#storm-control ?
   Action     Action to take for storm-control
   Broadcast  Broadcast address storm control
   Multicast  Multicast address storm control
   Unicast    Unicast address storm control
```

For each traffic type listed, the option level will follow. When the specified traffic type reaches that level, Storm Control acts. We'll use IOS Help to explore our options for broadcast storm control.

```
SW1(config-if)#storm-control broadcast ?
  Level      Set storm suppression level on this interface

SW1(config-if)#storm-control broadcast level ?
  pps        Enter suppression level in packets per second
  <0 - 100>  Enter Integer part of storm suppression level

SW1(config-if)#storm-control broadcast level 45 ?
  <0 - 100>  Enter Integer part of lower suppression level
  <cr>

SW1(config-if)#storm-control broadcast level 45 35 ?
  <cr>

SW1(config-if)#storm-control broadcast level 45 35
```

I'm using bandwidth usage percentage in this command, which can also be configured using packets per second.

It might surprise you that we have the option for one or two levels! If you specify only the storm suppression level (the first value), Storm Control takes action when the traffic type goes above that level, and stops that action when the traffic type goes below that level. (Makes sense, right?)

At times, you may want to set a different level at which Storm Control should cease action. The line storm-control broadcast level 45 35 means Storm Control will take action when broadcasts are taking up over 45% of available bandwidth and will stop that action when the level of broadcasts drops below 35% of that available bandwidth. It's not right or wrong to choose one option over the other – just choose the one that fits your situation.

Now, about that action...

```
SW1(config-if)#storm-control action ?
  Shutdown   Shutdown this interface if a storm occurs
  trap       Send SNMP trap if a storm occurs
```

What isn't shown here is Storm Control's default behavior of tossing the offending frames overboard. (That is, they're dropped.) Choosing shutdown or trap adds the configured behavior to this default.

Verify your config with *show storm-control*, which will show you information on all ports on the switch, or *show storm-control interface* to see the info for just that interface!

```
SW1#show storm-control fast 0/1
 Interface    Filter State Trap State      Upper    Lower    Current  Traps Sent
 ------       ------------ -----------     ------   ------   ------
 Fa0/1        Forwarding   inactive        45.00%   35.00%   0.00%    0
```

VLAN ACLs

Let's take a look at some Cisco switch security features that were developed specifically with VLANs in mind, starting with VLAN ACLs.

You'll certainly be familiar with ACLs and a few of their seemingly endless uses at this point in your Cisco studies! The ACL we've come to know and love has some limitations though. While an ACL can filter traffic travelling between VLANs...

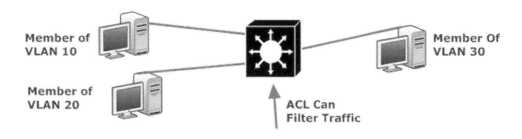

... it can't do anything about traffic from one host in a VLAN to another host in the same VLAN.

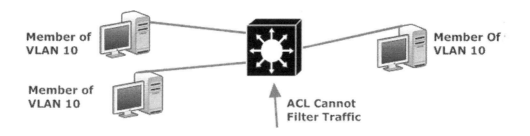

Why not, you ask? It relates to the application of ACLs on a multilayer switch. The CAM table holds the dynamically and statically learned MAC addresses, but it's the TCAM table – the *Ternary Content-Addressable Memory* table – that cuts down on the number of lookups required to compare a packet against an ACL. This packet filtering via the switch hardware speeds up the overall process, but it limits ACL capability. An ACL can be used to filter inter-VLAN traffic, but not intra-VLAN traffic. Filtering between hosts in the same VLAN requires the use of a VLAN Access List (VACL).

Even though a VACL will do the actual filtering, we'll still need to write an ACL. The ACL will be used as the match criterion within the VACL. You'll see what I mean in the following lab!

We want to stop these three hosts from communicating with any host in the 10.1.1.0 /24 subnet, and we mean any host – even among each other! Right now, each host can ping the other (results not shown).

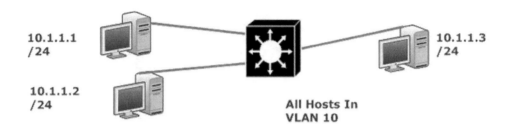

10.1.1.1 /24

10.1.1.2 /24

10.1.1.3 /24

All Hosts In VLAN 10

```
MLS _ 1(config)#ip access-list extended BLOCK _ FIRST _ THREE
MLS _ 1(config-ext-nacl)#permit ip ?
  A.B.C.D    Source address
  any        Any source host
  host       A single source host

MLS _ 1(config-ext-nacl)#permit ip 10.1.1.0 ?
  A.B.C.D    Source wildcard bits

MLS _ 1(config-ext-nacl)#permit ip 10.1.1.0 0.0.0.3 ?
  A.B.C.D    Destination address
  any        Any destination host
  host       A single destination host

MLS _ 1(config-ext-nacl)#permit ip 10.1.1.0 0.0.0.3 10.1.1.0 0.0.0.255 ?
  A.B.C.D    Destination wildcard bits

MLS _ 1(config-ext-nacl)#permit ip 10.1.1.0 0.0.0.3 10.1.1.0 0.0.0.255
```

I'm sure you noticed that the three source addresses named in the ACL are the ones that won't be allowed to communicate with other hosts on that subnet, but the ACL statement is a *permit*, not a deny. No worries, the deny is coming!

We'll write the VACL with *vlan access-map*, with any traffic matching that ACL to be dropped while allowing all other traffic.

```
MLS _ 1(config)#vlan access-map ?
  WORD       Vlan access map tag

MLS _ 1(config)#vlan access-map NO _ 123 ?
  <0-65535>    Sequence to insert to/delete from existing vlan access-map entry
  <cr>
```

```
MLS_1(config)#vlan access-map NO_123
MLS_1(config-access-map)#match ?
  Ip           IP based match
  Mac          MAC based match

MLS_1(config-access-map)#match ip ?
  Address      Match IP address to access control.

MLS_1(config-access-map)#match ip address ?
  <1-199>      IP access list (standard or extended)
  <1300-2699>  IP expanded access list (standard or extended)
  WORD         Access-list name

MLS_1(config-access-map)#match ip address BLOCK_FIRST_THREE
MLS_1(config-access-map)#action ?
  drop         Drop packets
  forward      Forward packets

MLS_1(config-access-map)#action drop
MLS_1(config-access-map)#exit
MLS_1(config)#vlan access-map NO_123 ?
  <0-65535>    Sequence to insert to/delete from existing vlan access-map
  entry
  <cr>

MLS_1(config)#vlan access-map NO_123
MLS_1(config-access-map)#action forward
```

No match was configured for the second VACL statement, meaning the action of "forward" will be applied to any and all traffic that didn't match previous statements.

I didn't enter a sequence number for those two VACL statements because I wanted to demo the default for you via *show vlan access-map*:

```
MLS_1#show vlan access-map
Vlan access-map "NO_123" 10
  Match clauses:
     ip address: BLOCK_FIRST_THREE
  Action:
     drop
Vlan access-map "NO_123" 20
  Match clauses:
  Action:
     Forward
```

The "10" and "20" shown are the default sequence numbers. If you follow my lead and don't define them as you go, they'll increment by 10. Sequence numbers are fantastic for those situations where you later need to add an action. If you needed to add an action that involved dropping traffic, you'd need to give it a sequence number between 10 and 20. Adding it at the end wouldn't do any good, since VACL sequence number 20 permits all traffic.

Hey, we need to apply this thing! Don't try to apply a VACL to a specific interface; we have to apply it in global configuration mode. The VLAN to be filtered is specified at the end of the command with the *vlan-list* option. We can specify individual VLANs or go with the *all* option. Be careful to specify the VACL name in this command, not the ACL name.

```
MLS_1(config)#vlan filter ?
   WORD        VLAN map name

MLS_1(config)#vlan filter NO_123 ?
   vlan-list   VLANs to apply filter to

MLS_1(config)#vlan filter NO_123 vlan-list ?
   <1-4094>    VLAN id
   all         Add this filter to all VLANs

MLS_1(config)#vlan filter NO_123 vlan-list 10
```

Verify with *show ip access-list* and *show vlan access-map*, and then test!

```
MLS_1#show ip access-list
Extended IP access list BLOCK_FIRST_THREE
     10 permit ip 10.1.1.0 0.0.0.3 10.1.1.0 0.0.0.25
MLS_1#show vlan access-list
                          ^
% Invalid input detected at '^' marker.

MLS_1#show vacl
              ^
% Invalid input detected at '^' marker.

MLS_1#show vlan access-map
Vlan access-map "NO_123" 10
   Match clauses:
      ip address: BLOCK_FIRST_THREE
   Action:
      drop
Vlan access-map "NO_123" 20
   Match clauses:
   Action:
      Forward
```

Hosts that could previously ping each other now cannot, thanks to our VACL!

```
HOST_2#ping 10.1.1.3
Success rate is 0 percent (0/5)
HOST_1#ping 10.1.1.3
Success rate is 0 percent (0/5)
```

Private VLANs

Want to put a host in such a secret place that you yourself may never be able to find it?

Private VLANs aren't quite that private, but if you want to hide a host from the rest of your network – even going as far as hiding a host from other hosts in the same subnet – private VLANs are the way to go.

This concept can throw you a bit at first, since a private VLAN is truly unlike any other VLAN concept. The terminology is unique as well, so hang in there and it'll be second nature before you know it.

Private VLANs give us all of the following:

Three port types – one type talks to everybody, one type talks to some, and one type talks to practically no one.

Two types of private VLANs, *primary* and *secondary*.

In turn, we have two types of secondary VLANs, *community* and *isolated*.

As always, we'll take this concept one step at a time, starting with those three port types.

Hosts that need to talk to everyone will be connected to *promiscuous ports*. This port type can communicate with any host connected to any of the other two port types. *When you have a router or multilayer switch that serves as a default gateway, that device must be connected to a promiscuous port for the network to function correctly.*

Hosts that just need to talk to some other devices are connected to *community ports*. These hosts can communicate with other community ports in the same private VLAN as well as any device connected to a promiscuous port.

Hosts that just don't want anything to do with anybody are connected to the aptly named *isolated ports*. Hosts connected to isolated ports can only communicate with hosts connected to promiscuous ports. Even if you have two isolated ports in the same private VLAN, those hosts can't intercommunicate.

Now let's have a brief, powerful look at the private VLAN types.

The "parent" private VLAN is the primary private VLAN, and the "child" private VLAN is the secondary private VLAN. That's it!

In our config, we'll map primary private VLANs to secondary private VLANs. A primary private VLAN can be mapped to multiple secondary VLANs, but a secondary private VLAN can be mapped to only one primary.

About those secondary VLAN types...

Ports in a *community private VLAN* can communicate with other ports in the same community as well as promiscuous ports in the primary.

Ports in an *isolated private VLAN* can only communicate with promiscuous ports in the parent private VLAN.

Each of these concepts is illustrated here:

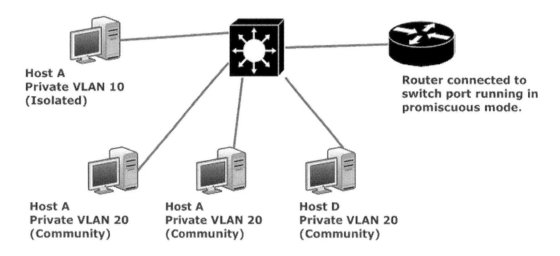

Host A
Private VLAN 10
(Isolated)

Router connected to
switch port running in
promiscuous mode.

Host A
Private VLAN 20
(Community)

Host A
Private VLAN 20
(Community)

Host D
Private VLAN 20
(Community)

Host A has been placed into an isolated private VLAN, and will be able to communicate only with the router, which is connected to a promiscuous port. If we placed another host in the same isolated private VLAN that Host A is in now, those two hosts could not communicate with each other.

The other hosts are in a community private VLAN, so they can communicate with each other as well as the router. They cannot communicate with Host A.

In the following configuration, we'll use the following VLANs and VLAN types:

VLAN 100 is a secondary private VLAN (community). Ports are Fa0/1 – 5.

VLAN 200 is a secondary private VLAN (isolated). Ports are Fa0/6 – 10.

VLAN 300 will be the primary private VLAN. Our router is off fast0/12.

Creating the first VLAN with VLAN config mode is no problem, but look what happens when we try to make it a community private VLAN – or for that matter, any kind of private VLAN!

```
MLS_1(config)#vlan 100
MLS_1(config-vlan)#private-vlan ?
  association  Configure association between private VLANs
  community    Configure the VLAN as a community private VLAN
  isolated     Configure the VLAN as an isolated private VLAN
  primary      Configure the VLAN as a primary private VLAN

MLS_1(config-vlan)#private-vlan community
%Private VLANs can only be configured when VTP is in transparent/off mode.
```

Private VLANs can only be configured with VTP is in transparent mode. (Yes, like it says right there.) Once we do that, configuring VLAN 100 as a community private VLAN and VLAN 200 as an isolated private VLAN is no problem.

```
MLS_1(config)#vtp mode transparent
Setting device to VTP Transparent mode for VLANS.
MLS_1(config)#vlan 100
MLS_1(config-vlan)#private-vlan ?
  association  Configure association between private VLANs
  community    Configure the VLAN as a community private VLAN
  isolated     Configure the VLAN as an isolated private VLAN
  primary      Configure the VLAN as a primary private VLAN

MLS_1(config-vlan)#private-vlan community
MLS_1(config-vlan)#vlan 200
MLS_1(config-vlan)#private-vlan isolated
```

Now we'll configure VLAN 300 as the primary private VLAN, and then associate those two secondary private VLANs with this primary private VLAN. (This association is *not* the mapping I mentioned earlier.)

```
MLS_1(config)#vlan 300
MLS_1(config-vlan)#private-vlan primary
MLS_1(config-vlan)#private-vlan association ?
  WORD    VLAN IDs of the private VLANs to be configured
  add     Add a VLAN to private VLAN list
  remove  Remove a VLAN from private VLAN list

MLS_1(config-vlan)#private-vlan association 200,100
```

We've accomplished the following:

Configured VTP to run in transparent mode (very important!)

Created our secondary private VLANs, both isolated and community

Created our primary private VLAN

Created an association between the secondary and primary private VLANs

217

Just two more things to do – place the ports into the proper VLAN and get that mapping done! The switch leading to the router is Fa0/12, and that port must be made promiscuous.

```
MLS _ 1(config)#int fast 0/12
MLS _ 1(config-if)#switchport mode ?
  access         Set trunking mode to ACCESS unconditionally
  dot1q-tunnel   set trunking mode to TUNNEL unconditionally
  dynamic        Set trunking mode to dynamically negotiate access or trunk
                 mode
  private-vlan   Set private-vlan mode
  trunk          Set trunking mode to TRUNK unconditionally

MLS _ 1(config-if)#switchport mode private-vlan ?
  host           Set the mode to private-vlan host
  promiscuous    Set the mode to private-vlan promiscuous

MLS _ 1(config-if)#switchport mode private-vlan promiscuous
```

We'll also need the *primary vlan mapping* command on that interface:

```
MLS _ 1(config-if)#switchport private-vlan ?
  Association       Set the private VLAN association
  host-association  Set the private VLAN host association
  mapping           Set the private VLAN promiscuous mapping

MLS _ 1(config-if)#switchport private-vlan mapping ?
  <1006-4094>    Primary extended range VLAN ID of the private VLAN promiscuous
                 port mapping
  <2-1001>       Primary normal range VLAN ID of the private VLAN promiscuous
                 port mapping

MLS _ 1(config-if)#switchport private-vlan mapping 300 ?
  WORD           Secondary VLAN IDs of the private VLAN promiscuous port
                 mapping
  add            Add a VLAN to private VLAN list
  remove         Remove a VLAN from private VLAN list

MLS _ 1(config-if)#switchport private-vlan mapping 300 100,200 ?
  <cr>

MLS _ 1(config-if)#switchport private-vlan mapping 300 100,200
```

Ports Fa0/1 – 5 are in VLAN 100. We'll use our buddy *interface range* to configure that port range with the *private-vlan host* and *private-vlan host-association* commands.

```
MLS _ 1(config)#int range fast 0/1 - 5
MLS _ 1(config-if-range)#switchport mode private-vlan ?
```

```
   host          Set the mode to private-vlan host
   promiscuous   Set the mode to private-vlan promiscuous

MLS_1(config-if-range)#switchport mode private-vlan host
```

We'll use *interface range* on Fa0/6 – 10 as well, using VLAN 200 instead of 100.

```
MLS_1(config)#int range fast 0/6 - 10
MLS_1(config-if-range)#switchport mode private-vlan host
MLS_1(config-if-range)#switchport private-vlan ?
   association       Set the private VLAN association
   host-association  Set the private VLAN host association
   mapping           Set the private VLAN promiscuous mapping

MLS_1(config-if-range)#switchport private-vlan host-association ?
   <1006-4094>       Primary extended range VLAN ID of the private VLAN host
                     port association
   <2-1001>          Primary normal range VLAN ID of the private VLAN port
                     association

MLS_1(config-if-range)#switchport private-vlan host-association 300 ?
   <1006-4094>       Secondary extended range VLAN ID of the private VLAN host
                     port association
   <2-1001>          Secondary normal range VLAN ID of the private VLAN host
                     port association

MLS_1(config-if-range)#switchport private-vlan host-association 300 200
```

Verify your private VLAN config with the tricky-to-type show vlan private-vlan command, and on an interface level with show interface switchport.

DHCP And Multilayer Switches

I'm sure you're wondering why DHCP is smack in the middle of a CCNP SWITCH exam discussion of switch security features. There are two really good reasons for this:

1. DHCP is a topic on your CCNP SWITCH exam.

2. Securing DHCP is a vital part of our overall Cisco switch security strategy, and the better our knowledge of DHCP, the better our security will be.

Let's jump right in with a quick review of the overall DHCP process. First, the client broadcasts a DHCP Discover packet, and its purpose is to discover the network's DHCP servers. The DHCP servers that receive that Discover packet respond with a broadcast in the form of a DHCP Offer packet. This includes an IP address the client can use, along with notification on how long the client can keep that address (the lease), the default gateway, and other info as desired and configured by you and I, the network admins.

The client will accept the first Offer received, ignoring the others. The client uses a broadcast *DHCP Request* message to indicate acceptance of the offer. The Request includes the IP address of the DHCP Server whose address offer is being accepted. When a DHCP Server sees a Request that does not include its own IP address, that server knows that its offer was not accepted.

The DHCP server whose offer is being accepted sends a DHCP Acknowledgement message back to the client, and that's it! (This ACK can be a unicast or a broadcast depending on the circumstances. Some books say it's a unicast, some say it's a broadcast, and technically they're both right.)

Generally speaking, you'll have a traditional server for your DHCP server, but a Cisco router or multilayer switch can handle the role nicely! The syntax may seem a little odd at first, but like all things Cisco, take it one command at a time and you'll be fine.

We're going to do something a bit unusual in this section and have a Cisco router acquire an IP address via DHCP from a Cisco multilayer switch. Here's the setup:

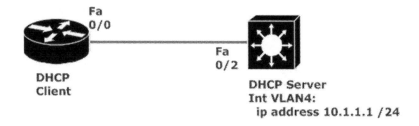

Using a multilayer switch as a DHCP server requires that switch to have an IP address on any subnet that it's offering addresses from. No problem there, but we do need to exclude that particular address from the DHCP pool. This can drive you a bit crazy at first, since the *ip dhcp excluded-address* command we use for that purpose is configured globally, not as part of the general DHCP configuration.

We can specify a single address to be excluded, an entire range or both. Here, we're going to assign addresses from 10.0.0.0 /8 via DHCP, but we don't want to use the addresses 10.0.0.0 – 10.1.1.0, nor do we want to assign the IP address already assigned to the SVI int VLAN 4. *ip dhcp excluded-address* gets the job done. I could have used one command with the range 10.0.0.0 – 10.1.1.1, but I want to illustrate that you can use this command to exclude a single address.

```
MLS _ 1(config)#ip dhcp excluded-address ?
   A.B.C.D    Low IP address
   Vrf        VRF name for excluded address range

MLS _ 1(config)#ip dhcp excluded-address 10.0.0.0 10.1.1.0 ?
   A.B.C.D    High IP address
   <cr>

MLS _ 1(config)#ip dhcp excluded-address 10.1.1.1 10.1.1.0?
   <cr>

MLS _ 1(config)#ip dhcp excluded-address 10.0.0.0 10.1.1.0
MLS _ 1(config)#ip dhcp excluded-address 10.1.1.1
```

With those tasks completed, we're now ready to create the DHCP pool with *ip dhcp pool*.

```
MLS _ 1(config)#ip dhcp pool CCNP
MLS _ 1(dhcp-config)#
```

We'll use *network* to define the range of addresses to be assigned to DHCP clients. For the mask, we're given the rare option of entering the value in either prefix notation or the more familiar dotted decimal.

```
MLS _ 1(dhcp-config)#network 10.0.0.0?
A.B.C.D

MLS _ 1(dhcp-config)#network 10.0.0.0 ?
   /nn or A.B.C.D Network mask or prefix length
   <cr>

MLS _ 1(dhcp-config)#network 10.0.0.0 /8
```

Other options include specifying a domain name with *domain-name*, using *dns-server* to give the DNS server location to clients, and specifying the IP address of the default router with *default-router*. Both the default router and DNS servers can be referred to by either their hostname or IP address.

```
MLS _ 1(dhcp-config)#domain-name ?
WORD Domain name

MLS _ 1(dhcp-config)#domain-name bryantadvantage.com
MLS _ 1(dhcp-config)#
MLS _ 1(dhcp-config)#dns-server ?
Hostname or A.B.C.D Server's name or IP address

MLS _ 1(dhcp-config)#dns-server 10.3.3.3

MLS _ 1(dhcp-config)#default-router ?
Hostname or A.B.C.D Router's name or IP address

MLS _ 1(dhcp-config)#default-router 10.1.1.1
```

Define the lease length with *lease*, or set it to never expire with *infinite*. Use IOS Help to check the units of time!

```
MLS _ 1(dhcp-config)#lease ?
  <0-365>   Days
  Infinite  Infinite lease

MLS _ 1(dhcp-config)#lease 10 ?
  <0-23>    Hours
  <cr>

MLS _ 1(dhcp-config)#lease 10 10 ?
  <0-59>    Minutes
  <cr>

MLS _ 1(dhcp-config)#lease 10 10 10 ?
  <cr>

MLS _ 1(dhcp-config)#lease 10 10 10
```

A Cisco router acting as a DHCP server will check for IP address conflicts before assigning an address. The conflict check takes the form of two pings sent to that address, and those pings will time out in 500 milliseconds. If they time out, we're good and that address can be sent to the client. If we get pings back, well, we can't assign that address!

This is a value you won't adjust often, but if you want to change the number of pings sent and/or the timeout duration during the conflict check, use *ip dhcp ping packets* and *ip dhcp ping timeout*. Setting the number of ping packets to zero disables the conflict check. Note that these are globally configured commands.

```
MLS _ 1(config)#ip dhcp ping ?
  packets        Specify number of ping packets
  timeout        Specify ping timeout

MLS _ 1(config)#ip dhcp ping packets ?
  <0-10>         Number of ping packets (0 disables ping)
  <cr>

MLS _ 1(config)#ip dhcp ping timeout ?
  <100-10000>   Ping timeout in milliseconds
```

Let's enable DHCP IP address acquisition on the router's Fast0/0 interface and then verify the addressing with *show int fast 0/0* on the router and *show ip dhcp binding* on the multi-layer switch.

```
HOST _ 2(config)#int fast 0/0
HOST _ 2(config-if)#ip address dhcp

HOST _ 2#show int fast 0/0
FastEthernet0/0 is up, line protocol is up
  Hardware is Gt96k FE, address is 001b.d4c2.0990 (bia 001b.d4c2.0990)
  Internet address is 10.1.1.2/8

MLS _ 1#show ip dhcp binding
Bindings from all pools not associated with VRF:
IP address        Client-ID/                   Lease expiration        Type
                  Hardware address/
                  User name
10.1.1.2          0063.6973.636f.2d30.         Mar 26 2015 01:16 AM    Automatic
                  3031.622e.6434.6332.
                  2e30.3939.302d.4661.
                  302f.30
```

On occasion we just might need some help with our DHCP broadcast messages... some helper addresses, perhaps!

IP Helper Addresses

Routers accept broadcasts, and routers create broadcasts, but routers do not forward broadcasts by default. That can present an issue with DHCP messages when a router is between the requesting host and the DHCP server. After all, the first message in the entire process is a broadcast!

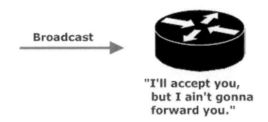

Using *ip helper-address* on a router or multilayer switch allows the device to translate certain broadcasts to a unicast, making forwarding possible.

The command should be configured on the interface that will be receiving the broadcasts, not the interface closest to the destination. The command syntax is exactly the same whether you're configuring this command on a multilayer switch SVI or a router's physical interface.

```
MLS_1(config)#int vlan 10
MLS_1(config-if)#ip address 10.1.1.1 255.255.255.0
MLS_1(config-if)#ip helper-address ?
  A.B.C.D    IP destination address
  global     Helper-address is global
  vrf        VRF name for helper-address (if different from interface VRF)

MLS_1(config-if)#ip helper-address
MLS_1(config-if)#ip helper-address 10.5.1.1 ?
  <cr>

MLS_1(config-if)#ip helper-address 10.5.1.1


R1(config)#int fast 0/0
R1(config-if)#ip helper-address ?
  A.B.C.D    IP destination address
  global     Helper-address is global
  vrf        VRF name for helper-address (if different from interface VRF)
```

Got multiple DHCP servers your switch needs help reaching? No worries, just configure multiple *ip helper-address* statements and verify with *show ip helper-address*.

```
HOST _ 1#show ip helper-address
Interface                 Helper-Address
FastEthernet0/0           10.5.5.5
                          10.6.6.6
```

A device running ip helper-address to help with DHCP server reachability is said to be a DHCP relay agent. That's accurate, but not entirely accurate, as nine common UDP service broadcasts are helped in this manner by this command. TIME, TACACS, DNS, BOOTP/ DHCP Server, BOOTP/DHCP Client, TFTP, NetBIOS name service, NetBIOS datagram service, and IEN-116 name service all benefit from this command.

The Dynamic Shall Become Static

On rare occasions, you may need to create a static IP address binding (also called a "manual" binding) in your network. That rare occasion is when you need DHCP to give a client the same address every single time. I'm saying "rare" in a hopeful voice, because configuring these suckers can be a real pain in the butt. (The voice of experience speaks!)

Before we start a manual binding, we need the client identifier of the client in question. The Cisco identifier is going to look a lot like a MAC address. If the client uses Ethernet, as our router does, the identifier is simply a "01" in front of the MAC. Here, we'll configure a manual binding for our router. Since that client already has an IP address from us, we can get the client ID from the DHCP binding table.

```
MLS _ 1#show ip dhcp binding
IP address            Client-ID/
                      Hardware address/
                      User name
10.1.1.2              0063.6973.636f.2d30.
                      3031.622e.6434.6332.
                      2e30.3939.302d.4661.
                      302f.30
```

Holy crap. That's a lot of ID, and even I don't want to start typing all those numbers! Luckily, we don't have to, as this is the ASCII string representing the client ID. To get the classic representation of that ID, use the client-id option with ip address dhcp. Note that the next address in the pool is assigned as a result of this change.

```
HOST _ 2(config)#int fast 0/0
HOST _ 2(config-if)#ip address dhcp ?
  client-id     Specify client-id to use
  hostname      Specify value for hostname option
<cr>
```

```
HOST _ 2(config-if)#ip address dhcp client-id ?
  FastEthernet   FastEthernet IEEE 802.3

HOST _ 2(config-if)#ip address dhcp client-id fastethernet 0/0 ?
  Hostname        Specify value for hostname option
  <cr>

HOST _ 2(config-if)#ip address dhcp client-id fastethernet 0/0
HOST _ 2(config-if)#
%DHCP-6-ADDRESS _ ASSIGN: . Interface  FastEthernet0/0  assigned  DHCP  address
10.1.1.3, mask 255.0.0.0, hostname HOST _ 2


MLS _ 1#show ip dhcp binding
Bindings from all pools not associated wit
IP address           Client-ID/
                     Hardware address/
                     User name
10.1.1.3             0100.1bd4.c209.90
```

Now there's a value we can work with! For a manual binding, start in DHCP pool mode, using the *host* command. We're going to bind that client ID to the IP address 10.1.1.3, so that interface will receive the same IP address every time. Let's go into our previous DHCP pool and make that happen.

```
MLS _ 1(config)#ip dhcp pool CCNP
MLS _ 1(dhcp-config)#host 10.1.1.3
% This command may not be used with network, origin, vrf or relay pools.
```

Hmmmm. Well, frankly, that doesn't leave a lot of ways to use it! How about *client-identifier*, the other required command for a DHCP manual binding?

```
MLS _ 1(dhcp-config)#client-identifier 0100.1bd4.c209.90
% This command may not be used with network, origin, vrf or relay pools.
```

With this, perhaps you're starting to feel manual bindings are too much of a pain to bother with. I'm about to make you feel better about them by telling you something that a lot of books / study guides / PDFs / websites leave out – manual bindings have to be put into their *own* DHCP pool.

```
MLS _ 1(config)#ip dhcp pool STATIC _ BINDINGS
MLS _ 1(dhcp-config)#host 10.1.1.3
MLS _ 1(dhcp-config)#client-identifier 0100.1bd4.c209.90
% A binding for this client already exists.
```

You also have to end any bindings that client currently has. I did so by closing the fast0/0 interface on R2. The binding was then gone, so I finished that config, reopened the interface on R2, and soon saw...

```
05:54:55: %DHCP-6-ADDRESS_ASSIGN: Interface FastEthernet0/0 assigned DHCP
address 10.1.1.3, mask 255.0.0.0, hostname HOST_2
```

All riiiiiiiiiiight! Verify on MLS_1 with *show ip dhcp binding,* and you're done! Note that this is described as a manual binding and the lease is infinite.

```
MLS_1#show ip dhcp binding
Bindings from all pools not associated with VRF:
IP address             Client-ID/              Lease expiration        Type
                       Hardware address/
                       User name
10.1.1.3               0100.1bd4.c209.90       Infinite                Manual
```

Now for just a bit of DHCP for IPv6, and then it's on to DHCP Snooping!

DHCP - IP Version 6 Style

IPv6 brings us *autoconfiguration,* both stateless and stateful. *Stateful autoconfiguration* is used when the host obtains an IPv6 address and other related information from a server. If that sounds like DHCP to you, well, it is – DHCPv6, to be exact!

The key phrase in that description is "from a server". If the DHCPv6 server goes down, we're out of luck and up that well-known creek. With *stateless autoconfiguration,* there's no dependency on a server, and the entire process starts with the IPv6 host configuring its own link-local address.

Our 128-bit IPv6 address is created in this manner with stateless autoconfiguration:

The first 64 bits of this self-generated address will be 1111 1110 10 (FE80), followed by 54 zeroes.

The last 64 bits are the interface identifier, which consists of (in order) the first half of the interface's MAC address, then the hex string FFFe, then the second half of the MAC address.

You'll usually see that hex string referred to as "FFFE". I personally like to write the "e" in lower case, since it's easy to read FFFE as FFFF.

Technically, the address is tentative at this point. It's been successfully calculated, but we need to make sure that no other host is using the same address. That's a remote possibility, but it never hurts to check, and that's where the Duplicate Address Detection (DAD) feature comes in.

DAD starts with a Neighbor Solicitation (NS) message asking if any other host on the link is using the same link-local address the NS-transmitting host just created for itself.

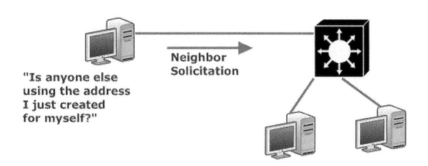

If another host on the link *is* using that address, that host will respond with a Neighbor Advertisement (NA). When the host that sent the NS receives the NA, it will disable its link-local address. If no response to the NS is received, the local host is satisfied that it has a unique link-local address. The local host will then send a Router Solicitation (RS) message with a destination of FF02::2, the "all-routers" multicast address.

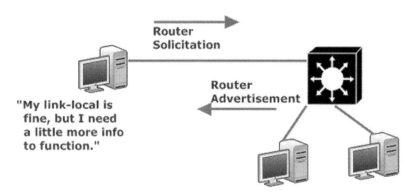

What's the host soliciting? It needs additional config information from a router in the form of a Router Advertisement (RA). Routers generally send these RAs periodically without an express request from a host, but even though the host would only have to wait 10 seconds or so for an RA, polling the router with an RS does speed up the overall process.

Information in the RA includes flags indicating whether the host should use DHCP for addressing information, and if DHCP is in use, the RA gives the location of the DHCP server. If DHCP is not in use, the router attaches the network prefix to the host's link-local address, which results in the host's full IPv6 address, complete with network prefix!

We can assign an IPv6 address to an SVI in almost the same way we've been assigning it an IPv4 address throughout the course. Just don't forget the "ipv6" in the command. I kid you not, one of the hardest things about learning IPv6 is getting used to entering "ipv6" over and over again in the commands.

```
ROUTER1(config)#int fast 0/0
ROUTER1(config-if)#ipv6 address ?
   WORD                General prefix name
   X:X:X:X::X          IPv6 link-local address
```

```
    X:X:X:X::X/<0-128>      IPv6 prefix

ROUTER1(config)#ipv6 dhcp pool CCNP
ROUTER1(config-dhcpv6)#?
IPv6 DHCP configuration commands:
    address             IPv6 address allocation
    default             Set a command to its defaults
    dns-server          DNS servers
    domain-name         Domain name to complete unqualified host names
    exit                Exit from DHCPv6 configuration mode
    import              Import options
    information         Information refresh option
    link-address        Link-address to match
    nis                 NIS server options
    nisp                NISP server options
    no                  Negate a command or set its defaults
    prefix-delegation   IPv6 prefix delegation
    sip                 SIP server options
    sntp                SNTP server options
    vendor-specific     Configure Vendor-specific option
```

Many of the commands and concepts are carried straight over from IPv4. The options for *host* and *client-identifier* are missing, and for good reason. We don't have the option to create manual bindings in IPv6 DHCP.

There's also an option missing from our *ipv6 dhcp* list that we did have in IPv4:

```
ROUTER1(config)#ipv6 dhcp ?
    database            Configure IPv6 DHCP database agents
    ping                Configure IPv6 DHCP pinging
    pool                Configure IPv6 DHCP pool
    server              Configure IPv6 DHCP server
```

There's no *ipv6 dhcp excluded-address* command, and that's for the simple reason that you can't exclude addresses in IPv6 DHCP!

DHCP Snoooooooooop (ing)

It's hard to believe that something as innocent and commonplace as DHCP can be used against our network, but the trouble can start as early as the host sending out a DHCP Discovery packet. Once that happens, the host listens for replies in the form of DHCP Offers. The host isn't particularly discriminating about the offer it accepts. Actually, the host accepts the very first offer it sees come in!

Part of the Offer is the address the host should use as its default gateway. No problem here, since only one DHCP Server is on the network. The host will receive the offer and set its default gateway accordingly. BUT – what if a DHCP server not under our administrative control, a DHCP rogue server, joins our network?

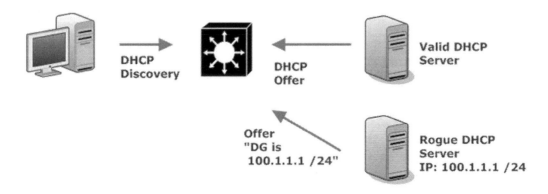

The host will use the info in the first Offer packet it receives, and if the host uses the Offer from the rogue DHCP server, the host will set its default gateway to the rogue server's IP address! The rogue server's accepted Offer could set the host's DNS server address to the rogue's IP address as well, which opens the host and the network up to all kinds of nasty attacks.

DHCP Snooping allows the switch to serve as a firewall between hosts and untrusted DHCP servers. Basically, the switch snoops on DHCP conversations between those devices and makes decisions on which conversations are between trusted devices and which ones are *not*.

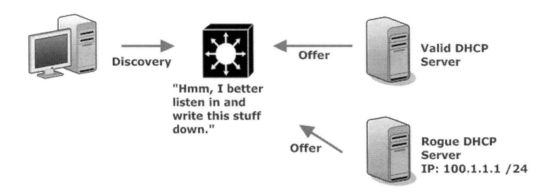

DHCP Snooping classifies switch interfaces as either trusted or untrusted. DHCP messages received on trusted interfaces will be allowed to pass through the switch, while DHCP messages received on untrusted interfaces will be dropped by the switch AND the interface will go into err-disabled state.

You're now asking yourself whether there's some automagical way for the switch to detect valid DHCP servers. Sorry, no. Trusted ports must be configured manually and explicitly by the network admin.

By default, the switch considers *all* ports untrusted, so we better remember to trust some ports when running this feature. Otherwise, we'll have no dynamic IP addressing and a lot of err-disabled ports!

First step: Enable DHCP Snooping on the switch.

```
MLS_1(config)#ip dhcp snooping ?
  database       DHCP snooping database agent
  information    DHCP Snooping information
  verify         DHCP snooping verify
  vlan           DHCP Snooping vlan
  <cr>

MLS_1(config)#ip dhcp snooping
```

Next step: Identify the VLANs that will use DHCP Snooping.

```
MLS_1(config)#ip dhcp snooping vlan ?
  WORD           DHCP Snooping vlan first number or vlan range, example:
                 1,3-5,7,9-11

MLS_1(config)#ip dhcp snooping vlan 4
```

With our trusted DHCP server on port Fa0/10, we'll now trust that individual port:

```
MLS_1(config)#int fast 0/10
MLS_1(config-if)#ip dhcp snooping ?
  information    DHCP Snooping information
  limit          DHCP Snooping limit
  trust          DHCP Snooping trust config
  vlan           DHCP Snooping vlan

MLS_1(config-if)#ip dhcp snooping trust
```

When used with DHCP Snooping, the sinister-sounding *Option 82* basically extends Snooping's trust boundary. When DHCP packets with Option 82 set come in on untrusted ports that have this option enabled, those packets are not dropped. Instead, the switch injects its own DHCP relay info into the Option-82 field (including its MAC address), and the packet is then forwarded to a DHCP Server.

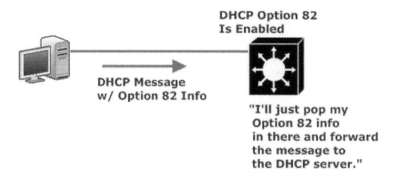

To enable this option, use *ip dhcp snooping information option.*

```
MLS_1(config)#ip dhcp snooping information ?
  option DHCP Snooping information option

MLS_1(config)#ip dhcp snooping information option
```

When the reply to that DHCP message comes back, the switch validates the message by checking to see if its own Option 82 info was included in the reply. If so, that info is removed and the packet is forwarded. If not, the packet is dropped.

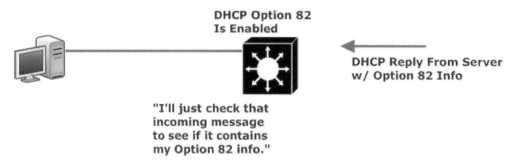

This validity check is enabled by default. If you want to turn it off for some reason, use *no ip dhcp relay information check.*

```
MLS_1(config)#no ip dhcp relay ?
  bootp         BOOTP specific configuration
  information   Relay agent information option
  prefer        Relay agent server selection approach

MLS_1(config)#no ip dhcp relay information ?
  Check        Validate relay information in BOOTREPLY
  Option       Insert relay information in BOOTREQUEST
  Policy       Define reforwarding policy
  trust-all    Received DHCP packets may contain relay info option with zero
               giaddr
```

Verify your config with *show ip dhcp snooping.*

```
MLS _1#show ip dhcp snooping
Switch DHCP snooping is enabled
DHCP snooping is configured on following VLANs:
4
DHCP snooping is operational on following VLANs:
4
Smartlog is configured on following VLANs:
none
Smartlog is operational on following VLANs:
none
DHCP snooping is configured on the following L3 Interfaces:

Insertion of option 82 is enabled
  circuit-id default format: vlan-mod-port
  remote-id: 0017.9466.f780 (MAC)
Option 82 on untrusted port is not allowed
Verification of hwaddr field is enabled
Verification of giaddr field is enabled
DHCP snooping trust/rate is configured on the following Interfaces:

Interface                 Trusted    Allow option   Rate limit (pps)
---------------------     ------     -----------
FastEthernet0/10          yes        yes            unlimited
```

Note the "rate limit" for the untrusted port is "unlimited". That refers to the number of DHCP packets the interface can accept in one second. Use *ip dhcp snooping limit rate* to set a limit for this value. IOS Help doesn't mention the measuring unit in this command, so it's a good idea to know it's packets per second.

```
MLS _1(config)#int fast 0/9
MLS _1(config-if)#ip dhcp snooping ?
  information  DHCP Snooping information
  limit        DHCP Snooping limit
  trust        DHCP Snooping trust config
  vlan         DHCP Snooping vlan

MLS _1(config-if)#ip dhcp snooping limit ?
  rate DHCP Snooping limit

MLS _1(config-if)#ip dhcp snooping limit rate ?
  <1-2048>     DHCP snooping rate limit

MLS _1(config-if)#ip dhcp snooping limit rate 1000 ?
  <cr>
```

Dynamic ARP Inspection

If you can't trust DHCP, who can you trust?

Well, not ARP, because the Address Resolution Protocol can turn on us in a minute! A rogue device on our network can overhear part of the ARP conversation and make itself look like a legitimate part of the action. This happens through ARP Cache Poisoning, also known as ARP Spoofing.

Here, Host A is sending an ARP Request, requesting the host with the IP address 172.12.12.2 respond with its MAC address.

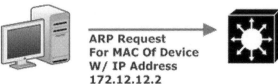

Host A
IP: 172.12.12.1 /24
MAC: aa-aa-aa-aa-aa-aa

ARP Request
For MAC Of Device
W/ IP Address
172.12.12.2

Host B
IP: 172.12.12.2 /24
MAC: bb-bb-bb-bb-bb-bb

Before responding, Host B makes an entry in its local ARP cache mapping the source IP address of the Request, 172.12.12.1, to the mac address aaaa.aaaa.aaaa. The ARP Reply is then sent.

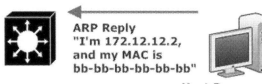

Host A
IP: 172.12.12.1 /24
MAC: aa-aa-aa-aa-aa-aa

ARP Reply
"I'm 172.12.12.2,
and my MAC is
bb-bb-bb-bb-bb-bb"

Host B
IP: 172.12.12.2 /24
MAC: bb-bb-bb-bb-bb-bb

Once Host A receives the ARP Reply, both hosts have a MAC address – IP address mapping for the other. However, if a rogue host responds to the original ARP Request, we have a problem.

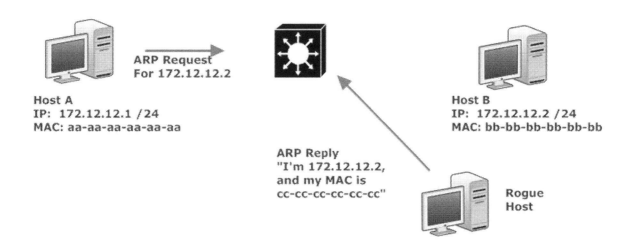

As a result of this man-in-the-middle attack, Host A makes an entry in its ARP cache mapping 172.12.12.2 to cccc.cccc.cccc. Meanwhile, the rogue host acquires Host B's true MAC address via ARP, leading to these two negative results:

1. When H   The rogue host can do the same for an ARP Request sent by Host B for Host A, and at that point, all communications between A and B are going through the rogue host.

Dynamic ARP Inspection (DAI) prevents this behavior by building a database of trusted IP – MAC address mappings. This database is the same one built by the DHCP Snooping process, and static ARP configurations can be also be used by DAI.

Watch this one: DAI uses the concepts of trusted and untrusted ports, just as DHCP Snooping does, but DAI has some *major* differences in how messages are treated by these port types. DAI is performed as ARP messages are received, not transmitted.

Once the IP – MAC address database is built, every single ARP Request and ARP Reply received on an untrusted interface is examined. If the ARP message has an approved MAC – IP address mapping, the message is forwarded appropriately. If no such mapping exists, the ARP message is dropped.

On trusted interfaces, DAI allows the ARP message to pass without checking the database at all.

With DAI using the DHCP Snooping Database to get the job done, it follows that DHCP Snooping must be enabled before DAI is configured. Verify with *show ip dhcp snooping*.

```
MLS _ 1#show ip dhcp snooping
Switch DHCP snooping is enabled
```

The next step in configuring DAI is to name the VLANs that will be using this feature.

```
MLS _ 1(config)#ip arp inspection ?
  filter      Specify ARP acl to be applied
  log-buffer  Log Buffer Configuration
```

```
smartlog    Smartlog all the logged pkts
validate    Validate addresses
vlan        Enable/Disable ARP Inspection on vlans

MLS_1(config)#ip arp inspection vlan ?
  WORD vlan range, example: 1,3-5,7,9-11


MLS_1(config)#ip arp inspection vlan 4
```

The *validate* option gives us the option to go beyond DAI's default inspection.

```
MLS_1(config)#ip arp inspection ?
  filter       Specify ARP acl to be applied
  log-buffer   Log Buffer Configuration
  smartlog     Smartlog all the logged pkts
  validate     Validate addresses
  vlan         Enable/Disable ARP Inspection on vlans

MLS_1(config)#ip arp inspection validate ?
  dst-mac    Validate destination MAC address
  ip         Validate IP addresses
  src-mac    Validate source MAC address
```

Here's what happens with these enabled:

"src-mac" compares the source MAC address in the Ethernet header and the MAC address of the source of the ARP message.

"dst-mac" compares the destination MAC in the Ethernet header and the MAC destination address of the ARP message.

"ip" compares the ARP Request's source IP against the destination IP of the ARP Reply.

Let's use the *ip* option and verify with *show ip arp inspection*.

```
MLS_1#show ip arp inspection


Source Mac Validation      : Disabled
Destination Mac Validation : Disabled
IP Address Validation      : Enabled


Vlan   Configuration     Operation    ACL Match          Static ACL
--     ------------      ---------    ---------
  4    Enabled           Active


Vlan   ACL Logging       DHCP Logging          Probe Logging
--     ----------        -----------
  4    Deny              Deny                  Off
```

Vlan	Forwarded	Dropped	DHCP Drops	ACL Drops
4	0	0	0	0

Vlan	DHCP Permits	ACL Permits	Probe Permits	Source MAC Failures
4	0	0	0	0

Vlan	Dest MAC Failures	IP Validation Failures	Invalid Protocol Data
4	0	0	0

If you see those validation failures start to add up, you just might have a rogue device on your network.

Now, about our ports! DAI considers all ports untrusted by default. To trust one (or remove trust from one that was trusted), use *ip arp inspection.*

```
MLS_1(config)#int fast 0/10
MLS_1(config-if)#ip arp inspection ?
  Limit  Configure Rate limit of incoming ARP packets
  Trust  Configure Trust state

MLS_1(config-if)#ip arp inspection trust ?
  <cr>

MLS_1(config-if)#ip arp inspection trust
```

Verify with show *ip arp inspection interface.* To see this DAI info for all interfaces, run that command; for just one, name the interface at the end of the command.

```
MLS_1#show ip arp inspection int fast 0/10

Interface          Trust State   Rate (pps)   Burst Interval
---------------    -----------   ---------    --------------
Fa0/10             Trusted          None          N/A
```

Should you run DAI in your network, you'll likely run it on all of your switches, and it's a good idea to avoid unnecessary inspection. Cisco's recommended trusted / untrusted port config is to have all ports connected to hosts run as untrusted and all ports connected to switches as trusted. Since DAI runs only on ingress ports, this scheme ensures that every ARP packet has to pass one checkpoint but no more than that.

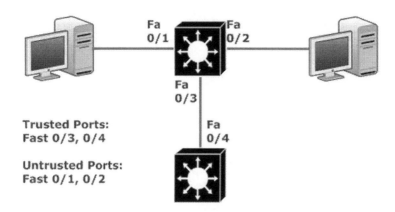

Trusted Ports:
Fast 0/3, 0/4

Untrusted Ports:
Fast 0/1, 0/2

IP Source Guard

Another "the name is the recipe" feature, IP Source Guard prevents a host on the network from using another host's IP address. IP Source Guard works in tandem with DHCP Snooping and uses the same database to carry out this operation, so we need to have DHCP Snooping up and running before configuring IP Source Guard.

With this feature enabled, a host that comes online and is connected to an untrusted port can receive only DHCP-related traffic. Once that host successfully acquires an IP address via DHCP, the switch takes note of that IP address assignment.

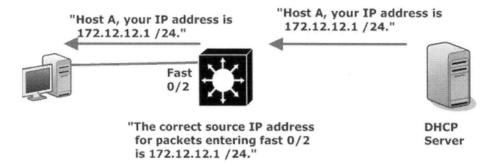

The switch then creates a VLAN ACL (VACL) that will only allow traffic to be processed by a port if the previously noted source IP address is present on incoming traffic. This IP address-to-switchport mapping is generally referred to as *binding*.

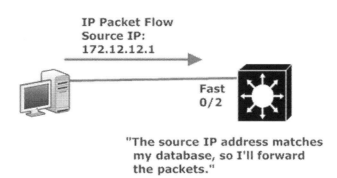

IP Packet Flow
Source IP:
172.12.12.1

Fast
0/2

"The source IP address matches
my database, so I'll forward
the packets."

Should the host pretend to be another host on that subnet – that is, to *spoof* that other host's IP address – the switch will simply drop that incoming traffic, since the source IP address of that incoming traffic will not match the database's entry for that port.

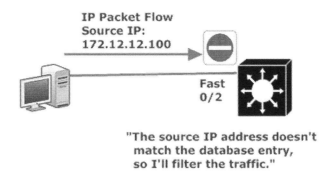

IP Packet Flow
Source IP:
172.12.12.100

Fast
0/2

"The source IP address doesn't
match the database entry,
so I'll filter the traffic."

Once DHCP Snooping is enabled and verified, use *ip verify source* to enable IP Source Guard at the interface level.

```
MLS _ 1(config)#int fast 0/3
MLS _ 1(config-if)#ip verify source ?
  port-security   port security
  smartlog        Smartlog denied packets
  <cr>

MLS _ 1(config-if)#ip verify source
```

The default value checked is the IP source address. After all, this is *IP Source Guard!* There are two important options to go with that, *port-security* and *smartlog*. The port-security option enables an extra level of security, as the source MAC address of incoming packets on that port will be checked against the local switch's MAC address table. If those addresses match, all is well; if not, the packets are dropped.

Smartlog enables the switch to send dropped packets to a NetFlow collector. If you don't need this feature, leave it alone, and be prepared to see "disabled" for "log" in the output of *show ip verify source.*

I'll go with the default setting here and leave those options off.

```
MLS _ 1#show ip verify source
Interface      Filter-type    Filter-mode IP-address   Mac-address      Vlan
Log
-------    ----------   ------------  -------------  ----------------

Fa0/3    ip           active      deny-all                           1
```

If the device off fast 0/3 was getting its IP address via DHCP, we'd see a secure MAC address under IP-address, rather than *deny-all*. That router is using a static address instead, so we have to create a manual binding for it with *ip source binding* in order to use IP Source Guard here.

The command is long-winded, but not difficult. You can get the MAC address of this host from the local switch's MAC address table or from the device itself. In the output of show ip verify source, note that "log" is disabled – that's Smartlog.

```
MLS _ 1(config)#ip source binding ?
    H.H.H      binding MAC address

MLS _ 1(config)#ip source binding 001f.ca96.2754 ?
    Vlan       binding VLAN

MLS _ 1(config)#ip source binding 001f.ca96.2754 vlan ?
    <1-4094>   binding VLAN number

MLS _ 1(config)#ip source binding 001f.ca96.2754 vlan 1 ?
    A.B.C.D     binding IP address

MLS _ 1(config)#ip source binding 001f.ca96.2754 vlan 1 10.1.1.3 ?
    Interface binding interface

MLS _ 1(config)#ip source binding 001f.ca96.2754 vlan 1 10.1.1.3 int fast 0/3 ?
    <cr>

MLS _ 1(config)#ip source binding 001f.ca96.2754 vlan 1 10.1.1.3 int fast 0/3
MLS _ 1#show ip verify source
Interface Filter-type Filter-mode   IP-address      Mac-address    Vlan
Log
------    ----------   ------------  -------------  ----------------
Fa0/3    ip           active        10.1.1.3                        1
disabled
```

VLAN Hopping

How can something that sounds so much fun be so evil?

VLAN Hopping techniques use dot1q tagging against us, and we love dot1q tagging! We get the native VLAN, we have less overhead... we LOVE dot1q tagging and we're not letting it go!

And if we follow a few simple network security tips, we don't have to! Let's have a look at how VLAN Hopping attacks work.

One form of hopping is double tagging, where an intruder transmits frames that are tagged with two separate VLAN IDs. Some very specific circumstances have to exist for this attack to bear fruit:

The intruding device *must* be attached to an access port.

The VLAN used by that access port *must* be the native VLAN.

ISL wouldn't work at all for this attack, so dot1q *must* be in use.

When that rogue host transmits a frame, the frame will have two tags – one indicating native VLAN membership, the other carrying the VLAN number of the VLAN to be attacked. We'll assume that VLAN 100 is the ultimate target.

The trunk receiving this double-tagged frame sees the tag for the native VLAN, and as usual that tag is removed and then sent across the trunk. Problem is, the tag for VLAN 100 is still there!

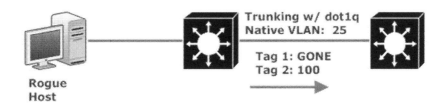

When the remote switch receives that frame, it sees the tag for VLAN 100 and forwards the frame to ports in that VLAN. The rogue has now successfully hopped from one VLAN to the other.

Big deal, right? Right! It *is* a big deal! It seems innocent enough, but VLAN Hopping has been used for a huge variety of network attacks, ranging from Trojan horse virus propagation to stealing bank account numbers and passwords.

Classic solution: Make your native VLAN a VLAN that *no* hosts are actually a member of. You may have a little more overhead as a result, but that stops double tagging in its tracks! You can also go the extra mile (or extra command) and prune that native VLAN from the trunk.

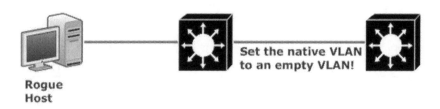

Rogue
Host

Set the native VLAN
to an empty VLAN!

Switch spoofing is a VLAN Hopping variation that's even worse than double tagging. Switch spoofing allows the rogue to pretend to be a member of all VLANs in our network.

Some Cisco switch ports run in dynamic desirable mode by default, which means a port is sending out Dynamic Trunking Protocol frames in an aggressive effort to form a trunk. Problem is, the switch just knows it's sending DTP frames – it has no idea who's actually receiving them. The switch is basically hoping nothing bad happens as a result of sending these frames blindly.

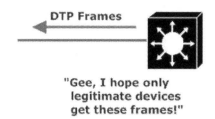

DTP Frames

"Gee, I hope only
legitimate devices
get these frames!"

"Remember Red, hope is a good thing, maybe the best of things, and no good thing ever dies." – Andy Dufresne, **The Shawshank Redemption**

"Hope is a good thing, but a lousy network security strategy." -- Chris Bryant, **The Book You're Reading**

Many well-meaning network admins will put this kind of port into Auto mode, meaning the port will trunk but isn't actively looking to do so. This solution leads to another problem, because a rogue host connected to a port in Auto mode can pretend it's a switch and send DTP frames of its own, which leads to a trunk between our switch and someone else's switch. (This is also a security vulnerability for Cisco switches whose default port trunking mode is Auto.)

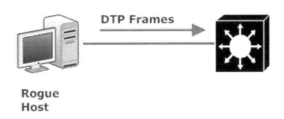

Not good!

There's a classic defense for this attack. Every port on your switch that doesn't lead to another switch known to be under your administrative control should be placed into access mode. Doing so disables the port's ability to create a trunk and the rogue host's ability to switch spoof!

These simple network security tips – using an empty VLAN as the native VLAN, disabling dynamic and auto trunking modes – will score points for you in the exam room and save you serious troubles in your server room!

The Cisco Discovery Protocol

Many companies have clear, concise network maps that show every physical connection in their network, and these maps are regularly updated as their network changes.

Some networks do not.

A big part of network troubleshooting is quietly verifying what a client has told you. Just because someone is looking over your shoulder and saying "That switch is connected to the other one at fast0/12!", they're not necessarily correct. We can use the Cisco Discovery Protocol (CDP) to see what Cisco devices are directly connected to the Cisco device we're currently working on. This Layer 2 protocol runs globally and on a per-interface level by default on Cisco routers and switches, and is Cisco-proprietary.

When you have interface-level and globally-configured commands enabling and disabling the same protocol, you just know that's going to show up on your exam in some fashion. Before we get to those commands, let's run *show cdp* to see if CDP is enabled in the first place. It's on by default but often disabled in production networks. If you get global info, it's on, and if you don't, it's not!

```
MLS _ 1#show cdp
Global CDP information:
        Sending CDP packets every 60 seconds
        Sending a holdtime value of 180 seconds
        Sending CDPv2 advertisements is enabled
```

```
MLS_1#show cdp
% CDP is not enabled
```

To enable CDP globally, use *cdp run* (and *no cdp run* to turn it off globally).

```
MLS_1(config)#cdp run
MLS_1(config)#^Z
MLS_1#show
*Mar 1 00:18:54.542: %SYS-5-CONFIG_I: Configure
MLS_1#show cdp
Global CDP information:
        Sending CDP packets every 60 seconds
        Sending a holdtime value of 180 seconds
        Sending CDPv2 advertisements is enabled
```

CDP sends its announcements every 60 seconds to the destination MAC address 01:00:0c:cc:cc:cc, and the holdtime is 180 seconds. To change either of those, use *cdp timer* and/or *cdp holdtime*.

```
MLS_1(config)#cdp ?
  advertise-v2  CDP sends version-2 advertisements
  holdtime      Specify the holdtime (in sec) to be sent in packets
  run           Enable CDP
  timer         Specify the rate at which CDP packets are sent (in sec)
  tlv           Enable exchange of specific tlv information

MLS_1(config)#cdp timer ?
  <5-254>       Rate at which CDP packets are sent (in sec)

MLS_1(config)#cdp holdtime ?
  <10-255>      Length of time (in sec) that receiver must keep this packet
```

For that all-important info on directly connected Cisco devices, run *show cdp neighbor*.

```
MLS_1#show cdp neighbor
Capability Codes: R - Router, T - Trans Bridge, B - Source Route Bridge
                  S - Switch, H - Host, I - IGMP, r - Repeater, P - Phone,
                  D - Remote, C - CVTA, M - Two-port Mac Relay

Device ID       Local Intrfce    Holdtme    Capability  Platform  Port ID
HOST_3          Fas 0/3          122            R S I   2801      Fas 0/0
HOST_1          Fas 0/1          176            R S I   2801      Fas 0/0
```

From left to right, we see...

Device ID, the remote device's hostname.

Local interface, the local switch's interface that is directly connected to the remote host.

Holdtime, the number of seconds the local device will retain the contents of the last CDP advertisement received from that remote host.

Capability, the type of device the remote device is! In this case, we have two devices that can run as both routers and switches, so it's a good guess that those are L3 switches!

Platform, the remote device's hardware platform. Both connections here are to Cisco 2801 switches.

Port ID, the remote device's interface involved in the direct connection.

Real-world courtesy tip: If your client has CDP turned off, and you turn it on for trouble-shooting, turn it back off before you leave, just as you would turn off debugs before leaving.

You may want to leave CDP on globally but disable / reenable it on a particular interface. At the interface level, use the commands *no cdp enable* and *cdp enable* to get the job done. We'll disable CDP on the interface leading directly to Host 1.

```
MLS _ 1(config)#int fast 0/1
MLS _ 1(config-if)#cdp ?
  enable   Enable CDP on interface
  tlv      Enable exchange of specific tlv information

MLS _ 1(config-if)#cdp enable ?
  <cr>

MLS _ 1(config-if)#no cdp ?
  enable   Enable CDP on interface
  tlv      Enable exchange of specific tlv information

MLS _ 1(config-if)#no cdp enable
```

About 3 minutes after disabling CDP on that interface, Host_1 disappears from the CDP table.

```
MLS _ 1#show cdp neighbor
Capability Codes: R - Router, T - Trans Bridge, B - Source Route Bridge
                  S - Switch, H - Host, I - IGMP, r - Repeater, P - Phone,
                  D - Remote, C - CVTA, M - Two-port Mac Relay

Device ID          Local Intrfce     Holdtme     Capability  Platform  Port ID
HOST _ 3           Fas 0/3           148              R S I  2801      Fas 0/0
```

For more details on those neighbors, run *show cdp neighbor detail*. This command gives you both the IP address and IOS version run by each neighbor.

```
MLS _ 1#show cdp neighbor detail

Device ID: HOST _ 3
Entry address(es):
   IP address: 10.1.1.3
Platform: Cisco 2801, Capabilities: Router Switch IGMP
Interface: FastEthernet0/3, Port ID (outgoing port): FastEthernet0/0
Holdtime : 125 sec

Version :
Cisco IOS Software, 2801 Software (C2801-ADVENTERPRISEK9 _ IVS-M), Version 15.1(2
T2, RELEASE SOFTWARE (fc1)
Technical Support: http://www.cisco.com/techsupport
Copyright (c) 1986-2010 by Cisco Systems, Inc.
Compiled Sat 23-Oct-10 00:43 by prod _ rel _ team

advertisement version: 2
VTP Management Domain: ''
Duplex: full
Management address(es):
```

CDP gives you a lot of great info, so why do many networks disable it? CDP offers no authentication, nor does it use any kind of encryption – all CDP info is sent in clear text. You can see by the info in the *show cdp neighbor detail* output that we don't want this information accessible to everyone.

The issue with disabling CDP is that many network management tools use info gathered by CDP. To minimize the risk of running CDP, determine where it really needs to be running, where you can do without it, and use the interface-level commands to make that happen.

I'm sure you noticed that the CDP commands referred to a "version 2", which brings up the musical question, "What happened to CDP version 1?" v1 is still available, and like the non-encrypted-by-default enable password, it's being kept around for backward compatibility. CDP v2 has greatly enhanced error-reporting capabilities (Cisco's terms for this include "rapid reporting mechanism" or "enhanced reporting mechanism"). CDPv2 recognizes the native VLAN concept, where v1 doesn't, and can report mismatched native VLANs.

In case you run into networks that (shudder) run non-Cisco devices, the Link Layer Discovery Protocol may come in handy. LLDP is the vendor-independent equivalent of CDP and is defined by IEEE 802.1ab. LLDP is also known as the Station and Media Access Control Connectivity Discovery. For obvious reasons, we prefer "LLDP".

You likely noted the term "tlv" in some of the CDP command options. "tlv" refers to Type-Length-Value, a series of informational messages sent by an LLDP-enabled device. (TLVs are not exclusive to LLDP though.)

There's a very helpful extension, LLDP for Media Endpoint Devices (LLDP-MED), which comes into play when VoIP is in use. According to Cisco's website, "LLDP-MED is specified to operate only between endpoint devices such as IP phones and network connectivity devices such as switches."

CDP does carry info that LLDP-MED doesn't, including the following:

MTU sizeVLAN Trunking Protocol information

IP network prefix support (for ODR, On-Demand Routing)

I've included a link to a Cisco PDF with a great deal of helpful info comparing LLDP-MED and CDP. While not required reading for the CCNP exams, I do recommend it for greater understanding of LLDP-MED in particular.

http://www.cisco.com/en/US/technologies/tk652/tk701/technologies_white_paper0900a-ecd804cd46d.html

Telnet vs. SSH

Telnet's a great way to communicate with remote routers and switches, but there's just one problem – all of the data sent to the remote host, including passwords, is transmitted in clear text. Any would-be network intruder who intercepts that transmission can easily enter our network and cause all kinds of trouble.

We *really* hate that.

Secure Shell (SSH) is basically encrypted Telnet, since the basic operation of SSH is similar to that of Telnet, but all data (and the password!) is encrypted.

SSH requires a little more config than Telnet, which is no problem, but it may also require a stronger IOS image and/or hardware that you don't have in your network, which *is* a problem. For SSH authentication, you'll need to configure a local database on the router or use AAA. Telnet allows the configuration of a one-size-fits-all password on the VTY lines ("password CCNP"), but SSH does not. To limit authentication to SSH and disallow Telnet authentication, run *transport input ssh* on the VTY lines.

```
MLS_1(config)#line vty 0 4
MLS_1(config-line)#login local
MLS_1(config-line)#transport input ?
  all     All protocols
  none    No protocols
  ssh     TCP/IP SSH protocol
  telnet  TCP/IP Telnet protocol

MLS_1(config-line)#transport input ssh
```

Be careful with your switch VTY line configs, as the one I just wrote limited those five VTY lines to SSH connections. Problem is, Cisco switches have 16 lines:

```
line vty 0 4
  login local
  transport input ssh
line vty 5 15
  login
```

Whoops! Easily fixed, though. After entering VTY line config mode with *line vty 0 15*, running *transport input ssh* and *login local* again applies that command to all lines.

```
MLS_1(config)#line vty 0 15
MLS_1(config-line)#login local
MLS_1(config-line)#transport input ssh

line vty 0 4
  login local
  transport input ssh
line vty 5 15
```

```
   login local
   transport input ssh
```

A local user database is created with the *username /password* command. Each individual user is assigned a password of their own, and the username/password combination must match a database entry for authentication to be successful.

```
   MLS _ 1(config)#username tarrant password tarantula
   MLS _ 1(config)#username signal password gasoline
   MLS _ 1(config)#username homer password beeeeeeer
```

SSH configuration also requires a domain name to be specified with *ip domain-name* and crypto key creation with *crypto key generate rsa*.

```
   MLS _ 1(config)#crypto key generate rsa
   The name for the keys will be: MLS _ 1.bryantadvantage.com
   Choose the size of the key modulus in the range of 360 to 4096 for your
      General Purpose Keys. Choosing a key modulus greater than 512 may take a
      few minutes.

   How many bits in the modulus [512]:
   % Generating 512 bit RSA keys, keys will be non-exportable...
   [OK] (elapsed time was 1 seconds)
```

Telnet and SSH do share an important option, and that's the use of ACLs to determine who should be able to connect. Create the ACL defining the source IP addresses of trusted users – or as I've done here, block untrusted addresses and allow everyone else in - and apply the ACL to the VTY lines with *access-class*.

```
   MLS _ 1(config)#ip access-list standard STOPTHATGUY
   MLS _ 1(config-std-nacl)#deny host 3.3.3.3
   MLS _ 1(config-std-nacl)#permit any
   MLS _ 1(config-std-nacl)#line vty 0 15
   MLS _ 1(config-line)#access-class STOPTHATGUY ?
     in    Filter incoming connections
     out   Filter outgoing connections

   MLS _ 1(config-line)#access-class STOPTHATGUY in
```

Let's take a *deep* breath and move from security to monitoring!

Chapter 10:

MONITORING THE SWITCHES

Syslog delivers messages regarding network events, along with a timestamp that helps you determine when the event occurred. These messages can be quite helpful in figuring out what the heck just happened in your network – you just have to remain calm and read the message carefully. I say that because some network admins panic more than a little when these messages show up, and in that panic they miss the message that's right in front of them.

Logging is straightforward, but the *logging* command itself can be a little tricky. Let's take a look at the *logging* options .

```
MLS_1(config)#logging ?
    Hostname or A.B.C.D IP address of the logging host
```

That one's simple enough! We just need to follow *logging* with the hostname or IP address of that host. The *trap* option is a bit more complex:

```
MLS_1(config)#logging trap ?
    <0-7>           Logging severity level
    alerts          Immediate action needed          (severity=1)
    critical        Critical conditions              (severity=2)
    debugging       Debugging messages               (severity=7)
    emergencies     System is unusable               (severity=0)
    errors          Error conditions                 (severity=3)
    informational   Informational messages           (severity=6)
    notifications   Normal but significant conditions (severity=5)
    warnings        Warning conditions               (severity=4)
    <cr>
```

When you select a trap level, all messages of the numeric severity you choose *and all those with a lower numeric value* are sent to the logging server specified with *hostname*. Therefore, to send all log messages to the server, you need only specify level 7. You can use the name of the level or the numeric value – just set it high enough so you get all the messages you need sent to that server.

Deciphering syslog messages takes a little practice, so let's get that practice with the latest syslog message on my L3 switch.

```
*Mar 1 02:50:32.465: %SYS-5-CONFIG _ I: Configured from console by console
```

You can change the beginning of syslog messages to the timestamp format of your choice with *service timestamps log*. I personally find the milliseconds to be annoying, so let's keep the *datetime* format but leave the *msec* option off.

```
MLS _ 1(config)#service timestamps ?
  debug          Timestamp debug messages
  log            Timestamp log messages
  <cr>


MLS _ 1(config)#service timestamps log ?
  datetime        Timestamp with date and time
  uptime          Timestamp with system uptime
  <cr>


MLS _ 1(config)#service timestamps log datetime ?
  localtime       Use local time zone for timestamps
  msec            Include milliseconds in timestamp
  show-timezone   Add time zone information to timestamp
  year            Include year in timestamp
  <cr>


MLS _ 1(config)#service timestamps log datetime
```

As a result, the next syslog message gives the date and time without the msecs.

```
*Mar 1 02:52:28: %SYS-5-CONFIG _ I: Configured from console by console
```

If you prefer to have the device uptime reflected in syslog messages, just choose that option!

```
MLS _ 1(config)#service timestamps log uptime ?
  <cr>


MLS _ 1(config)#service timestamps log uptime
```

The next syslog message indicates this device has been up for 2 hours, 54 minutes, and 56 seconds.

```
02:54:56: %SYS-5-CONFIG_I: Configured from console by console
```

The "5" bolded above indicates the severity level, followed by the mnemonic for this message and the message text itself.

The switch console is set to display all syslog messages by default, and I've kept it there throughout the course. To change this value, use *logging console*.

```
MLS_1(config)#logging console ?
   <0-7>            Logging severity level
   alerts           Immediate action needed           (severity=1)
   critical         Critical conditions               (severity=2)
   debugging        Debugging messages                (severity=7)
   emergencies      System is unusable                (severity=0)
   errors           Error conditions                  (severity=3)
   informational    Informational messages            (severity=6)
   notifications    Normal but significant conditions (severity=5)
   warnings         Warning conditions                (severity=4)
```

To send log messages to the local device's internal buffer, run *logging buffered* followed by the severity level; to change the internal buffer from its default of 4096 bytes, run this same command followed by the number of bytes desired.

```
MLS_1(config)#logging buffered ?
   <0-7>               Logging severity level
   <4096-2147483647>   Logging buffer size
   alerts           Immediate action needed           (severity=1)
   critical         Critical conditions               (severity=2)
   debugging        Debugging messages                (severity=7)
   discriminator    Establish MD-Buffer association
   emergencies      System is unusable                (severity=0)
   errors           Error conditions                  (severity=3)
   filtered         Enable filtered logging
   informational    Informational messages            (severity=6)
   notifications    Normal but significant conditions (severity=5)
   warnings         Warning conditions                (severity=4)
```

To view the log along with log settings, run *show logging*.

```
MLS_1#show logging
Syslog logging: enabled (0 messages dropped, 0 messages rate-limited, 0 flushes,
0 overruns, xml disabled, filtering disabled)
    Console logging: level debugging, 36 messages logged, xml disabled,
    filtering disabled
```

```
    Monitor logging: level debugging, 0 messages logged, xml disabled,
    filtering disabled
    Buffer logging: level debugging, 36 messages logged, xml disabled,

filtering disabled
    Exception Logging: size (4096 bytes)
    Count and timestamp logging messages: disabled
    File logging: disabled
    Persistent logging: disabled

No active filter modules.

    Trap logging: level informational, 39 message lines logged

Log Buffer (4096 bytes):

*Mar 1 00:00:32.505: %LINEPROTO-5-UPDOWN: Line protocol on Interface Vlan1, cha
nged state to downAuth Manager registration failed
*Mar 1 00:00:36.146: %DC-6-DEFAULT _ INIT _ INFO: Default Profiles DB not loaded.
*Mar 1 00:00:38.352: %SYS-5-CONFIG _ I: Configured from memory by console
*Mar 1 00:00:39.183: %SYS-5-RESTART: System restarted --
Cisco IOS Software, C3560 Software (C3560-IPSERVICESK9-M), Version 15.0(1)SE, RE
(truncated for clarity at this point)
```

Before we move to another topic, let me show you a nifty little trick. Throughout the book, you've seen log messages regarding ports opening and closing, such as this one:

```
03:12:30: %SYS-5-CONFIG _ I: Configured from console by console
03:12:31: %LINK-3-UPDOWN: Interface FastEthernet0/0, changed state to up
03:12:32:  %LINEPROTO-5-UPDOWN:  Line  protocol  on  Interface  FastEthernet0/0,
changed state to down
03:12:35:  %LINEPROTO-5-UPDOWN:  Line  protocol  on  Interface  FastEthernet0/0,
changed state to up
```

I like seeing these message in lab environments, but in production networks, you can fill up a log pretty quickly with these messages. To prevent these particular messages from logging, run the interface-level command *no logging event link-status*. On routers, you may see only these two options:

```
ROUTER1(config)#int fast 0/0
ROUTER1(config-if)#no logging event ?
    link-status          UPDOWN and CHANGE messages
    subif-link-status       Sub-interface UPDOWN and CHANGE messages

ROUTER1(config-if)#no logging event link-status
ROUTER1(config-if)#shut
ROUTER1(config-if)#no shut
03:14:33: %SYS-5-CONFIG _ I: Configured from console by console
```

We received only the configuration message; the syslog messages regarding link and line protocol status are gone. To get those logging messages back, run *logging event link-status*.

```
ROUTER1(config)#int fast 0/0
ROUTER1(config-if)#logging event link-status
ROUTER1(config-if)#shut
03:16:27: %LINK-5-CHANGED: Interface FastEthernet0/0, changed state to adminis-
tratively down
03:16:28: %LINEPROTO-5-UPDOWN: Line protocol on Interface FastEthernet0/0,
changed state to down
ROUTER1(config-if)#no shut
03:16:37: %LINK-3-UPDOWN: Interface FastEthernet0/0, changed state to up
03:16:38: %LINEPROTO-5-UPDOWN: Line protocol on Interface FastEthernet0/0,
changed state to up
```

You'll have more options for this command on switches.

```
MLS_1(config)#int fast 0/1
MLS_1(config-if)#no logging event ?
  bundle-status          BUNDLE/UNBUNDLE messages
  link-status            UPDOWN and CHANGE messages
  nfas-status            NFAS D-channel status messages
  spanning-tree          Spanning-tree Interface events
  status                 Spanning-tree state change messages
  subif-link-status      Sub-interface UPDOWN and CHANGE messages
  trunk-status           TRUNK status messages
```

Getting rid of the link up-down messages is a good way to keep the log size down and make the log easier to read, but I'd be careful about turning too many log messages off. You might just miss one you really need to see!

Timestamping

If your timestamps reflect an era long gone, it's time to get another time source.

```
MLS_1#show clock
*04:55:05.037 UTC Mon Mar 1 1993
```

Yeah, like that! We can set the local device's time with *clock set*, then fine-tune that setting with *clock timezone* and *clock summer-time*. Note where *clock set* is run as opposed to the other clock commands.

```
MLS_1#clock ?
  set    Set the time and date

MLS_1#clock set ?
  hh:mm:ss    Current Time
```

```
MLS_1#clock set 13:43:00 ?
   <1-31>        Day of the month
   MONTH         Month of the year

MLS_1#clock set 13:43:00 March ?
   <1-31>        Day of the month

MLS_1#clock set 13:43:00 March 25 ?
   <1993-2035>   Year

MLS_1#clock set 13:43:00 March 25 2015 ?
   <cr>

MLS_1#clock set 13:43:00 March 25 2015

04:59:01: %SYS-6-CLOCKUPDATE: System clock has been updated from 23:59:01 EST Sun
Feb 28 1993 to 13:43:00 EDT Wed Mar 25 2015, configured from console by console

MLS_1(config)#clock timezone ?
   WORD          name of time zone

MLS_1(config)#clock ?
   initialize    Initialize system clock on restart
   save          backup of clock with NVRAM
   summer-time   Configure summer (daylight savings) time
   timezone      Configure time zone

MLS_1(config)#clock timezone ?
   WORD          name of time zone

MLS_1(config)#clock timezone EST ?
   <-23 - 23>    Hours offset from UTC

MLS_1(config)#clock timezone EST -5

MLS_1(config)#clock summer-time ?
   WORD          name of time zone in summer

MLS_1(config)#clock summer-time EDT ?
   date          Configure absolute summer time
   recurring     Configure recurring summer time

MLS_1(config)#clock summer-time EDT recurring ?
   <1-4>         Week number to start
   first         First week of the month
   last          Last week of the month
   <cr>

MLS_1(config)#clock summer-time EDT recurring
```

The *clock timezone* command doesn't list every time zone in the world, nor the Coordinated Universal Time (UCT), so you gotta know yours! I live on the East Coast in the United States, so I put Eastern Standard Time (EST) in for the time zone and -5 for the offset. For your personal reference, here's the Wikipedia page listing all offsets:

http://en.wikipedia.org/wiki/List_of_UTC_time_offsets

clock set is okay for one or two routers, but in our networks, we're going to have a lot more routers and switches, and it's vital they have the same time. The Network Time Protocol (NTP) helps us make that happen.

The Network Time Protocol

It's vital for our routers and switches to have a central time source that allows our network devices to synchronize their clocks. Doing so allows our syslog timestamps to have accurate and synced time throughout the network, making troubleshooting a lot less frustrating. Synced time is important for our digital certificates as well, and if you're using any kind of accounting in your network, accurate and synced time is a necessity. You haven't lived until you bill a department for 67 days' usage of a network resource – in a single month.

NTP allows us to specify time sources for our switches and routers, whether that time source is another router in the same network or an external time source.

At the very top of our NTP hierarchy are stratum-0 devices, typically atomic clocks. You can't configure a Cisco router to get its time directly from a stratum-0 server.

Stratum-0

Our Network MLS
Can't Get Time Directly
From Stratum-0 Clock

The number following "stratum" in non-stratum-0 devices indicates how many hops away the device is from a stratum-0 device. (And you thought you were done with hops in RIP!)

Stratum-1 servers are generally referred to as *time servers*, and we *can* configure a Cisco router to get its time from a stratum-1 device.

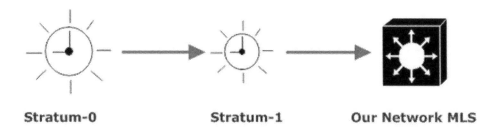

Stratum-0   Stratum-1   Our Network MLS

It's strongly recommended that your network's "outside" router receive its time from a public NTP timeserver. For the latest IP addresses of these servers, just run a search on the term public NTP servers. Be sure not to block UDP port 123 on that or other routers in your network – that's the port NTP uses.

Cisco routers can serve as NTP servers, clients, or peers. They can also depend on NTP broadcasts for the correct time. The NTP server-client relationship is as you'd expect, with the server giving the correct time to clients.

NTP Server   **NTP Client**
("Master")

Clients accept the time synch message from the server and set their internal clock accordingly. Clients do NOT sent NTP time synch messages back to the server.

We're not limited to the traditional Server/Client relationship with NTP. NTP peers send NTP messages to each other, and either peer can send time synch messages to the other.

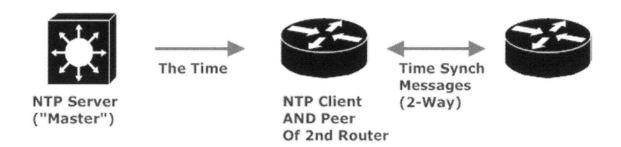

NTP Server   **The Time**   **NTP Client**   **Time Synch**
("Master")   **AND Peer**   **Messages**
                           Of 2nd Router   **(2-Way)**

We can choose to run NTP in broadcast mode or multicast mode as well. With these methods, the server broadcasts or multicasts its NTP messages, which the clients must be able to receive – otherwise, we're wasting our time! Remember that routers don't forward broadcasts or multicasts, NTP-based or otherwise.

It's highly recommended an NTP public timeserver be used as your NTP Master time source. Should you choose to use one of your network routers as the NTP Master, it's imperative you use NTP authentication and/or ACLs to prevent routers from outside your network from attempting to synch with one of your routers.

In our lab, we'll configure MLS_1 as our NTP Master and a timeserver, with ROUTER_3 configured as a client of MLS_1. As always, the router number serves as the last octet of each IP address.

NTP Server
10.1.1.4

NTP Client
10.1.1.3

The Time

Let's check the clock on our NTP-Master-to-be:

```
MLS _ 1#show clock
09:25:29.167 EST Wed Mar 25 2015
```

It ain't 1993, so we'll take it! Our NTP options:

```
MLS _ 1(config)#ntp master ?
   <1-15> Stratum number
   <cr>
```

On R3, I'll use *ntp server* to point R3 to this switch as its time source.

```
ROUTER _ 3(config)#ntp server ?
   A.B.C.D                  IP address of peer
   Hostname or A.B.C.D      IP address of supervisor (127.0.0.x)
   WORD                     Hostname of peer
   X:X:X:X::X               IPv6 address of peer
   ip                       Use IP for DNS resolution
   ipv6                     Use IPv6 for DNS resolution
   vrf                      VPN Routing/Forwarding Information

ROUTER _ 3(config)#ntp server 10.1.1.4
```

The commands *show ntp status* and *show ntp association* verify NTP's operation. There's a lot of info here, and the phrase we're looking for is "clock is synchronized". We're also looking for that asterisk next to the address in *show ntp association*, which indicates that the synch is complete. Here's the output from the server's point of view, which includes the reference address 127.127.1.1, indicating the time source is the switch's internal clock.

```
MLS _ 1#show ntp association
address        ref clock    st    when   poll   reach   delay   offset    disp
*~127.127.1.1  .LOCL.        7      8      16     377    0.000   0.000    0.243
* sys.peer, # selected, + candidate, - outlyer, x falseticker, ~ configured

MLS _ 1#show ntp status
Clock is synchronized, stratum 8, reference is 127.127.1.1
```

```
nominal freq is 119.2092 Hz, actual freq is 119.2092 Hz, precision is 2**17
reference time is D8BD46F7.46BF9352 (09:38:47.276 EST Wed Mar 25 2015)
(Output truncated for clarity)
```

And from the client's point of view:

```
ROUTER _ 3#show ntp status
Clock is synchronized, stratum 9, reference is 10.1.1.4
nominal freq is 250.0000 Hz, actual freq is 250.0000 Hz, precision is 2**24
reference time is D8BD47D4.F3858835 (14:42:28.951 UTC Wed Mar 25 2015)
(Output truncated for clarity)

ROUTER _ 3#show ntp association
address        ref clock    st   when   poll   reach   delay   offset   disp
*~10.1.1.4     127.127.1.1   8    64     64      37     2.348   -66.425 439.77
 * sys.peer, # selected, + candidate, - outlyer, x falseticker, ~ configured
```

If we're fortunate and smart enough to have NTP Master redundancy, we can configure our NTP clients to have more than one time server to choose from. We can also prefer one server over the other! Just use multiple *ntp server* commands while also using the *prefer* option to indicate the preferred server.

```
ROUTER _ 3(config)#ntp server 10.1.1.4 prefer
ROUTER _ 3(config)#ntp server 10.1.1.7
```

The NTP process likely strikes you as wide open to attack, since the only thing we're really telling the client is "Hey, here's the IP address of the time server." Let's use NTP authentication to tie things down a bit. We'll enable this feature with *ntp authenticate*, then define a key and link that key to the *ntp server* command.

```
ROUTER _ 3(config)#ntp authenticate
ROUTER _ 3(config)#ntp authentication-key ?
  <1-4294967295> Key number

ROUTER _ 3(config)#ntp authentication-key 1 ?
  md5 MD5 authentication

ROUTER _ 3(config)#ntp authentication-key 1 md5 ?
  WORD Authentication key
ROUTER _ 3(config)#ntp authentication-key 1 md5 CCNP
ROUTER _ 3(config)#ntp trusted-key ?
  <1-4294967295> Key number

ROUTER _ 3(config)#ntp trusted-key 1
ROUTER _ 3(config)#ntp server 10.1.1.4 ?
  burst      Send a burst when peer is reachable
  iburst     Send a burst when peer is unreachable
  key        Configure peer authentication key
```

```
maxpoll      Maximum poll interval
minpoll      Minimum poll interval
prefer       Prefer this peer when possible
source       Interface for source address
version      Configure NTP version
<cr>
```

```
ROUTER _ 3(config)#ntp server 10.1.1.4 key ?
  <0-4294967295> Peer key number
```

```
ROUTER _ 3(config)#ntp server 10.1.1.4 key 1
```

We'll need the same commands on the server (except the *ntp server* command, of course!):

```
MLS _ 1(config)#ntp authentication-key 1 md5 CCNP
MLS _ 1(config)#ntp authenticate
MLS _ 1(config)#ntp trusted-key 1
```

Verify NTP authentication with *show ntp association detail*. I've left out most of the output of this command, because when it says "detail", it means detail! The authentication verification is right at the top of the output:

```
ROUTER _ 3#show ntp association detail
10.1.1.4 configured, authenticated, our_master, sane, valid, stratum 8
ref ID 127.127.1.1 , time D8BE4169.4569D946 (08:27:21.271 UTC Thu Mar 26 2015)
```

That's all well and good, but NTP authentication isn't quite what it seems. I've just added another router to our lab, and it's able to get time from MLS_1 with no problem – and no authentication, either!

```
ROUTER _ 1(config)#ntp server 10.1.1.4
```

```
ROUTER _ 1#show ntp assoc
Address      ref clock      st    when    poll   reach    delay    offset    disp
*~10.1.1.4   127.127.1.1    8      26      64      17      2.790    ⌐8.124   939.53
* sys.peer, # selected, + candidate, - outlyer, x falseticker, ~ configured
```

```
ROUTER _ 1#show ntp assoc detail
10.1.1.4 configured, our_master, sane, valid, stratum 8
ref ID 127.127.1.1 , time D8BE4561.46322015 (08:44:17.274 UTC Thu Mar 26 2015)
our mode client, peer mode server, our poll intvl 64, peer poll intvl 64
```

NTP authentication really just assures the client that it's talking to an NTP server that's under our administrative control. Enabling NTP authentication on the server does NOT require NTP clients to use authentication, as we've seen.

To further protect our NTP deployment, we'll configure an ACL on the server and use ntp access-group to apply it to NTP. Our ACL will permit only the source IP address 10.1.1.3 (Router_3), and we'll call that ACL in *ntp access-group*.

```
MLS_1(config)#access-list 22 permit host 10.1.1.3
MLS_1(config)#
MLS_1(config)#ntp access-group ?
   Peer            Provide full access
   query-only      Allow only control queries
   serve           Provide server and query access
   serve-only      Provide only server access

MLS_1(config)#ntp access-group serve ?
   <1-99>          Standard IP access list
   <1300-1999>     Standard IP access list (expanded range)
   WORD            Named access list

MLS_1(config)#ntp access-group serve 22
```

debug ntp packets illustrates that when MLS_1 receives an NTP message from the permitted IP address of 10.1.1.3, an NTP message is sent in reply. The debug shows an NTP message coming in from 10.1.1.1 as well, but that message is not answered due to the ACL and *ntp access-group* command.

```
MLS_1#debug ntp packet
NTP packets debugging is on
NTP message received from 10.1.1.3 on interface 'Vlan13' (10.1.1.4)
NTP message sent to 10.1.1.3, from interface 'Vlan13' (10.1.1.4)
NTP message received from 10.1.1.1 on interface 'Vlan13' (10.1.1.4)
NTP message received from 10.1.1.3 on interface 'Vlan13' (10.1.1.4)
NTP message sent to 10.1.1.3, from interface 'Vlan13' (10.1.1.4)
NTP message received from 10.1.1.1 on interface 'Vlan13' (10.1.1.4)
MLS_1#u all
All possible debugging has been turned off
```

With our time all synched up, let's do some network monitoring!

SNMP

The Simple Network Management Protocol is used to carry network management info from one network device to another, and you'll find it in just about every network out there today. An SNMP deployment has three main parts:

The SNMP Manager, the actual monitoring device.

The SNMP Agents, the devices being monitored (and running an SNMP instance).

The Management Information Base (MIB), the database on the Agent that contains important information ("variables") about the Agent.

SNMP Managers *poll* Agents over UDP port 161, and these messages take the form of GETs and SETs. A "GET" is a request for information...

... and a "SET" is a request from the Manager to the Agent, requesting a certain variable be set to the value indicated in the SET.

Seems like a good approach, but there's one glaring issue. The only way for the Manager to receive immediate or even near-immediate notice of a critical network event is to poll the Agents quite often, which in turn sucks up bandwidth and is a hit on the Manager's CPU.

Let's say our Manager is polling our Agent every 10 minutes regarding one particular variable. Three seconds after the Agent answers one such GET, that variable undergoes a critical change. It would then take 9 minutes and 57 seconds for the Manager to find out about the change!

To get a quick notification on such an event without overloading the Manager, we configure *SNMP traps* on the managed devices, allowing the Agents to send a message to the Manager when such a variable changes.

We still have three versions of SNMP out there – versions 1, 2c, and 3 – and there are some serious security concerns with the earlier versions. V3 has both authentication and encryption capabilities; the earlier versions do not. For that reason alone, you should use

V3 whenever possible, and the use of the other versions should be restricted to allowing read-only access via the use of *community strings.*

SNMP community strings, found in SNMP v1 and 2c, are a kind of password / authority level combination that allow you to set the strings as read-only or read-write.

```
MLS_1(config)#snmp-server community ?
   WORD SNMP community string

MLS_1(config)#snmp-server community CCNP ?
   <1-99>        Std IP accesslist allowing access with this community string
   <1300-1999>   Expanded IP accesslist allowing access with this community
                 string
   WORD          Access-list name
   ro            Read-only access with this community string
   rw            Read-write access with this community string
   view          Restrict this community to a named MIB view
   <cr>

MLS_1(config)#snmp-server community CCNP ro ?
   <1-99>        Std IP accesslist allowing access with this community string
   <1300-1999>   Expanded IP accesslist allowing access with this community
                 string
   WORD          Access-list name
   ipv6          Specify IPv6 Named Access-List
   <cr>

MLS_1(config)#snmp-server community CCNP ro 15
```

This configuration would allow hosts identified by ACL 15 to have read-only access to all SNMP objects specified by this community string.

With SNMP v3, things are much more secure and just a tad more complex. Let's use IOS Help to venture through some of the most long-winded commands you're ever going to see. Let's start with creating an SNMP group and then assigning a user to that group.

```
MLS_1(config)#snmp-server group BULLDOGS ?
   v1      group using the v1 security model
   v2c     group using the v2c security model
   v3      group using the User Security Model (SNMPv3)

MLS_1(config)#snmp-server group BULLDOGS v3 ?
   auth      group using the authNoPriv Security Level
   noauth    group using the noAuthNoPriv Security Level
   priv      group using SNMPv3 authPriv security level
```

A quick word about those three security levels – they look intimidating, but when you break them down they're easy to remember.

authNoPriv – You have **auth**entication, but no **priv**acy (no encryption)

noAuthNoPriv – You're really asking for it. You have no **auth**entication and no **priv**acy (encryption).

authPriv – Your SNMP packets are both **auth**enticated and **priv**acy is assured via encryption.

```
MLS _ 1(config)#snmp-server group BULLDOGS v3 priv ?
    access       specify an access-list associated with this group
    context      specify a context to associate these views for the group
    match        context name match criteria
    notify       specify a notify view for the group
    read         specify a read view for the group
    write        specify a write view for the group
    <cr>

MLS _ 1(config)#snmp-server group BULLDOGS v3 priv
```

The views mentioned in the last IOS Help readout aren't required, and creating them is out of the CCNP SWITCH exam scope, but I do want you to know the defaults:

If no read view is defined, all objects can be read.

If no write view is defined, no objects can be written.

If no notify view is defined, group members are not sent notifications.

Now let's create our user, using SHA for authentication and AES 128-bit encryption, which are both excellent choices when your hardware allows them.

```
MLS _ 1(config)#snmp-server user CHRIS ?
    WORD        Group to which the user belongs

MLS _ 1(config)#snmp-server user CHRIS BULLDOGS ?
    Remote      Specify a remote SNMP entity to which the user belongs
    v1          user using the v1 security model
    v2c         user using the v2c security model
    v3          user using the v3 security model

MLS _ 1(config)#snmp-server user CHRIS BULLDOGS v3 ?
    Access      specify an access-list associated with this group
    Auth        authentication parameters for the user
    Encrypted   specifying passwords as MD5 or SHA digests
    <cr>

MLS _ 1(config)#snmp-server user CHRIS BULLDOGS v3 auth ?
    md5         Use HMAC MD5 algorithm for authentication
    sha         Use HMAC SHA algorithm for authentication
```

```
MLS_1(config)#snmp-server user CHRIS BULLDOGS v3 auth sha ?
   WORD          authentication pasword for user

MLS_1(config)#snmp-server user CHRIS BULLDOGS v3 auth sha CCNP ?
   Access        specify an access-list associated with this group
   Priv          encryption parameters for the user
   <cr>

MLS_1(config)#snmp-server user CHRIS BULLDOGS v3 auth sha CCNP priv ?
   3des          Use 168 bit 3DES algorithm for encryption
   aes           Use AES algorithm for encryption
   des           Use 56 bit DES algorithm for encryption

MLS_1(config)#snmp-server user CHRIS BULLDOGS v3 auth sha CCNP priv aes ?
   128           Use 128 bit AES algorithm for encryption
   192           Use 192 bit AES algorithm for encryption
   256           Use 256 bit AES algorithm for encryption

MLS_1(config)#snmp-server user CHRIS BULLDOGS v3 auth sha CCNP priv aes 128 ?
   WORD          privacy pasword for user

MLS_1(config)#$S BULLDOGS v3 auth sha CCNP priv aes 128 TIREDOFTYPING ?
   access        specify an access-list associated with this group
   <cr>

MLS_1(config)#$S BULLDOGS v3 auth sha CCNP priv aes 128 TIREDOFTYPING
MLS_1(config)#^Z
MLS_1#
Mar 26 10:16:25.467: Configuring snmpv3 USM user, persisting snmpEngineBoots.
```

Finally, we'll define the host to which we'll send traps.

```
MLS_1(config)#snmp-server host ?
   WORD IP/IPV6 address of SNM
                                                    notification host
     http://<Hostname or A.B.C.D>[:<port number>][/<uri>] HTTP address of XML
                                                    notification host

MLS_1(config)#snmp-server host 10.1.1.3 ?
   WORD          SNMPv1/v2c community string or SNMPv3 user name
   informs       Send Inform messages to this host
   traps         Send Trap messages to this host
   version       SNMP version to use for notification messages
   vrf           VPN Routing instance for this host

MLS_1(config)#snmp-server host 10.1.1.3 traps ?
   WORD          SNMPv1/v2c community string or SNMPv3 user name
   version       SNMP version to use for notification messages
```

```
MLS _ 1(config)#snmp-server host 10.1.1.3 traps version ?
  1              Use SNMPv1
  2c             Use SNMPv2c
  3              Use SNMPv3

MLS _ 1(config)#snmp-server host 10.1.1.3 traps version 3 ?
  auth           Use the SNMPv3 authNoPriv Security Level
  noauth         Use the SNMPv3 noAuthNoPriv Security Level
  priv           Use the SNMPv3 authPriv Security Level

MLS _ 1(config)#snmp-server host 10.1.1.3 traps version 3 priv ?
  WORD           SNMPv1/v2c community string or SNMPv3 user name

MLS _ 1(config)#snmp-server host 10.1.1.3 traps version 3 priv CHRIS ?

<about 45 options, too many to list here>
<cr>

MLS _ 1(config)#snmp-server host 10.1.1.3 traps version 3 priv CHRIS
```

Whew! You obviously have to do some serious planning for SNMPv3, including the encryption type and bit level of same you'll be able to use, but it pays off in the end with security that's far superior to earlier versions.

Service Level Agreements

During your Frame Relay studies in your CCNA days, you were introduced to the Committed Information Rate (CIR). The CIR is basically a guarantee given to the customer by the Frame Relay service provider, where the provider says "For X dollars, we guarantee you'll get "Y" amount of bandwidth. You may get more, but we guarantee you won't get less." Given that guarantee of minimum performance, the customer can then plan the WAN appropriately.

The SLA is based on the concept of minimum, guaranteed performance, but this agreement is between different parties. It can be much like the CIR, where a service provider guarantees a certain level of overall network uptime and performance, or it can be between the internal clients of a company and the network team at that same company.

The SLA can involve just about any quality-measurable value in your network, from available bandwidth and acceptable levels of jitter in voice networks, to DNS lookup time, trouble notification and resolution time. Here's a sneak peek of the available tests:

```
MLS _ 1(config)#ip sla 5
MLS _ 1(config-ip-sla)#?
IP SLAs entry configuration commands:
  dhcp              DHCP Operation
  dns               DNS Query Operation
```

```
exit              Exit Operation Configuration
ftp               FTP Operation
http              HTTP Operation
icmp-echo         ICMP Echo Operation
path-echo         Path Discovered ICMP Echo Operation
path-jitter       Path Discovered ICMP Jitter Operation
tcp-connect       TCP Connect Operation
udp-echo          UDP Echo Operation
udp-jitter        UDP Jitter Operation
video             Video Operation
```

An SLA setup consists of a source and a responder. To kick off the festivities, the source sends control packets to the responder via UDP port 1967 in an attempt to create a control connection similar to that in FTP. This connection isn't the actual SLA test, but is an agreement on the rules of communication. In this case, the rules sent to the responder are the port number to be listened to during the test and the time limit on that listening.

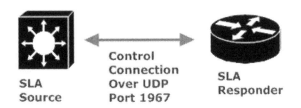

Should the responder be kind enough to agree, it'll send a message back to the source indicating the same, and then the responder starts listening to the indicated port. (If the responder doesn't agree, it'll send a message back indicating that decision, and our story ends prematurely.)

We now go from controlling to probing, as the source sends test packets to the responder. The source wants to see if the packets are echoed back *and* how long the overall process takes.

The responder adds timestamps to those packets both as the packets are accepted and then returned. This gives the sender a better idea of the overall time the responder took to process the packets as well as the overall round-trip time. (Of course, this timestamping only helps if the devices have synched time – NTP, anyone?)

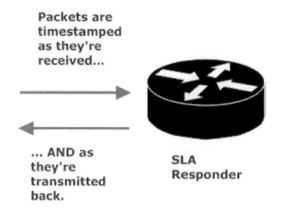

Packets are timestamped as they're received...

... AND as they're transmitted back.

SLA Responder

Let's tackle an SLA lab! MLS_1 will be the SLA source, with ROUTER_3 serving as the responder. Here are the first options for the *ip sla* command:

```
MLS _ 1(config)#ip sla ?
   <1-2147483647>             Entry Number
   enable                     Enable Event Notifications
   group                      Group Configuration or Group Scheduling
   key-chain                  Use MD5 Authentication for IP SLAs Control Messages
   logging                    Enable Syslog
   low-memory                 Configure Low Water Memory Mark
   reaction-configuration     IP SLAs Reaction-Configuration
   reaction-trigger           IP SLAs Trigger Assignment
   read                       Read data for use with IP SLA
   reset                      IP SLAs Reset
   responder                  Enable IP SLAs Responder
   restart                    Restart An Active Entry
   schedule                   Entry Scheduling
```

We'll go with SLA entry number 5, and accepting that value drops us into SLA entry config mode. We'll then choose the *icmp-echo* test, using 10.1.1.3 as the target of the test. Note the option to configure the source interface and IP address – those options can come in handy in larger networks. Since we only have one path from source to responder, we'll leave those alone here.

```
MLS _ 1(config)#ip sla 5
MLS _ 1(config-ip-sla)#?
IP SLAs entry configuration commands:
   dhcp            DHCP Operation
   dns             DNS Query Operation
   exit            Exit Operation Configuration
   ftp             FTP Operation
   http            HTTP Operation
   icmp-echo       ICMP Echo Operation
```

```
    path-echo           Path Discovered ICMP Echo Operation
    path-jitter         Path Discovered ICMP Jitter Operation
    tcp-connect         TCP Connect Operation
    udp-echo            UDP Echo Operation
    udp-jitter          UDP Jitter Operation
    video               Video Operation

  MLS_1(config-ip-sla)#icmp-echo ?
    Hostname or A.B.C.D Destination IP address or hostname, broadcast disallowed

  MLS_1(config-ip-sla)#icmp-echo 10.1.1.3 ?
    source-interface    Source Interface (ingress icmp packet interface)
    source-ip     Source Address
    <cr>

  MLS_1(config-ip-sla)#icmp-echo 10.1.1.3
```

We then drop into SLA ICMP Echo config mode (!), where I'll set a frequency of 60 seconds between tests. That also happens to be the default!

```
  MLS_1(config-ip-sla)#icmp-echo 10.1.1.3
  MLS_1(config-ip-sla-echo)#?
  IP SLAs Icmp Echo Configuration Commands:
    default             Set a command to its defaults
    exit                Exit operation configuration
    frequency           Frequency of an operation
    history             History and Distribution Data
    no                  Negate a command or set its defaults
    owner               Owner of Entry
    request-data-size   Request data size
    tag                 User defined tag
    threshold           Operation threshold in milliseconds
    timeout             Timeout of an operation
    tos                 Type Of Service
    verify-data         Verify data
    vrf                 Configure IP SLAs for a VPN Routing/Forwarding instance

  MLS_1(config-ip-sla-echo)#frequency ?
    <1-604800>          Frequency in seconds

  MLS_1(config-ip-sla-echo)#frequency 60
```

Finally, we get to schedule this sucker! I'll use IOS Help to show you the options and then start the test immediately. Note the option to grant the test eternal life.

```
  MLS_1(config)#ip sla schedule ?
    <1-2147483647>          Entry number
```

```
MLS _ 1(config)#ip sla schedule 5 ?
    ageout              How long to keep this Entry when inactive
    life                Length of time to execute in seconds
    recurring           Probe to be scheduled automatically every day
    start-time          When to start this entry
    <cr>

MLS _ 1(config)#ip sla schedule 5 life ?
    <0-2147483647>      Life seconds (default 3600)
    forever             continue running forever

MLS _ 1(config)#ip sla schedule 5 start-time ?
    after               Start after a certain amount of time from now
    hh:mm               Start time (hh:mm)
    hh:mm:ss            Start time (hh:mm:ss)
    now                 Start now
    pending             Start pending

MLS _ 1(config)#ip sla schedule 5 start-time now
```

Verify your config with *show ip sla config*. I'll show you the entire output here, and the most important info to us is near the top.

```
MLS _ 1#show ip sla config
IP SLAs Infrastructure Engine-III
Entry number: 5
Owner:
Tag:
Operation timeout (milliseconds): 5000
Type of operation to perform: icmp-echo
Target address/Source address: 10.1.1.3/0.0.0.0
Type Of Service parameter: 0x0
Request size (ARR data portion): 28
Verify data: No
Vrf Name:
Schedule:
    Operation frequency (seconds): 60 (not considered if randomly scheduled)
    Next Scheduled Start Time: Start Time already passed
    Group Scheduled : FALSE
    Randomly Scheduled : FALSE
    Life (seconds): 3600
    Entry Ageout (seconds): never
    Recurring (Starting Everyday): FALSE
    Status of entry (SNMP RowStatus): Active
Threshold (milliseconds): 5000
Distribution Statistics:
    Number of statistic hours kept: 2
```

```
    Number of statistic distribution buckets kept: 1
    Statistic distribution interval (milliseconds): 20
Enhanced History:
History Statistics:
    Number of history Lives kept: 0
    Number of history Buckets kept: 15
    History Filter Type: None
```

To view SLA statistics, run *show ip sla statistics*. I ran the command twice, and we can see that the tests are running a minute apart and they've both been successful. The default TTL is 3600 seconds, and we can see that's ticking away.

```
MLS_1#show ip sla stat
IPSLAs Latest Operation Statistics

IPSLA operation id: 5
    Latest RTT: 1 milliseconds
Latest operation start time: 06:11:35 EST Thu Mar 26 2015
Latest operation return code: OK
Number of successes: 1
Number of failures: 0
Operation time to live: 3552 sec

MLS_1#show ip sla stat
IPSLAs Latest Operation Statistics

IPSLA operation id: 5
    Latest RTT: 1 milliseconds
Latest operation start time: 06:12:35 EST Thu Mar 26 2015
Latest operation return code: OK
Number of successes: 2
Number of failures: 0
Operation time to live: 3528 sec
```

An interesting thing about SLA tests – you can't edit one that's in progress. Here, I tried to go back and set this test to live forever rather than time out, and here's what happened:

```
MLS_1(config)#ip sla 5
Entry already running and cannot be modified
    (only can delete (no) and start over)
    (check to see if the probe has finished exiting)
```

It's always *something*!

Hey, did you notice I never configured anything on the responder? Since I was running a simple ICMP echo test, I didn't need to, since I know the responder can handle pinging. For some of those other tests, though, you may need *ip sla responder.* It doesn't hurt anything to enable SLA capabilities for the simpler tests.

```
ROUTER _ 3(config)#ip sla responder
```

We can secure our SLA config with a key-chain and the *ip sla key-chain* command.

```
ROUTER _ 3(config)#key chain CCNP
ROUTER _ 3(config-keychain)#key 1
ROUTER _ 3(config-keychain-key)#key-string SPIDERS

ROUTER _ 3(config)#ip sla key-chain CCNP

MLS _ 1(config)#key chain CCNP
MLS _ 1(config-keychain)#key 1
MLS _ 1(config-keychain-key)#key-string SPIDERS

MLS _ 1(config)#ip sla key-chain CCNP
```

Just one more SLA thing... I want to show you what the statistics output is when something's gone wrong. Here, I shut ROUTER_3's port down that leads to the switch. Here's the result of the very next echo test:

```
MLS _ 1#show ip sla stat
IPSLAs Latest Operation Statistics

IPSLA operation id: 5
    Latest RTT: NoConnection/Busy/Timeout
Latest operation start time: 06:53:35 EST Thu Mar 26 2015
Latest operation return code: Timeout
Number of successes: 42
Number of failures: 1
Operation time to live: 1024 sec
```

After reopening the interface, the successes start incrementing again!

```
MLS _ 1#show ip sla stat
IPSLAs Latest Operation Statistics

IPSLA operation id: 5
    Latest RTT: 1 milliseconds
Latest operation start time: 06:54:35 EST Thu Mar 26 2015
Latest operation return code: OK
Number of successes: 43
Number of failures: 1
Operation time to live: 989 sec
```

AAA

Those As stand for authentication, authorization, and accounting. Each "A" is a separate function and requires separate configuration. Before we deal with configs though, let's look at each "A" and see exactly what's going on with each.

Authentication is the process of deciding if a given user should be allowed to access the network (or network service). As a CCNA and future CCNP, you've already configured authentication in the form of a local database of usernames and passwords. This is sometimes called a self-contained AAA deployment, since no external device is involved.

username chris password bryant
username tictac password dough

aaa authentication login default local

Self-Contained AAA

As your network grows and you need a more scalable authentication scheme, it's likely you'll turn to one of the following protocols for your AAA deployment.

TACACS+, a Cisco-proprietary TCP-based protocol (port 49, that is).

RADIUS, an open-standard UDP-based protocol (ports 1812 and 1813, that is) originally developed by the IETF.

You just might be asking yourself what happened to the original TACACS if we're now using TACACS+. TACACS was the original version of the protocol and is rarely used today, so we don't have to concern ourselves with that version. We do need to concern ourselves with these differences between TACACS+ and RADIUS:

TACACS+ encrypts the entire packet, where RADIUS encrypts only the password in the initial client-server packet.

RADIUS actually combines the authentication and authorization processes. That might sound like a good thing, but it makes it very difficult to run one process without running the other. TACACS+ runs each "A" as a separate process, allowing another method of authentication to be used while still using TACACS+ for authorization and/ or accounting.

RADIUS cannot control the authorization level of users, but TACACS+ can.

Regardless of the "A" you're configuring, AAA must first be enabled with the global command aaa new-model. The location of the TACACS+ and/or RADIUS server must then be configured, along with a shared encryption key that must be agreed upon by both client and server.

**TACACS+ Server
10.1.1.3**

**RADIUS Server
10.1.1.5**

```
MLS _ 1(config)#aaa new-model
MLS _ 1(config)#tacacs-server host 10.1.1.3 key CCNP
MLS _ 1(config)#radius-server host 10.1.1.5 key CCIE
```

aaa new-model not only enables AAA, it also overrides every previously configured authentication method for the router lines – especially the vty lines!

We have our TACACS+ server at 10.1.1.3 and our RADIUS server at 10.1.1.5, with the switch configured as a client of both. We now need to determine which servers will be used for authentication, and in what order, with aaa *authentication*. Let's have a look at the options.

```
MLS _ 1(config)#aaa authentication login ?
   WORD        Named authentication list (max 31 characters, longer will be
               rejected).
   default     The default authentication list.
```

We have to create either a named authentication list or a default list that will be used for all authentications that don't reference a named list. We'll go with the default list.

```
MLS _ 1(config)#aaa authentication login default ?
   cache         Use Cached-group
   enable        Use enable password for authentication.
   group         Use Server-group
   krb5          Use Kerberos 5 authentication.
   krb5-telnet   Allow logins only if already authenticated via Kerberos V
                 Telnet.
   line          Use line password for authentication.
   Local         Use local username authentication.
   local-case    Use case-sensitive local username authentication.
   none          NO authentication.
   passwd-expiry enable the login list to provide password aging support
```

Some choices might surprise you! We can configure authentication to use the enable password, and we could also use a line password. The local and local-case options allow us to use the local username/password database. A quick review on how to build one of those:

```
MLS_1(config)#username bruno password wwwf
MLS_1(config)#username thesz password nwa
MLS_1(config)#username gagne password awa
```

And that's that! However, instead of using the local database, we'll use our TACACS+ and RADIUS servers by drilling a little deeper with *aaa authentication*. If you don't see those options in the above config, there's a good reason – they're not there! To use TACACS+ or RADIUS in *aaa authentication*, choose *group* and all will be revealed!

```
MLS_1(config)#aaa authentication login default group ?
  WORD          Server-group name
  ldap          Use list of all LDAP hosts.
  radius        Use list of all Radius hosts.
  tacacs+       Use list of all Tacacs+ hosts.
```

I'll go with TACACS+ and then check the options.

```
MLS_1(config)#aaa authentication login default group tacacs+ ?
  cache         Use Cached-group
  enable        Use enable password for authentication.
  group         Use Server-group
  krb5          Use Kerberos 5 authentication.
  line          Use line password for authentication.
  local         Use local username authentication.
  local-case    Use case-sensitive local username authentication.
  none          NO authentication.
  <cr>
```

Hmm. The tacacs+ choice is legal, and this command is fine on its own – but why do I have the option to list more authentication choices, including "none"?

We can actually name up to four methods, and they'll be used in the order listed, from left to right. If you try to list a fifth method as I did below, the IOS will not let you enter the 5th method. IOS Help won't even show you the remaining options once you hit four! The following statement lists TACACS+ as the first method, a line password second, the local database third, and finally, the enable password. IOS Help will not show me the remaining options since my statement is already at the legal limit.

```
MLS_1(config)#$ication login default group tacacs+ line local enable ?
  <cr>
```

Let's go back to an *aaa authentication* line with just one method listed.

```
MLS _ 1(config)#aaa authentication login default group tacacs+ ?
    cache           Use Cached-group
    enable          Use enable password for authentication.
    group           Use Server-group
    krb5            Use Kerberos 5 authentication.
    line            Use line password for authentication.
    local           Use local username authentication.
    local-case      Use case-sensitive local username authentication.
    none            NO authentication.
    <cr>
```

Here's the most important rule of this entire section. In this line, TACACS+ will be the first authentication method used. If the TACACS+ authentication attempt times out or an error is encountered, the next method we choose in this line will be used.

Next method in aaa auth statement will be used.

If TACACS+ actively refuses the authentication attempt, the second method is not used. That's the end of the authentication try!

Next method in aaa auth statement will NOT be used.

You're likely wondering why the heck "none" is an AAA authentication option. After all, are we doing all this work just to have no authentication? In some cases – yes!

It's *always* a good idea to list at least one authentication method that doesn't require an external device. That way, if the external devices aren't available, you can still authenticate! Some admins like to use *none* at the end of their authentication method list, so no authentication is necessary if the external servers are down. The enable password is also a good choice.

Always leave yourself a back door to get in, and *always* stay logged in while you test your authentication setup with a separate connection. You don't want to log out and then find out you can't log back in!

This authentication method list will try our defined TACACS+ server first, then our RADIUS server, and will then use the local username/pw database if those servers are unavailable or return errors.

MLS_1(config)#aaa authentication login default group tacacs+ group radius local

Finally, apply the authentication method list to the appropriate lines with *login authentication*. I'll apply the default list to the switch's VTY lines.

```
MLS _ 1(config)#line vty 0 15
MLS _ 1(config-line)#login authentication ?
   WORD   Use an authentication list with this name.
   DefaultUse the default authentication list.

MLS _ 1(config-line)#login authentication default ?
   <cr>

MLS _ 1(config-line)#login authentication default
```

And now... a word to the wise.

Don't Get Cute

Don't get cute with passwords. Never set a password that you don't want to say out loud at a meeting, particularly a meeting with high-ranking sensitive folk.

(Didn't happen to me, but I was there to see it. Ugly. Real ugly.)

Another time not to get cute is when you're naming an AAA authentication list. For some reason, admins like to use AAA for the name of the list, resulting in this command:

```
MLS _ 1(config)#aaa authentication login PASSWORD group tacacs+ local
```

That command confuses the uninitiated. Above all, don't call it *login, tacacs+, radius,* or *group*, because then you end up with one of these:

```
MLS _ 1(config)#aaa authentication login login group tacacs+ local

MLS _ 1(config)#aaa authentication login tacacs+ group tacacs+ local

MLS _ 1(config)#aaa authentication login radius group tacacs+ local

MLS _ 1(config)#aaa authentication login group group tacacs+ local
```

Don't get cute. When you give something a name on a router or switch, make the name intuitive. At the very least, don't use a word already in the command!

Authorization

While authentication decides whether a given user should be allowed into our network, *authorization* dictates what users can do once they're in.

aaa authorization creates a user profile that's checked when a user attempts to use a particular command or service. As with authentication, we'll have the option of creating a default list or a named list – and as always, AAA must be enabled with *aaa new-model* if you haven't already done so! We did just that in the last lab, along with defining the RADIUS and TACACS+ server IP addresses, so we'll dive straight into the authorization options.

```
MLS _ 1(config)#aaa authorization ?
    auth-proxy           For Authentication Proxy Services
    cache                For AAA cache configuration
    commands             For exec (shell) commands.
    config-commands      For configuration mode commands.
    configuration        For downloading configurations from AAA serve
    console              For enabling console authorization
    credential-download  For downloading EAP credential from Local/RAD
    exec                 For starting an exec (shell).
    multicast            For downloading Multicast configurations from server
    network              For network services. (PPP, SLIP, ARAP)
    policy-if            For diameter policy interface application.
    prepaid              For diameter prepaid services.
    radius-proxy         For proxying radius packets
    reverse-access       For reverse access connections
    subscriber-service   For iEdge subscriber services (VPDN etc)
    template             Enable template authorization

MLS _ 1(config)#aaa authorization exec ?
    WORD                 Named authorization list (max 31 characters, longer
                         will rejected).
    default              The default authorization list.

MLS _ 1(config)#aaa authorization exec default ?
    cache                Use Cached-group
    group                Use server-group.
    if-authenticated     Succeed if user has authenticated.
    krb5-instance        Use Kerberos instance privilege maps.
    local                Use local database.
    none                 No authorization (always succeeds).
```

```
MLS _ 1(config)#aaa authorization exec default group tacacs+ local
```

Frankly, I could write a whole book solely on the many different *aaa authorization* combinations, so we're not going to walk through every single one. Watch the *commands* and *config-commands* options, though – the first means the user must be authorized to run any command on the switch, while the second limits authorization to the use of configuration commands. If you're dealing with PPP (or ARAP or SLIP for that matter), go with the *network* option.

Also note the *if-authenticated* option. If the user's already authenticated, that method will (obviously) consider the user authorized.

Apply the authorization list to the appropriate lines with *authorization*.

```
MLS _ 1(config)#line vty 0 15
MLS _ 1(config-line)#authorization ?
   arap                  For Appletalk Remote Access Protocol
   commands              For exec (shell) commands
   exec                  For starting an exec (shell)
   reverse-access        For reverse telnet connections

MLS _ 1(config-line)#authorization commands ?
   <0-15>                Enable level

MLS _ 1(config-line)#authorization exec ?
   WORD                  Use an authorization list with this name
   default               Use the default authorization list

MLS _ 1(config-line)#authorization exec default
```

Accounting

Authentication decides who gets in and who doesn't; authorization decides what users can do once they get in; *accounting* tracks the resources used by that user. This tracking can be for security purposes (detecting users doing things they shouldn't be doing!) or for tracking network usage in order to bill other departments in your company.

Naturally, AAA must be enabled before proceeding with accounting.

We're not going to spend much time on accounting, but I do want to show you a sample config. This line would give us info on users who use commands while in privilege level 1, both when they start and stop. Getting that same info for privilege level 15 would be easy enough – just replace the "1" with "15".

```
MLS _ 1(config)#aaa accounting commands ?
   <0-15>          Enable level
```

```
MLS_1(config)#aaa accounting commands 1 ?
WORD            Named Accounting list (max 31 characters, longer will be
                rejected).
Default         The default accounting list.

MLS_1(config)#aaa accounting commands 1 default ?
None            No accounting.
start-stop      Record start and stop without waiting
stop-only       Record stop when service terminates.
<cr>

MLS_1(config)#aaa accounting commands 1 default start-stop ?
Broadcast       Use Broadcast for Accounting
Group           Use Server-group

MLS_1(config)#aaa accounting commands 1 default start-stop group ?
WORD            Server-group name
tacacs+         Use list of all Tacacs+ hosts.

MLS_1(config)#aaa accounting commands 1 default start-stop group tacacs+ ?
Group           Use Server-group
<cr>

MLS_1(config)#aaa accounting commands 1 default start-stop group tacacs+
```

AAA supports six different accounting formats:

Commands: Information regarding EXEC mode commands issued by a user.

Connection: Information regarding all outbound connections made from a network access server.

EXEC: Information about user EXEC terminal sessions.

Network: Info on all PPP, ARAP, and SLIP sessions.

Resource: Info regarding start and stop records for calls passing authentication, and stop records for calls that fail authentication.

System: Non-user-related system-level events.

Chapter 11:

NETWORK DESIGN AND MODELS

Blunt as always: This isn't the most exciting material in the course. Having said that, it is very important material, so grab some caffeine and let's dive right in!

During your CCNA studies, your only responsibilities concerning the Cisco 3-Layer Hierarchical Model was memorizing the layers and their location. The stakes are raised in your CCNP studies, as we need to know what should and should not occur at each layer. We'll start this section with a review of the model, and then delve into each layer in detail.

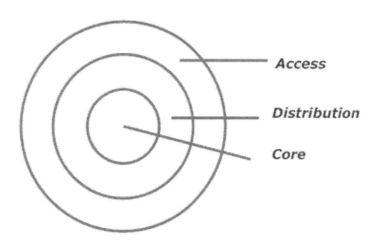

The Core Layer

Switches at the core layer allow distribution-layer switches to communicate, and this is more than a full-time job! It's vital that we keep extra, non-switching features off the core layer and let these switches do what they do best – switch. The core layer is the backbone of our entire network, so we're interested in high-speed data transfer, very low latency, and that's it!

Today's core switches are generally the multilayer switches we've worked with throughout this course. Be sure to examine your network's requirements and review the documentation on switch models carefully before making your purchase. Core layer switches are generally the most powerful in your network, capable of higher throughput than switches found at the other layers.

As you know, everything we do on a Cisco router or switch takes away from overall switch resources, so we'll leave most frame manipulation and filtering to other layers. With networking though, you know there's an exception to that rule, and that exception is Quality of Service (QoS). Advanced QoS is generally performed at the core layer. Leave your ACLs and other traffic filtering methods for other layers of this model.

We always want redundancy, but we want a lot of redundancy in the core layer. This is the nerve center of your entire network, so fault tolerance should be at the highest level possible.

The Distribution Layer

Not all the work is done at the core layer! The demands on distribution-level switches is very high. The access-layer switches will have their uplinks connecting to our distribution-level switches, so not only do the distribution-level switches need high-speed ports and links, they have to have quite a few in order to connect to both the access and core-layer switches.

Distribution-layer switches must be able to handle redundancy for all links. Examine your network topology closely and check vendor documentation before making purchasing decisions. It's a lot easier to get everything you need when you're buying than to go back and try to add it later.

When multilayer switches are in use, routing should take place at the distribution layer. The access layer's too busy with end users to handle routing, and we want the core layer to be concerned strictly with switching.

While QoS is configured at the core layer when possible, you'll find it in the distribution layer as well. The distribution layer also serves as a boundary for broadcasts and multicasts sent by access-layer devices.

The Access Layer

Here's where the end users communicate with the network! VLAN membership, traffic filtering, and some basic QoS features all run here. Redundancy is important at this layer (of course! It's important everywhere!), and you must plan for future network growth. A 12-port switch might be fine for your needs at present, but a month from now you'll wish you had bought a larger switch with more ports. A good rule of thumb for access-layer switches is "low cost, high switchport-to-user ratio". Today's sufficient port density is tomorrow's "Where the $%)$ am I gonna plug this user in?"

Collision domains are found at the access layer, and MAC address filtering can be performed here as well, although hopefully there are other ways to get the job done that you need done. (MAC filtering is a pain to configure, I kid you not.)

The Enterprise Composite Network Model

Before we dive into this topic, I want to remind you that network models are guidelines and should be used as such. That's particularly true of the Enterprise Composite Network Model, a very popular model used to design campus networks. (A campus network is basically a series of LANs interconnected via a network backbone.)

Switch blocks are units of access-layer and distribution-layer devices. These layers contain both the traditional L2 switches (found at the access layer) and multilayer switches, typically found in the distribution layer. Devices in a switch block work together to bring network access to a unit of the network, such as a single building on a college campus or business park.

Core blocks naturally consist of our high-powered core switches, and these core blocks allow the switch blocks to communicate. This is a tremendous responsibility, and it's the major reason I continue to mention that the access and distribution layers should handle many of the network services, leaving the core switches free to use all their resources to switch.

As you'd expect, there's no one right way to design an enterprise network. The number of LANs involved, the physical layout of the buildings as a unit and individually – these are just two important factors involved. These models are strictly guidelines. Helpful guidelines, but guidelines nonetheless.

The Enterprise Composite Network Model has three main parts:

The Enterprise Campus

The Enterprise Edge

The Service Provider Edge

In turn, the Enterprise Campus consists of these modules:

Campus Infrastructure

Server Farm

Network Management

Enterprise Edge (yes, again)

In turn again, the Campus Infrastructure model consists of these modules:

Building Access (access-layer devices)

Building Distribution (distribution-layer devices)

Campus Backbone (Interconnects multiple Distribution modules)

Let's take a look at a typical campus network and see how these block types work together.

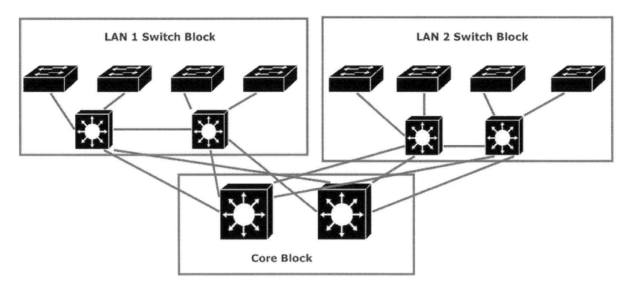

Our access- and distribution-layer switches are both found in this model's Switch Block. All four distribution-layer switches have connections to both switches in the Core Block, giving us as much redundancy as this topology can offer. The Core Block serves as the campus backbone, allowing switches in one Switch Block to communicate with switches in the other Switch Block. We love this setup, especially the *dual core*; if one of the core switches goes down, we still have total connectivity.

Reality does rear its ugly head on occasion, and that occasion may be not having the money to afford a setup like this. Smaller networks (and admins on a tight budget!) can use a collapsed core setup, where certain switches will perform as both Switch Block and Core Block switches. In a collapsed core, there is *no* dedicated core switch.

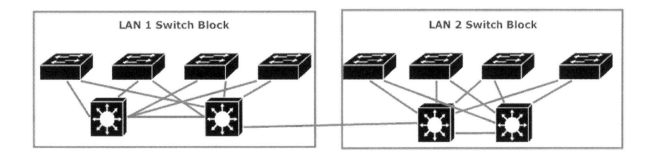

The four multilayer switches are working as both core-layer and distribution-layer switches. Note that each of the access switches have redundant uplinks to both distribution/core switches in their switch block.

There are times when we've wanted to throw a server or two (or twelve) straight out the window, but we're not going to have much of a network without them. In a campus network, the server farm block is a separate switch block, complete with access and distribution-layer switches. The combination of access, distribution, and core layers shown here is sometimes called the Campus Infrastructure.

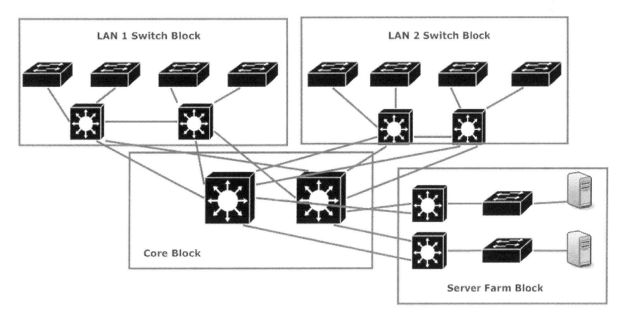

The distribution-layer switches again have redundant connections to the core switches. This is a relatively small campus network, but you already have a good idea of the sheer workload the core switches will be handling.

In today's world, network management tools are a necessity. AAA servers, syslog servers, intruder detection tools, and network monitoring tools are found in almost every campus network today. All of these devices can be placed in a switch block of their own, the *network management block*.

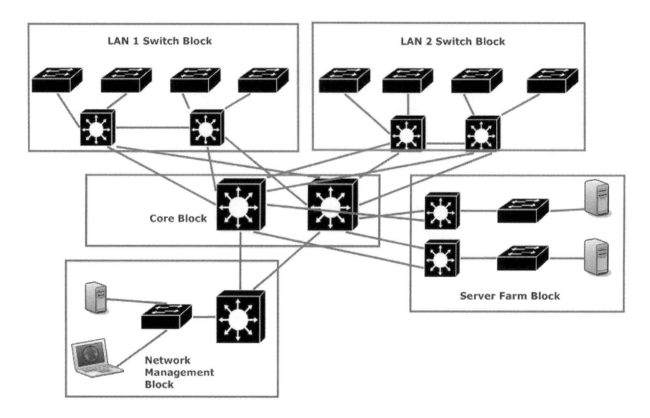

Our core switches have even more work to do not, but we're not quite done yet. Two blocks will team up to bring our users that all-important internet connectivity – the *Enterprise Edge Block* and the *Service Provider Edge Block*.

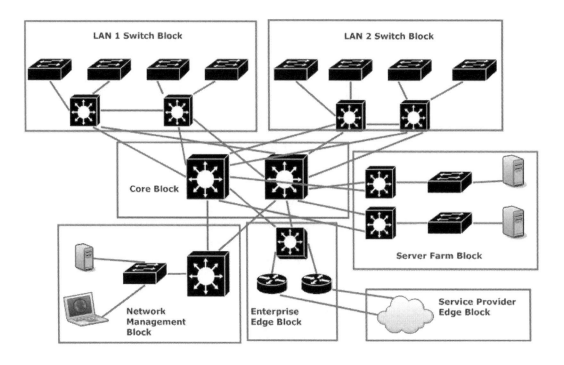

The Enterprise Edge Block is naturally found at the edge of the campus network, and this block of routers and switches brings WAN connectivity to the rest of the campus network. While the Service Provider Edge Block is considered part of the campus network model, we have no control over the actual structure of the block. And frankly, we don't care! The key is that this block borders the Enterprise Edge Block, and it's the final piece of the Internet connectivity puzzle for our campus network.

With all the lines leading to the core switches, it's easy to see why we want to dedicate as much of the switches' capabilities to pure switching – the workload is *huge!*

End-to-End And Local VLANs

"Oh no, not more VLANs!" Hey, I hear you, but these two VLAN types do fit in with our design chat. Let's spend a few minutes with each type...

As you'd expect from the name, end-to-end VLANs span the entire network. The physical location of the user doesn't matter. A user is assigned to a single VLAN, and that VLAN will remain the same no matter where the user is.

The very nature of an end-to-end VLAN and the fact that it spans the entire network makes working with one a challenge. ETE VLANs can come in handy as a security tool, or when the hosts have similar resource requirements – for example, if you had certain hosts across the network that needed access to a particular network resource, but you didn't want your other hosts to even know of the existence of that resource.

ETE VLANs should be designed with the 80/20 rule in mind, where 80% of the local traffic stays within the local area, and the other 20% will traverse the network core en route to a non-local destination. ETE VLANs must be accessible on every access-layer switch in order to accommodate mobile users.

Many of today's networks don't lend themselves well to this type of VLAN. The following network diagram is very simple, but even this network would be difficult to configure with ETE VLANs when the hosts need Internet connectivity or Cloud access. This level of access is more of a necessity than a luxury today, so 80/20 traffic patterns are becoming increasingly rare.

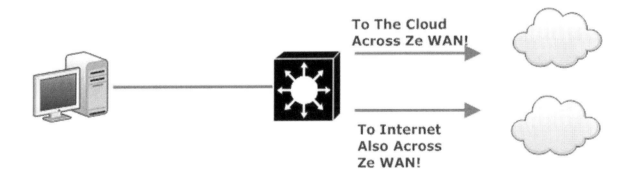

Local VLANs use the 20/80 rule, assuming that 20% of traffic is local in scope and the other 80% will cross the network core. Physical location is unimportant in ETE VLANs, but users are grouped by location in Local VLANs.

Well, shoot. That's it! The end of the book! Thanks for reading, and I wish you all the best on your CCNP SWITCH exam and in your future studies.

Chris B.

Made in the USA
San Bernardino, CA
06 July 2016